Wasser Water

Gestalten mit Wasser: Von Uferpromenaden zu Wasserspielen
Designing with water: Promenades and water features

Edition Topos

Callwey Verlag
München

Birkhäuser
Basel · Boston · Berlin

Inhalt
Table of contents

Parque de Catalunya, Sabadell, Spain
Design: Enric Battle and Joan Roig
with Lluis Gibert
Photo: Luis On

Robert Schäfer

Wasser in der Stadt ist eine ambivalente Sache. Einerseits: Treten Flüsse über die Ufer, laufen Keller voll und die Menschen merken, dass sie nah am Wasser gebaut haben. In Venedig wie in Köln arrangieren sich die Bürger mit den saisonalen Hochwassern. Anderswo verursachen die unverhofften Starkregen Überflutungen in Serie und rücken das Thema Wasser in den Mittelpunkt der Gespräche und der Planung. Versickerung, Rückhaltung, Ablaufverzögerung gewinnt mehr Gewicht in der Bauleitplanung. Ingenieure und Landschaftsarchitekten entwickeln Konzepte für den, auch ästhetisch ansprechenden Umgang mit dem Wasser. So im Hochwasser-Park von le Pecq an der Seine, in Amiens Stadtpark Saint-Pierre oder im Erholungsgebiet mit Wasserkraftwerk an der Donau in Wien. Sogar Ökologie und Gestaltung schließen sich nicht aus, wenn man der Dynamik der Prozesse Rechnung trägt, wie die Beispiele Dehesa del Saler bei Valencia oder die Planungen für Duindoornstad bei Hoek van Holland zeigen.

Andererseits: Seit Abwässer gereinigt und Flüsse nicht mehr als Schmutzwasserkanäle missbraucht werden, führt die Gestaltung der Uferbereiche die Hitliste der Stadtentwicklungsprojekte an. Flüsse und Strände werden ins Stadtbild zurückgeholt. Barcelona wandte sich ganz entschieden dem Meer zu, eroberte mit Promenaden und Parks den Horizont zurück und richtet für die nächste Etappe bis 2004 das Hauptaugenmerk auf die Sanierung der Flüsse Besòs und Llobregat sowie deren Mündungsbereiche. In vielen Städten entstehen Wohngebiete und neue Arbeitsplätze, Kulturstätten, Parks und Promenaden direkt am Wasser, auf attraktiven Gebieten, wo vor kurzem noch Werften und Lagerhäuser sich breit machten. In Kopenhagen ist dies nicht nur Christiansbro, fast das gesamte Hafenareal wandelt sein Gesicht. Ähnlich in Göteborg und natürlich in Malmö, auf der anderen Seite des Öresunds. Über eine Internationale Bauausstellung gelang es, mit der Sundspromenade und dem Daniapark zwei Freizeitanlagen direkt am Strand einzurichten, die sich innerhalb kürzester Zeit eines erstaunlichen Zuspruchs erfreuten.

Der kulturhistorisch bedeutenden Themselandschaft widmet sich Greater London seit einem Jahrzehnt mittels einer strategischen Planung. Hamburg, Berlin, Lyon, Bordeaux, Lissabon und Porto entdecken erneut den Wert der Flüsse, die ja einst maßgeblich zu ihrer Entwicklung beigetragen haben. Alles fließt...und in neuen Parks kräuseln sich die Wellen im Wind. Ob im Parque de Catalunya von Sabadell oder im Parque Juan Carlos I in Madrid: großzügige Teiche und Becken erlauben auch im Binnenland den weiten Blick über den Wasserspiegel. Natürlich sprudelt Wasser auch auf den neuen Plätzen Europas, exemplarisch sei genannt die Place des Terreaux in Lyon. Unter dem Pflaster parken die Autos, oben schießen Fontänen aus den Rasterquadraten des Platzes. Wasserspiele, die auch auf die Lage der Stadt an Rhône und Saône anspielen. Dieser Band ist eine wasserreiche Sammlung von Beiträgen, die seit 1993 in Topos – European Landscape Magazine erschienen sind.

Water in the city is an ambivalent matter. On the one hand, rivers rise above banks, flood cellars, and show people how close they are to being inundated. In Venice as in Cologne, residents learn to live with seasonal high water levels. Elsewhere, unexpected heavy rains cause repeated floods and make the subject of water the main focus of discussion and planning. Seepage, retention, and drainage retardation acquire increased importance in project planning. Engineers and landscape architects develop technical and aesthetically pleasing concepts for dealing with water. Such realisations include the high-water park of le Pecq along the Seine, the Saint-Pierre urban park in Amiens, and the recreational grounds around the hydroelectric power plant on the Danube in Vienna. Even ecology and design are not mutually exclusive when we take the dynamics of processes into account, as demonstrated by Dehesa del Saler near Valencia or the planning for Duindoornstad near Hoek van Holland.

On the other hand, ever since sewage has been cleaned and rivers are no longer used as canals for waste water, the design of riverbanks tops the hits among urban development projects. Rivers and beaches are being brought back into the urban picture. Barcelona made a firm decision to face the sea and reconquered the horizon by means of promenades and parks. The city has made the decontamination and restoration of the area at the mouths of the rivers Besòs and Llobregat the main focus of the next phase up to 2004. In many cities new residential districts and workplaces, cultural venues, parks and promenades are being set up right next to the water in attractive sites where shipyards and warehouses had spread out only recently. In Copenhagen this applies not only to Christiansbro but also almost the entire harbour district. Similarly in Göteborg and of course in Malmö on the opposite bank of the Öresund. Under the auspices of the International Architecture Exhibition two recreational areas, the Sund promenade and Dania Park, were set up right on the beach. These became astoundingly popular in no time.

Greater London has applied strategic planning to the culturally and historically important Thames landscape for the last decade. Hamburg, Berlin, Lyon, Bordeaux, Lisbon and Porto are re-discovering the value of the rivers that had once contributed decisively to their development. All is flow... and in new parks there are waves rippling in the wind. Whether it be the Parque de Catalunya of Sabadell or Parque Juan Carlos I in Madrid: sizeable ponds and pools allow distant views across the water even inland. Of course water is also bubbling forth on the new squares of Europe. A good example is Place des Terreaux in Lyon: the cars are parked under the paved surface; jets of water shoot up from the grid of square setts. These fountains play on the city's location at the Rhône and Saône. This volume provides a wealth of water-related articles that have appeared in Topos – European Landscape Magazine since 1993.

Hochwasser-Park in Le Pecq

Flood park in Le Pecq

Pascale Hannetel

Im Westen von Paris windet sich die Seine in mehreren Flußschleifen durch die hügelige Region. Auf einem der Hügel thront der Ort Saint-Germain-en-Laye – mit dem berühmten Schloßpark Le Nôtres. Von hier aus blickt man über die Vorstadt-Landschaft bis nach Paris. Unterhalb des Schloßparks liegt Le Pecq, eine kleine Gemeinde, die von der Seine durchflossen wird. Ihre Bewohner hatten bisher nicht viel vom Fluß – Brückenkonstruktionen und -auffahrten verstellten die Ufer. Heute ist die Stadt wieder an ihren Fluß herangerückt. Im südlichen Stadtteil entsteht ein Freizeithafen, im nördlichen erstreckt sich von der Stadtgrenze bis zum Viadukt der RER-Stadtbahn ein neuer Park: der Parc Corbière.

Corbière ist der Name der Insel, die hier einst in der Seine lag. Sie wurde im Laufe der Zeit abgetragen. Übrig blieben acht Hektar Schwemmland zwischen den höhergelegenen Gemüsefeldern und dem Fluß – das Gelände für unseren Park. Wegen der Hochwassergefahr darf diese Ebene nicht bebaut werden. Ein Park aber läßt sich hier anlegen, vorausgesetzt man plant Überschwemmungen ein. Das machte die Stadt uns zur Auflage. Zudem verlangte sie, daß für Aufschüttungen nur Boden verwendet werden sollte, der vor Ort abgetragen wurde. Das neue Relief des Parks sollte die Strömung der Seine natürlich nicht behindern.

The Seine meanders through a region of hills in loops to the west of Paris. On one of these hills lies the town of Saint Germain-en-Laye and Le Nôtre's famous park, which affords views of the landscape of suburbs leading all the way into Paris. Below the park, the small settlement of Le Pecq is to be found, divided into two by the Seine. In recent years, its inhabitants have not had much pleasure from the river, its banks being obstructed by bridges and approach roads. In the meantime, however, the town has drawn closer to its river; a marina is undergoing construction to the south, for example, while a new park now extends from the town's northern perimeter to the viaduct of the RER suburban railway system.

Corbière is the name of the island that was once to be found at this part of the Seine but which has since been washed away, to be replaced by eight hectares of alluvial banks. These banks

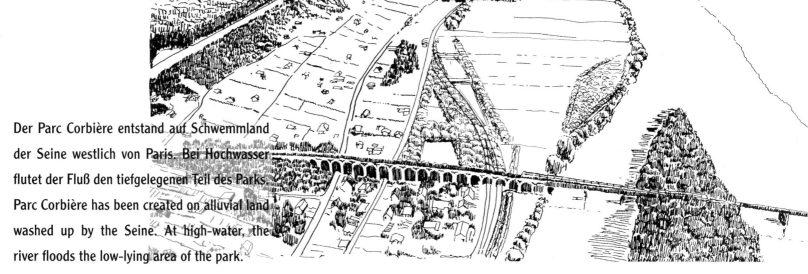

Der Parc Corbière entstand auf Schwemmland der Seine westlich von Paris. Bei Hochwasser flutet der Fluß den tiefgelegenen Teil des Parks

Parc Corbière has been created on alluvial land washed up by the Seine. At high-water, the river floods the low-lying area of the park.

Eine schnurgerade Eichenallee auf dem neugeschaffenen Deich grenzt die geschwungene Straße vom Park ab. Die Bauminsel am Ufer läßt die Umrisse der früheren Flußinsel wiedererstehen.
Skizze: Pascale Hannetel

The straight oak avenue on the new embankment sets off the park from the curving road behind it, while the irregular circle of trees near the river traces the perimeter of the former island.
Sketch: Pascale Hannetel

Auf acht Hektar ungenutztem Schwemmland im Hochwasserberich der Seine entstand ein Park, der für die Gemeinde Le Pecq den Zugang zum Fluß öffnete ohne sie zugleich der Hochwassergefahr auszusetzen.

Created on eight hectares of unused alluvial land where the Seine floods is a park that provided the community of Le Pecq with access to the river without exposing the population to the danger of flooding at the same time.

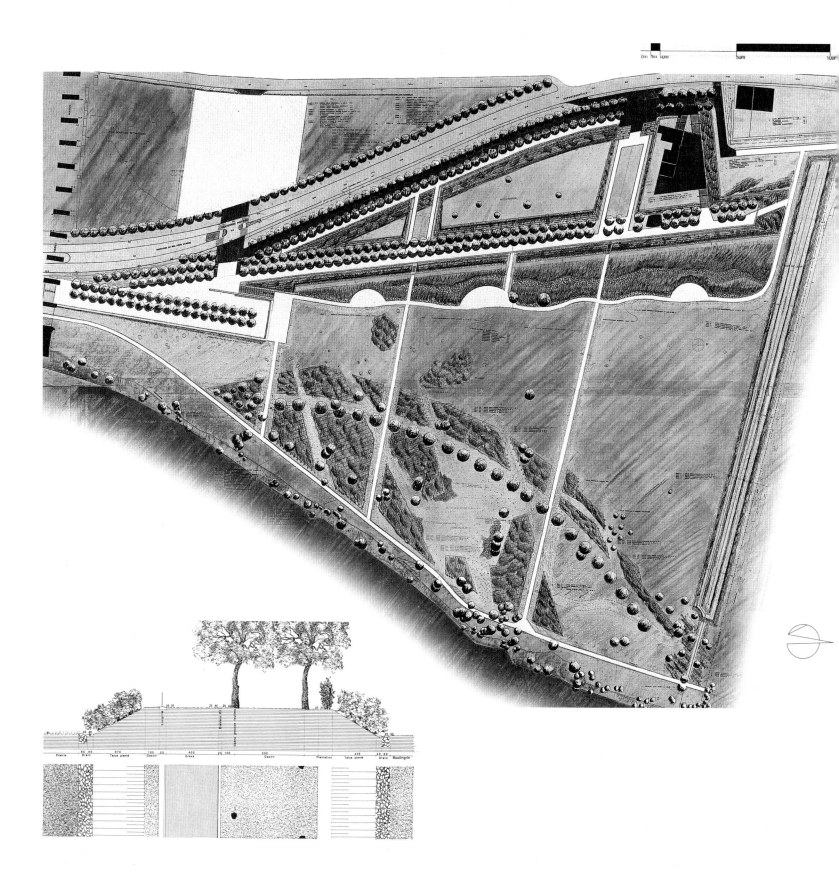

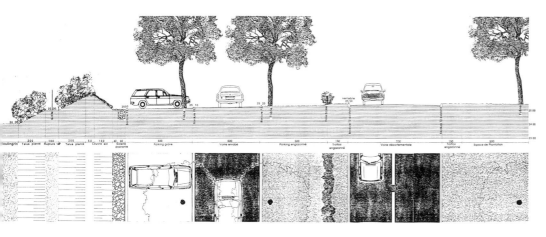

Im Süden betritt man den Parc Corbière durch die Arkaden eines Bahnviadukts. Von der lindenbestandenen Aussichtsplattform eröffnet sich der Blick auf die tiefergelegenen Feuchtwiesen. Sie können überschwemmt werden. Im Osten begrenzen die Silberweiden der Bauminsel den Park, im Westen die Eichenallee auf dem Deich (im Schnitt gegenüber). Treppen leiten von einer geschwungenen Promenade aus befestigtem Sand hinauf. Rasenbewachsene Senken trennen die Eichenallee von der zweispurigen Straße (im Schnitt oben). Die Autos parken entlang einer dritten, baumbestandenen Spur. Statt eines Zaunes begrenzt ein breiter Graben den Park im Norden. Der Zaun ist in den Graben integriert. So bleibt der Blick ins Umland frei.

Parc Corbière is entered from the south through the arches of a railway viaduct. The outlook platform, which is planted with linden trees, provides a view to the wet meadows below, designed with the very likely possibility of flooding in mind. The white willows that recall the former island mark off the park to the east, while the embankment and oak avenue confine it to the west (see cross-section on the opposite page). Steps lead upwards from a curved path of compacted sand. Grass-covered hollows divide the avenue off from the two-lane road (see cross-section above). A third lane dotted with trees is provided for visitor parking. The park is delineated to the north by a fence hidden in a wide trench to provide unobstructed views of the fields beyond.

Unsere Lösung: Wir schufen einen Park mit einem oberen und einem unteren Teil. Der hochgelegene Bereich liegt wie ein Balkon über der Seine, ähnlich dem Schloßpark von Saint Germain-en-Laye. Das Relief des Parks tüftelten wir so aus, daß der obere Teil immer zugänglich bleibt, der untere je nach Wasserstand des Flusses überschwemmt werden kann.

Den oberen Teil des Parks gestalteten wir als großzügige Promenade. Dazu legten wir einen Deich parallel zur Nationalstraße an. Er schirmt den tiefergelegenen Park vom Lärm der Nationalstraße ab. Die Promenade hielten wir bewußt klassisch: als eichenbestandene, langgestreckte Allee mit schlichten Bänken und einem filigranen Metallgeländer, das die Linearität unterstreicht. Zwischen Eichen-Allee und Nationalstraße bildeten wir rasenbedeckte Senken und bepflanzte Böschungen aus.

Von der Allee blicken die Besucher über den tiefergelegenen Teil des Parks, der überschwemmt werden kann. An mehreren Stellen führen kurze Treppen hinunter auf die Flußebene. Formell steht die Ebene im Gegensatz zum oberen Park: Die Wege aus hellem, befestigtem Sand biegen sich sanft, sie folgen dem unregelmäßigen Flußverlauf, winden sich um die vorhandenen Bäume und weiten sich hier und da aus zu Sitz- oder Spielplätzen. In die weite Rasenfläche pflanzten wir feuchtigkeitsliebende Pflanzen: Wei-

are the site of our park, which is named for the island. Due to the danger of flooding, they are naturally unfit for development but are nevertheless suitable for a park, provided the possibility of inundation is taken into account. This last was one of the requirements made of us by the town council. The brief also stipulated that only soil excavated at the site was to be used for the earthworks, and that the riverside contours of the new park were not to obstruct the flow of the Seine.

Our solution was to create a park with an upper and a lower section. The top part lies above the Seine like a terrace, like the park of Saint Germain-en-Laye, and is always to remain accessible, no matter how high the water rises. We designed this area in the form of a generously sized promenade on top of an embankment laid out parallel to the nearby trunk road. The promenade is kept classic in appearance, and consists of a

Parc Corbière, Le Pecq, near Saint Germain-en-Laye
Client: Town of Le Pecq-sur-Seine
Landscape architect: Pascale Hannetel
Collaborators: Anne-Marie Werckle, engineering; Arnaud Yver, architecture and park furniture design; Anne Gaëlle Le Guillanton, landscape architecture assistant
Size: 84,000 square metres
Competition: July 1993
Planning: October 1994 – March 1995; Construction: July 1995 – May 1996
Costs: FRF 6.2 million (park), FRF 102.000 (park furniture)

ong, oak-lined avenue fitted out with simple benches and a filigree balustrade that underscores he linear character of the walkway. Grass-covered hollows and vegetation-covered embankments lie between the oak avenue and the arterial road.

The avenue provides visitors with views of the bottom section of the park, which has been consciously designed with the possibility of flooding n mind. Occasional short flights of steps lead down to the flood plain, which contrasts formally with the top section, featuring curving paths of pale, compacted sand that follow the irregular course of the river to their way around existing trees, leading up occasionally to seating and play areas. We planted hydrophilic species, such as willows, Cornus species and ash trees in the broad swathes of grass, and created groups of trees by removing poplars and leaving old maples where they were growing to articulate the space. At a wide curve of the river, densely planted white willows trace the outer perimeter of the former island, resurrecting it again as an arboreal circle at the edge of the water meadows.

In order to retain the views of the nearby vegetable fields situated a little higher, a broad trench terminates the park on one side. We installed the park fence at the bottom of the trench to ensure that it does not form a visual barrier; this makes the fields seem to be a continuation of the park and creates an illusion of greater space. Moreover, the trench not only serves as the boundary of the park but also collects seepage water and guides it into the Seine. On the opposite side, the park narrows out and ends at the railway viaduct, which is where the entrance gates are to be found – a filigree wrought iron construction fitted into one of the arches.

den, Hartriegel, Eschen. Wir haben alte Ahornbäume erhalten und einige Pappeln gefällt. Die Bäume stehen heute in Gruppen und gliedern so den Freiraum. Am Fluß zeichnen dicht gepflanzte Silberweiden in einem weiten Bogen den Umriß der einstigen Corbière-Insel nach – so lebt sie wieder auf, als Bauminsel in den Feuchtwiesen.

Um den Blick über die benachbarten Gemüsefelder freizuhalten, schließt ein breiter Graben den Park an einer Seite ab. Den Zaun haben wir im Graben versenkt, so daß man ihn nicht sieht. Durch diesen Kniff scheinen die Felder einfach in den Park überzugehen – wir haben optisch an Weite gewonnen. Zudem dient der Graben nicht nur als Parkgrenze, sondern er fängt auch Sickerwasser auf und leitet es in die Seine. An der gegenüberliegenden Seite läuft das Grundstück schmal zu und endet am Stadtbahn-Viadukt. Unter einen seiner Bögen plazierten wir ein filigranes schmiedeeisernes Tor – den Haupteingang des Parks. Eine lindenbestandene Aussichtsplattform ragt in den Park. Gabionenmauern rahmen die Plattform, ein breiter umlaufender Handlauf lädt ein zum Aufstützen.

Unten und oben bilden einen gestalterischen Gegensatz im Parc Corbière. Unten formen Hügel, Baumgruppen und Wege ein bewegtes Relief, oben betonen langgestreckte Parterres, ein filigranes Metallgeländer und Baumreihen die Linearität des neuen Deiches.

Parc Corbière is characterised by the contrast of above and below; above is marked by a long parterre, filigree metal railings and linear rows of trees, and below by the organic forms of hills, groups of trees and pathways.

Park an der Somme, Amiens

The park on the Somme at Amiens

Jacqueline Osty

In April, 1990 the municipality of Amiens launched a competition for the future Saint-Pierre Park. Seven teams were consulted to design a landscaped urban core, emphasizing the potential of the site: the water, the vegetation, and the city. It was also to re-establish the connection between the park and the "hortillonnages", unique local gardens with special features described below. A reception building suited to the activities in a park of twenty hectares was to be planned as well. Our project won the competition.

A design evolved which is concerned with basing the future Saint-Pierre Park in an area in the heart of town and extending it throughout the geography and poetry of the Somme river, while encompassing both the urban setting and the local activities.

A Water Landscape. The Saint-Pierre Park is in the heart of the city of Amiens on a site bound and traversed by the Somme, in a stretch with a very special garden landscape. The Somme is a sinuous river, avoiding obstacles, it winds around them, dividing into multiple arms which cut back into its main bed. The water, shimmering like metal, slow and silent, barely rippling from a gliding barge, here spreads out into ponds and swamps, dividing up the exploited territory. The Somme sketches a veritable labyrinth, like a mane of water with islands everywhere, creating a landscape with plant scenery hovering between land and water.

The plots of land emerging from the water are the result of successive exploitation of the soil. The extraction of peat and the planting of vegetable gardens lead to a peculiar division of the soil into long, narrow plots. They are called "hortillonnages", a name that derives from the Latin

Ein Labyrinth aus Wasserläufen läßt im Stadtpark Saint-Pierre in Amiens die Kulturlandschaft der Somme wiederauferstehen.

The labyrinth of waterways distinguishing the Saint-Pierre Park makes a cultural landscape arise in the heart of Amiens.

ord "hortus", meaning garden. On the banks
f the river, the narrow strips are known as
ours". One "jour" corresponds to the amount
f land that could be plowed in one day. In spite
f being separated from the site of the gardens by
n urban avenue perched atop an embankment,
he Saint-Pierre Park is indissolubly bound to the
omme, whose waters retain the memory and
lentity of place.

The Park. The park, close to the gardens dis-
nguished by their particular tradition of garden-
ng, acquires a certain increased value from the
andscape dimension of the river and the plant
orld intimately connected to it. To recover the
andscape identity was to assure the continuity of
his plant world by installing it in the heart of the
ark and taking advantage of the ecological re-
trictions in the watery and damp environment
f the peat bogs. This web in the shape of the
omme, weaving a net of water, is the major
ompositional element of the park. It relates both
he Rivery and Saint-Pierre ponds, and the gar-
lens and the park to each other. Consisting of
hree waterways winding through the site and
ejoining to blend in one sheet of water, it leads

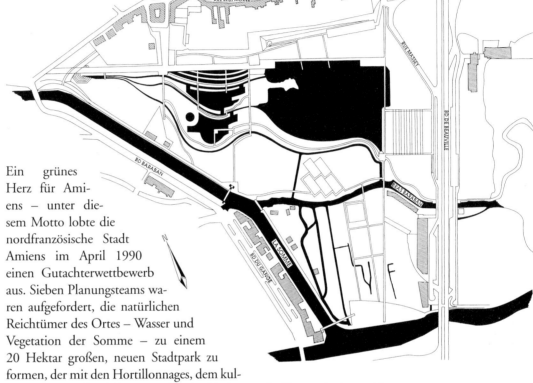

Ein grünes
Herz für Ami-
ens – unter die-
sem Motto lobte die
nordfranzösische Stadt
Amiens im April 1990
einen Gutachterwettbewerb
aus. Sieben Planungsteams waren aufgefordert, die natürlichen
Reichtümer des Ortes – Wasser und
Vegetation der Somme – zu einem
20 Hektar großen, neuen Stadtpark zu
formen, der mit den Hortillonnages, dem kul-
tivierten Sumpfland der Gegend, in Verbindung steht. Für uns bedeutete das,
den Park als ein Stück Kulturlandschaft zu entwerfen, das sich mitten in der
Stadt befindet. Dort, zwischen Einkaufstrubel, lautem Verkehr und städtischer Architektur, sollte man die Geographie und die Poesie der Flußlandschaft erleben können. Unser Projekt erhielt den ersten Preis.

Die Wasserlandschaft. Die Somme streift den neuen Parc Saint-Pierre,
bevor sie am Rande der Stadt in die charakteristische Landschaft der Hortillonnages übergeht, wo sie sich in vielfältige Nebenarme aufgliedert, in
ihr Hauptbett zurückkehrt, sich wieder verzweigt. Kaum von Schiffen
durchzogen, fließt das Wasser still und langsam dahin, gleißend wie Metall,
weitet sich hier zu Teichen und schafft dort Feuchtgebiete. Bündel von
Wasseradern mit Tausenden von Inseln bringen eine zwischen Wasser und
Land schwebende Landschaft hervor. Das bewirtschaftete Land, kaum über
dem Wasserspiegel, liegt dazwischen in einer Ordnung, die ihm das Laby-

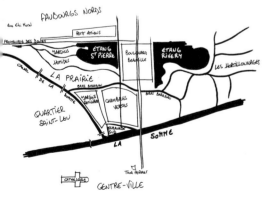

ber zwei Achsen erschließt
ich der Park Saint-Pierre in
miens. Die Nord-Süd-Rich-
ung verbindet das Stadt-
entrum mit der Nordstadt.
ie »Promenade des Jours«
olgt dem Verlauf der feinen
Vasserarme, die sich von
Vesten nach Osten durch den
ark ziehen. Sie münden in
inen See und gehen schließ-
ch in das bewirtschaftete
lortillonnages-Land über.

Two long paths open up Park
Saint-Pierre to visitors, with
the north-south axis linking
downtown Amiens with the
northern regions of the city.
The west-east axis is formed
by the Promenade des Jours,
accompanied by a fine system
of tributaries that leads
through the park to a lake
and from there to the hortillonnages.

rinth des Flusses diktierte. Lange, schmale Parzellen sind hier sukzessive entstanden, auf denen Torf gestochen und Obst und Gemüse gezogen wurde. Ihr Name – Hortillonnages – leitet sich vom lateinischen »hortus«, Garten, ab – zu Recht: Diese Landschaft ist ein Garten.

Der Park. Ein Stadtboulevard auf einem acht Meter hohen Damm trennt den Parc Saint-Pierre vom eigentlichen Flußlauf der Somme. Jedoch gelang es uns, nach dem Bild der Somme ein Wassergespinst anzulegen und den Park zu einer eigenen Wasserlandschaft werden zu lassen. Das Gewässernetz verbindet die Teiche Rivery und Saint-Pierre, die Hortillonnages und den Park miteinander. Durch den Park schlängeln sich drei Wasserbänder und vereinigen sich am Ende in einer weiten Wasserfläche.

Folgt man den Wasserläufen, gelangt man in die verschiedenen Parkbereiche. Am Anfang öffnet sich eine weite Rasenfläche der Stadtsilhouette. Die anschließenden kleinteiligen Gärten erinnern mit ihrer Feuchtvegetation an die Hortillonnages und geben dem Besucher das Gefühl, zwischen

the way to the interior of Saint-Pierre Park an organizes the division of spaces.

These spaces consist of the following. Th meadow provides wide, open areas directing th view towards the city's horizons and welcomin festivities and gatherings. The watery garden dense, varied, more intimate, and evoking th "hortillonnages", repeat the sensation of hoverin between the sky and the water. The first poc along a promenade is very designed and plante with water-lilies. Two other pools, lower dowr reintroduce a swamp to the heart of the park domesticated with riverside vegetation such a willows, poplars, reeds, and aquatic plants. Th Saint-Pierre pond's contours are repeated in th

Die platanengesäumte »Promenade des Jours« beginnt im Westen des Stadtparks Saint-Pierre in Amiens. 620 Meter lang, geleitet sie die Besucher durch die verschiedenen Bereiche des Parks. Vorbei an geometrischen Seerosen-Bassins, öffnet sich der Blick zur Kathedrale. Ein Feuchtgebiet mit Auenvegetation schließt sich an.

The plane-lined 620-metre-long Promenade des Jours begins at the western end of Park Saint-Pierre in Amiens and leads visitors past geometric water-lily pools, where it opens up to a view of the distant cathedral, and passes on by a wetland habitat with carr vegetation.

two broad promenades of the park and the rose trellis. It remains the heart, the subconscious of the place and of the city. Its calm surface reflects the famous gothic cathedral, the suburbs, and the vegetation of the park.

The City. Clearly marked by the river, the Saint-Pierre Park nevertheless comprises part of the city. It is a hinge, as it were, between various districts. It was by working on a kind of stitching, on scars, and on their tension that we developed the urban dimension of the park. The interface between the park and the city was determined individually according to the characteristics of each boundary. The city borders on the park in the north in the shape of compartments with suburban houses, thus extending the typology of the garden plots. In the west is the tow-path along the canal of the Somme, underlined by the rows of linden trees planted along it. In the south an urban plaza faces downtown.

Two large compositional axes, the promenade of the "jours" gardens and the north-south avenue, provide the scale for the area. The promenade, an urban line of mineral and light, 620 metres long, crosses the site from east to west. It begins in Place Bélidor with a belvedere overhanging the sheet of water, as if engraved into the labyrinth. It continues between the pools and the

Wasser und Himmel zu spazieren. Ein abgezirkeltes Seerosen-Bassin erstreckt sich am Rand des Spazierwegs. Zwei tiefer liegende Bassins im Zentrum des Parks schaffen eine Art Feuchtgebiet mit einer Auenvegetation aus Weiden, Pappeln, Erlen und Wasserpflanzen. Den Saint-Pierre-Teich schließlich umfassen zwei breite Promenaden. An seinem Rand wächst Röhricht und auf seiner glatten Oberfläche spiegeln sich Kathedrale, Häuserfassaden und Vegetation. Er bildet den wahren Kern des Parks, vielleicht sogar der Stadt, und hält den Geist des Ortes in sich bewahrt.

Die Stadt. Der Landschaft einbeschrieben, ist der Parc Saint-Pierre dennoch Teil der Stadt, gleichsam ein Scharnier zwischen den verschiedenen Stadtteilen. An den Übergängen von Stadt zu Park haben wir lange herumgefeilt, um die städtische Dimension des Parks herauszubilden. Im Norden schaffen schmale Parkparzellen den Übergang zu den Gärten der Vorstadthäuser, im Westen nimmt ein Treidelpfad die Linie des lindengesäumten Somme-Kanals auf, und im Süden vermittelt eine Esplanade zwischen dem Parc Saint-Pierre und der Innenstadt.

Zwei große Achsen, eine in Nord-Süd-Richtung, die andere, die von Ost nach West verlaufende »Promenade des Jours«, führen durch den Park. Das 620 Meter lange Band der »Promenade des Jours« beginnt am Place Bélidor, betont durch einen Aussichtsturm im Labyrinth der mäandrierenden Wasserläufe. Zwischen Bassins und Spielbereichen führt die Promenade auf den See zu und endet an der Gabelung zweier Uferwege. Auf der geneigten, im Norden gelegenen Rasenanlage strecken sich Hecken, Alleen und Obstbaumreihen der Promenade entgegen. Platanen flankieren den mit Marmorbruch gepflasterten Gehweg auf der einen Seite, auf der anderen reihen sich eigens entworfene Stadtmöbel aus Metall und Holz auf.

Die platanenbestandene Esplanade am Südende des Parks zeigt ein ähnliches Vokabular wie die Promenade. Hier werden über einen 60 Meter langen Metallsteg der Stadtteil Saint-Leu und die Kathedrale von Amiens an den Park angeschlossen. In die Landschaft der Hortillonnages führt ein weiterer Metallsteg, der am Brückenbauwerk des Boulevard Beauville verankert ist. Die Böschungen des Boulevard bestehen aus Rasenterrassen, die zum Teich hin abfallen. Ginkgos rahmen den Blick zur Kathedrale.

Seit der Eröffnung entwickelt sich der Park weiter, die Vegetation gedeiht. Auch die Einwohner von Amiens eignen sich seine verschiedenen Bereiche an. Sie schwimmen im See und waten im Schlamm der Bassins – was nicht vorgesehen war, aber den Park um so attraktiver macht.

playgrounds, and descends to water-level along the pond between two docks. On the sloping lawn, the hedges and avenues, as well as the rows of fruit trees extend the shape of the garden plots towards the promenade. Covered with reconstituted marble, ground and spread as gravel or laid out in patterns, the promenade is emphasized by a row of plane trees on one side and a metal and wood structure on the other. The latter was created especially for the Saint-Pierre Park by the architects Maurer & Orsi.

The formal vocabulary of this promenade is taken up in the treatment of the plaza with a mall of plane trees situated in the south of the park facing the city. It admits the elevated metal passage-way, sixty metres long, providing access to the park from the Saint Leu district to the North and the cathedral of Amiens.

The connection between the "hortillonnages" and the park is assured by an elevated metal passage-way, suspended like a drawbridge from the bridge of the boulevard overhanging the park, and by the special structure placed along this boulevard. The embankments of the boulevard are furnished with a series of lawn terraces leading to the pond. The ginkgos planted here frame the view of the cathedral.

Since the opening of the park in July 1994, the residents of Amiens have begun to appropriate the various areas, sometimes changing the usage. They bathe and wade in the pools, creating new activities. Plant life is gently settling in to its growth. The site of the Saint-Pierre pond, a composite place invested with multiple uses, has today become the Saint-Pierre Park, with its traditions preserved in the heart of a redesigned water landscape.

Client: City of Amiens
Design: Jacqueline Osty, landscape architect;
Antoine Calix, assistant; Maurer & Orsi, architects;
Yannick Jegado, assistant
Size: 20 hectares
Competition: 1990
Construction period: 1992–1994
Costs: 45 million Francs

Im Osten des Parks Saint-Pierre flankieren geneigte Rasenflächen die »Promenade des Jours«. Hecken, Alleen und Obstbaumreihen strecken sich ihr entgegen. Alle Wasserläufe des Parks entspringen aus einer Quelle inmitten eines geometrischen Motivs am westlichen Ende der Promenade. Der See bildet den Kern des Parks, vielleicht sogar der Stadt, und hält den Geist des Ortes in sich bewahrt.

Sloping areas of grass with hedges, avenues of trees and rows of fruit trees flank the Promenade des Jours at the eastern end of Park Saint-Pierre. All the watercourses in the park arise at a spring set in a geometric pattern of stones at the Promenade's western end. The lake they empty into is the heart of the park, if not of the whole city, and as such is an expression of the spirit of Amiens.

Erlebnisse im Park Juan Carlos I. in Madrid

Events at Juan Carlos I Park in Madrid

Susana Canogar

Unzweifelhaft gehört der Park Juan Carlos I. zu den bedeutendsten zeitgenössischen Parks im Raum Madrid. Er ist Teil der ambitionierten Stadtplanung für das Gebiet Campo de las Naciones, das ungefähr vier Millionen Quadratmeter umfaßt. Der Park nimmt etwa die Hälfte davon ein. Das Gelände liegt günstig am östlichen Stadtrand Madrids in der Nähe des Flughafens Barajas – hier befindet sich auch die neue Messe mit einem Dienstleistungszentrum, das ein Hotel, mehrere Bürogebäude und das neue, von Ricardo Bofill entworfene Kongreßzentrum umfaßt.

Der Park wurde 1992 eröffnet, in einem für Spanien symbolträchtigen Jahr. Mehrere internationale Veranstaltungen fanden damals statt: die Weltausstellung in Sevilla und die Olympischen Spiele in Barcelona; Madrid beging das nicht ganz so prachtvolle Jahr als europäische Kulturhauptstadt. Der Park war wohl der größte Beitrag zu dieser Feier. Anfänglich war das Presseecho nicht allzu gut. Damals herrschte Dürre in Spanien, und die endlosen Rasenflächen und Wasseranlagen schienen im Gegensatz zu den Beschränkungen im Wasserverbrauch zu stehen, die

Ende gut, alles gut! Der anfangs heftig kritisierte Park ist zum beliebten Freizeitziel für die Bewohner Madrids geworden.

All's well that ends well: The initially much-criticised park has become a favourite recreation place for the inhabitants of Madrid.

One of the most significant public parks buil recently in the Madrid area is undoubtedl Parque Juan Carlos I, which occupies approxima tely half of an ambitious urban planning schem some 4 million square meters in size. Known a the Campo de las Naciones, the scheme is situat ed between the eastern edge of Madrid and th Barajas airport, an ideal location for the city's ne exhibition grounds and service area, which in cludes hotels, office buildings and the new pos modern congress centre designed by Ricardo Bofil

The park was inaugurated in 1992, a sym bolic time for Spain because of diverse interna tional events taking place in the country tha year, namely the Universal Exhibition in Sevill the Olympic Games in Barcelona and Madrid less glamorous tenure as the Cultural Capital o Europe. The park was probably the largest con tribution to this latter celebration. Initial reac tions in the press were not exactly favourable Spain was suffering a severe drought at the tim and the endless lawns and extensive wate features seemed a contradiction to the water re strictions being imposed on the citizens. Reac tions from professionals in the field were no les critical, questioning the design of the park and it appropriateness as an urban park in an area tha is relatively inaccessible for the inhabitants o Madrid. Six years have since gone by, and th thousands of visitors that crowd the park eac weekend (35,000 were recorded recently) an jam the entrances due to insufficient parking fa cilities have proven the sceptics wrong.

Emilio Esteras and José Luis Esteban, a team of architects now working for the City of Madrid were commissioned to design the park. The found themselves faced with a blighted site tha was being used as an illegal dump but which also featured the remnants of a century-old olive grove, which they duly incorporated into their design. The site plan can be described as a gigantic circle or ring intersected by a water feature, with the circle (which contains the main areas of the park) representing the age-old theme of enclosure. In the design process, the architects drew on abstract art (the work of the Constructivist movement comes to mind) to create an overlay of different grids and planes, both conceptual and physical, as expressed by the superimposition of the existing grid of olive trees with that of new plantings, pedestrian paths crossed by vehicular tracks and water surfaces bridged by aerial paths.

The park is conceived as an urban experiment in search of the "ideal city", in which architecture is explored in the design of pavilions, landmarks, plazas, pergolas and a greenhouse currently under construction. It also contains references to garden history which are especially amusing to those from the profession, such as a labyrinth, several pyramids and a bridge with surprise showers of water reminiscent of Renaissance giochi d'acqua.

While the layout of the park can be grasped from its high points, this is practically impossible at ground level because of its sheer size. Indeed, given the park's proximity to the airport, the project manifesto talks of allotting significance to the way it is seen from the air, and it is thus a shame that aircraft making their way to Madrid's Barajas airport generally do not pass over the park.

The park makes a significant cultural contribution in that it shelters a number of sculptures, featuring the work of 16 internationally noted

den Bürgern von Madrid auferlegt worden waren. Nicht weniger kritisch äußerten sich die Fachleute zu diesem Park. Sie bezweifelten die Angemessenheit der Gestaltung und die Lage – in einer schlecht erreichbaren Gegend von Madrid. Nun sind sechs Jahre vergangen, und Tausende von Besuchern drängen an den Wochenenden in den Park. Kürzlich wurden an einem einzigen Wochenende 35 000 Besucher gezählt, und die Staus an den Eingängen, die durch ungenügende Parkplätze verursacht werden, widerlegen die Skeptiker.

Der Zuschlag für die Gestaltung des Parks ging an Emilio Esteras und José Luis Esteban, zwei Architekten, die heute im Stadtplanungsamt Madrid arbeiten. Sie fanden eine abgeräumte Brachfläche, die als illegale Müllkippe genutzt wurde, aber auch die Überreste eines alten Olivenhains, den sie in die Gestaltung einbezogen. Organisiert ist das Gelände durch einen riesigen Ring, der die wichtigsten Bereiche des Parks umschließt und symbolisch auf das uralte Thema der Umfriedung anspielt. Durchschnitten wird er von einem quer durch das Gelände laufenden Wassergraben. Im Gestaltungsprozeß ließen sich die Architekten von abstrakter Kunst inspirieren – man denkt an die Werke der Konstruktivisten – und es entstanden überlappende Raster und Ebenen, im Konzept wie in der Wirklichkeit. Augenfällig werden sie durch die Gegenüberstellung des Rasters der vorhan-

Zur beliebtesten Parkanlage Madrids avancierte mittlerweile der Park Juan Carlos I., am östlichen Stadtrand gelegen. Er wurde 1992 eröffnet, als Madrid das Jahr der europäischen Kulturhauptstadt feierte. Die Architekten Emilio Esteras und José Luis Esteban dachten sich den Park als urbanes Experiment, inspiriert von der abstrakten Kunst.

Parque Juan Carlos I, which is located at the east of Madrid, has become one of the city's favourite green spaces since its inauguration in 1992, when Madrid was the European Cultural Capital. Abstract art inspired the design put forward by the architects Emilio Esteras and José Luis Esteban.

19

denen Ölbäume mit dem der neuen Pflanzungen, durch Fußgängerwege, die von Fahrwegen gekreuzt und durch Wasserflächen, die von Stegen überbrückt werden.

Der Park ist als urbanes Experiment gedacht, auf der Suche nach der »idealen Stadt«: Die Möglichkeiten der Architektur werden ausgereizt durch die Gestaltung der Pavillons, der Aussichtspunkte, der Platzflächen, der Pergolen und den im Bau befindlichen Wintergarten. Auf dem Weg durch den Park finden die Besucher auch Anspielungen auf historische Gärten – was besonders Fachleute amüsieren wird. Erwähnenswert sind das Labyrinth, eine »Regenbrücke« mit Wasserspielen wie in der Renaissance, mehrere Pyramiden, terrassierte Hügel. Von den Aussichtspunkten aus überblicken die Besucher allmählich die Ordnung der Fläche, was schon wegen der schieren Größe des Parks ansonsten nicht möglich ist. Nicht umsonst erwähnt der Erläuterungsbericht für den Park die Bedeutung der Vogelschau: Beim Anflug auf den nahegelegenen Flughafen Madrids erhalten Flugreisende einen ersten Willkommensgruß. Pech auch, daß die meisten Flugzeuge den Park vor der Landung nicht überqueren!

Einer der wichtigsten Beiträge des Parks zum Kulturleben ist seine Funktion als Skulpturengarten. Werke von 16 international bekannten Künstlern sind zu sehen. Die meisten Künstler waren Teilnehmer des »International Symposium of Open Air Sculpture«, einer Veranstaltung im Rahmen des Kulturhauptstadt-Jahres. Unter ihnen firmieren Cruz Díez, Miguel Berrocal, Amadeo Gabino, Jorge du Bon und Dani Karavan. Einige Skulpturen wurden später dieser Sammlung zugefügt – was die Frage aufwirft, wie viele noch aufgestellt werden können, ohne den Park zu überfüllen.

Von den soeben beschriebenen Highlights abgesehen gibt es noch eine besondere Art der Nutzung, die den Charakter des Parks verstehen hilft: Aufgrund seiner ausgedehnten Asphalt- und Pflasterwege ist er zum Lieblingstummelplatz für Radfahrer und Skater geworden. Tatsächlich erlebt man ihn besser aus der Perspektive eines Radfahrers als aus der eines Fußgängers. Der Park besitzt den groben Rhythmus einer Landschaft, die man aus der Bewegung heraus wahrnehmen sollte, im Gegensatz zu den feinen Arrangements eines Gartens, der sich eher von einer Bank aus genießen läßt. So ist dieser Park der geeignete Rahmen für die Erholungswünsche einer schnellebigen Gesellschaft.

Der *Jardín de las Tres Culturas* ist einer der Bereiche in dem Park, in denen die Besucher zur Ruhe kommen können. Er soll an die außergewöhn-

artists, most of whom participated in the International Symposium of Open Air Sculpture organised as part of the European Cultural Capital celebrations. These include Cruz Díez, Miguel Berrocal, Amadeo Gabino, Jorge du Bon and Dani Karavan. Additions have been made to the collection since, raising the issue of how many more sculptures can be incorporated without cluttering the park.

Because of its endless circuit of paved and asphalted paths, the park is popular among cyclers and skaters, and is better appreciated from the viewpoint of a bicycle than on foot, having the rhythm of a landscape designed to be perceived in motion rather than from a park bench. In this respect, it is a suitable setting for the form of recreation favoured by a fast-paced society.

However, it also features areas that invite the visitor to slow down, such as the *Jardín de las Tres Culturas*, which commemorates the extraordinary coexistence of the Christian, Jewish and Muslim cultures in Spain before the expulsion of the Moors and the Jews. The author and landscape architect Myriam Silber sought to create a public space with a commendable message of tolerance, an important gesture in a world still troubled by wars and ethnic conflicts. The garden is full of symbols, such as the circle, the square and the cross, and a "paradise" is located on a hillock, and has to be reached along a long boardwalk and by passing through a gateway that represents the Tree of Life. From the top of this hillock, which is planted evocatively with palm trees, an excellent view can be had of the three theme gardens, namely the Christian "Cloister of Ballads", the Islamic "Garden of Delights" and the Jewish "Grove of Pomegranates". Although

PARQUE OLIVAR DE LA HINOJOSA

Parque Juan Carlos I, Campo de las Naciones, Madrid
Client: City of Madrid and Empresa Municipal Campo de las Naciones, S.A.
Architects: Emilio Esteras and José Luis Esteban
Size: 220 hectares
Construction: October 1989 – March 1992
Cost: ESP 7,000 million

ike the rest of the park, the Three-Culture Garden is already suffering from some deterioration, it provokes conversation among visitors.

A colourful activity which is unique to this park is kite flying. On approaching it on weekends, a myriad of kites of all colours and shapes can be seen dancing in the sky, and it is the site of regular events held by a local kiting association. Other activities that occur seasonally or periodically are catamaran rides in the canals, fishing competitions and boat modelling. The amphitheatre, an austere concrete structure with seating for 8,000 spectators, is located outside the main ring of the park, and is mainly used on summer nights for a popular light-and-sound-show. These activities all form part of a strategy to increase use and thus gain revenue for maintenance, and it is probable that more events and activities will be sponsored in the future.

One of the drawbacks would seem to be the lack of playgrounds for children. Admittedly, one area has been equipped with good-quality play facilities, but given the park's original intention to be an urban experiment, it could have contributed more imaginative playgrounds. This brings to mind some of Noguchi's wonderful proposals for contoured play spaces.

On the whole, the Juan Carlos I Park is a successful park experience. It caters to the new leisure demands of the population and features cultural symbols for those who want to see them. It is sufficiently open-ended to allow for evolution in recreational trends and act as a framework for human activity.

Time will also play a beneficial role as the trees begin to mature and the vegetation comes to share a leading role with the hardscape.

liche Koexistenz dreier Kulturen in Spanien erinnern – in den Jahrhunderten, bevor die Mauren und Juden vertrieben wurden: der christlichen, der jüdischen und der islamischen. Die Landschaftsarchitektin des Gartens, Myriam Silber, wollte einen öffentlichen Raum schaffen, der einen Appell an die Toleranz ausstrahlt – eine Botschaft, die nottut in einer immer noch von Kriegen und Zwistigkeiten zwischen den Volksgruppen verstörten Welt. Der Garten ist voller symbolischer Gesten: einem Kreis, einem Quadrat, einem Kreuz. Das »Paradies« ist auf einem Hügelchen zu finden, erschlossen über einen langen Holzsteg mit einem Tor, das den Baum des Lebens darstellt. Von diesem erhöhten Punkt aus, stimmungsvoll mit Palmen bepflanzt, genießen die Besucher den Blick über die drei Themengärten: das christliche »Balladenkloster«, den islamischen »Garten der Lüste« und den jüdischen »Granatapfel-Hain«. Leider fehlt dem Garten – wie überhaupt dem Park – ein wenig mehr Pflege, doch er stimuliert bei den Besuchern Gespräche über die drei Kulturen.

Schon auf dem Weg zum Park sieht man an Wochenenden unzählige Drachen in allen Farben und Formen am Himmel. Der Verein der Drachenfreunde trifft sich hier regelmäßig. Andere Events finden je nach Jahreszeit oder sporadisch statt, wie etwa das Floßfahren auf den Kanälen, das Wettfischen oder das Modellboot-Fahren. Außerhalb des Park-Rings liegt ein Amphitheater, eine strenge Betonkonstruktion mit Plätzen für 8 000 Zuschauer. Es wird in Sommernächten für eine beliebte Licht- und Ton-Schau genutzt. Diese Events sind Teil einer Strategie, um mit steigenden Besucherzahlen auch mehr Geld für die Pflege des Parks einzutreiben. Möglicherweise werden deshalb künftig noch mehr Veranstaltungen und Spektakel stattfinden.

Eine der Schattenseiten dieses Parks ist sicher der Mangel an Angeboten für das Kinderspiel. Ein einziger Spielbereich verfügt über Geräte in guter Qualität, aber es wären in diesem Park weit phantasievollere Spielanlagen möglich gewesen – im Sinne des beabsichtigten Idealstadt-Experiments.

Insgesamt ist der Park Juan Carlos I. eine erfolgreiche Anlage. Er geht auf die neuen Freizeitansprüche der Bevölkerung ein und bietet gleichzeitig mit seinen eingestreuten, eher kulturell geprägten Symbolen etwas für die Schaulust. Er ist hinreichend offen, um neue Trends in der Erholung aufzunehmen. Auch sein Erscheinungsbild wird sich noch wandeln, da die jungen Bäume allmählich ein Blätterdach entwickeln und ein Gegengewicht zu den harten Bodenbelägen bilden.

Der Park bietet für jeden etwas. Radfahrer und Skater nutzen die Asphaltwege, Kunstinteressierte erfreuen sich an den zahlreichen Skulpturen. Zur Ruhe kommen können die Besucher im Jardín de las Tres Culturas, der symbolisch an das friedliche Zusammenleben dreier Kulturen – der christlichen, jüdischen und islamischen – erinnert. Elemente historischer Gärten wie Labyrinthe, Wasserspiele, Pyramiden, Aussichtspunkte gestalten den Aufenthalt spannend und unterhaltsam.

The park has something for everyone. Cyclists and skaters frequent the asphalted paths, the numerous sculptures find the interest of art aficionados and historical garden elements, such as a labyrinth, water jokes, pyramids and a ziggurat, provide an entertaining and interesting touch. A quieter area is to be found at the Jardín de las Tres Culturas, which uses symbolic gestures to recall the peaceful co-existence of Christianity, Islam and Judaism.

Eine neue Uferpromenade für Christianshavn, Kopenhagen

Quayside solution in Christianshavn, Copenhagen

Sven-Ingvar Andersson

Christianshavn blickt auf eine historisch bedeutsame, aber auch wechselvolle Vergangenheit zurück: Auf dem Sund zwischen Seeland und der Insel Amager gelegen, wurde das heute zu Kopenhagen gehörende Viertel 1620 von Christian IV. zunächst als eigenständige Ansiedlung gegründet. Das Besondere daran war, dass sie bereits damals innerhalb der Stadtbefestigung Kopenhagens lag und dennoch unabhängig war. Im Laufe der Jahrhunderte entwickelte sich Christianshavn zu einem wichtigen Handelszentrum. Die Einwohnerzahl nahm zu, der Ort wuchs und entwickelte sich zu einer reichen und blühenden, vom Schiffsbau geprägten Stadt. Heute ist Christiansbro eines von vielen Vierteln in der Hauptstadt Dänemarks. Bis um 1970 herum war es durch die Schwerindustrie geprägt, die sich um die Christiansbro Schiffswerft, übrigens die größte Dänemarks, herum angesiedelt hatte. Rußgeschwärzte, fast verfallene Gebäude, elende und erbärmliche Slums, schmutzig und verwahrlost, kennzeichneten den Stadtteil. Hinzu kam der Lärm der zahlreichen Fabriken und Manufakturen.

Heute befindet sich Christiansbro im Umbruch – verursacht zum einen durch den Strukturwandel in der Industrie, der viele Flächen brachfallen lässt, zum anderen aber auch wegen des beachtlichen finanziellen Interesses, das diesen in den zentralen Hafenbecken freiwerdenden Flächen entgegengebracht wird. Alte Gebäude werden restauriert, neue entstehen und Christianshavn entwickelt sich wieder zu einer der besseren und geschätzten Adressen Kopenhagens, die es bereits im 18. Jahrhundert einmal gewesen war. Ermöglicht wurde diese Entwicklung durch ein städtisches Erneuerungsprogramm, das in den späten sechziger Jahren angestoßen wurde und ganz bewusst der Größe und Höhe, also den senkrechten Dimensionen der am Wasser liegenden Speicherhäuser und Docks Rechnung trägt.

Die neue Hauptgeschäftsstelle der Uni-Bank, bestehend aus vier Gebäudekomplexen, greift eben diese Höhenentwicklung auf. Henning Larsen gewann mit seinem Entwurf 1995 den Wettbewerb und bereits im Jahr 1999 konnten die Bauarbeiten abgeschlossen werden. Der Entwurf ist gekennzeichnet durch eine rationale architektonische Formensprache, die dem klassisch modernistischen Stil entspricht, die den Architekten Larsen auszeichnet. Doch ungeachtet dieses rationalen Ansatzes mündet der Entwurf in einem Element, das zum einen aus den Vorgaben des

Weiden und Buchsbaumhecken beleben die Innenhöfe einer Bank. Parallel zum Kai verlaufen Granitbänder und Wassertreppen.

Willows and box hedges wind their way through the courts at Uni-Bank, while straight granite strips and water steps run parallel to the quay.

Christianshavn, which is located on th Sound between Zealand and the island of Am ager, was founded in 1620 as an independen town by Christian IV within the circular fortifi cations of Copenhagen. The new town under went periods of growth combined with trade and shipbuilding, and later became a district o Copenhagen. Until 1970 or thereabouts, it wa dominated by heavy industry surrounding th Christiansbro shipyard – the largest in Denmar – and was characterised by a noisy environment smoke-stained buildings in a state of decay, and picturesque but squalid slums.

Today, Christiansbro is marked by radica change caused by the relocation of industry and considerable financial interest in the central por areas. Old buildings are being restored, new one are being built, and Christianshavn is again be coming the kind of highly estimated address i once was in the 18th century. This is due in par to an urban renewal scheme initiated in the late sixties, which echoed the perpendicular arrange ment of waterside storehouses and docks.

A similar arrangement also applies to the fou wings that constitute the new head office of th Uni-Bank. The respective competition held ir 1995 resulted in a design by Henning Larsen and construction work was completed in 1999 The rational office architecture is in the con trolled, classic modernistic style typical of Larsen and has a outstanding finish that was a require ment of the client while also being a Larsen trade mark. Despite the rational approach, the head of fice includes a lofty entrance hall that extends upwards over four stories, and features post-mod ern decoration in the form of copper-faced stee frames on the harbour-side facades.

Der rationalen architektonischen Formensprache wider-
setzen sich die niedrigen
Buchshecken, die zur Promenade zu drängeln scheinen.
Die Höfe des Verwaltungsbaus
öffnen sich nur zum Wasser.

Offsetting the rational architectural formal idiom are the
low boxwood hedges that
seem to urge us to go for a
walk. The courtyards of the
administration building open
only towards the water.

Die Gebäudekomplexe der Bank in Christiansbro sind so ausgerichtet wie die alten Lagerhäuser, die hier früher standen. Sie verbinden das Hafenareal mit der Eigtvedkirche. Um die Hafennähe auch in einem Hof zu demonstrieren, wurde eine Treppenanlage ersonnen, deren Granitstufen in gleichem Abstand von zwei Seiten zu einem Wasserbecken führen. Diese Wassertreppe unterstreicht, das war der Wunsch des Architekten, den leichten Charakter der Gebäude. Chatsworth Garden mit seinen Wassertreppen stand Pate für diese Entwurfsidee.

The buildings of the bank complex at Christiansbro are lined up like the old warehouses that once stood at the site, and flank the street opposite St. Eigtved church and the rest of the old docks quarter. The architects wanted the buildings to create the impression of rising directly from the water. In one of them, a sheet of water is approached on two different sides by steps placed at the same intervals as dark granite strips let into the paving. The cascades at Chatsworth Garden inspired this solution.

Klienten resultiert, zugleich aber auch ein Markenzeichen von Larsen ist: eine emporragende Eingangshalle, die sich bis in das vierte Stockwerk erstreckt und zusätzlich durch kupferüberzogene Stahlrahmen an der zum Hafen gerichteten Fassade betont wird.

Die vier neuen Gebäudekomplexe der Uni-Bank sind unterirdisch über eine Tiefgarage miteinander verbunden. Ein aus Glas gestalteter Übergang im dritten Stockwerk verbindet sie auch oberirdisch miteinander. Zwei ältere Gebäude weiter im Südwesten werden durch ein großes Gebäude verknüpft, das unmittelbar gegenüber der Kirche St. Eigtved (1755 erbaut) und den übrigen Fragmenten des alten Viertels liegt. Aber genau diese historischen Überreste, die die einstige städtische Situation widerspiegeln, waren bei der Gestaltung der Freiräume von elementarer Bedeutung.

Wie St. Petersburg ist Christianshavn vollkommen eben. Unter Anleitung von holländischen Ingenieuren war das Viertel im 17. Jahrhundert auf einem sumpfigen Strand errichtet worden. Nachdem wir mit der Gestaltung der Freiflächen der Uni-Bank beauftragt worden waren, begannen wir zunächst damit, die im Zuge der Bauarbeiten neu angelegten Straßen, Fußgängerbereiche, Wasserbecken und die Uferpromenade mit Granitbelag zu pflastern, so wie es die Tradition dieses Ortes vorgibt. Dabei überwiegen jedoch die Bereiche, in denen kleine Pflastersteine verwendet wurden. Wir wählten aus China importierten Granit, weil er die Farbe der Sandsteingebäude aufnimmt. Bänder aus dunklem finnischen Granit setzen einen Kontrast. Sie wurden in Abständen von sieben Metern parallel zum Ufer verlegt, aber in einem geringfügigen Winkel zu den Gebäuden. Die Granitbänder, die bis zu 300 Meter lang sind, mussten in absolut gerader Linie verlegt werden, um zu vermeiden, dass den Passanten schwindlig wird. Diese Präzision machte es jedoch notwendig, die Flächen zwischen den Bändern leicht abzuschrägen, um den sonst ebenen Boden zu entwässern. Der beabsichtigte horizontale Effekt kann deshalb längs

The four new wings are connected by an underground parking garage and a third-storey glass tube passage, while two older wings are linked by a full-size building that flanks the street opposite St. Eigtved church from 1755 and the rest of the old quarter. These details go to show that the urban situation was of vital importance in detailing the open spaces.

The greater district of Christianshavn is absolutely flat, and like St. Petersburg, was built on a swampy seashore with the help of Dutch engineers acting as consultants. Asked to design the open spaces at the bank, we paved the new roads, pedestrian areas, basins and quays in granite in the tradition of the locality, whereby areas with small paving stones predominate. The granite itself was chosen to echo the colour of the sandstone buildings, and was imported from China. In contrast to the light-coloured paving, strips of dark Finnish granite run throughout at seven-meter intervals, laid parallel to the quay but at a slight angle to the buildings. The strips, which are up to 300 metres in length, had to be laid in an absolutely straight line to prevent people from feeling seasick. This need for precision made it

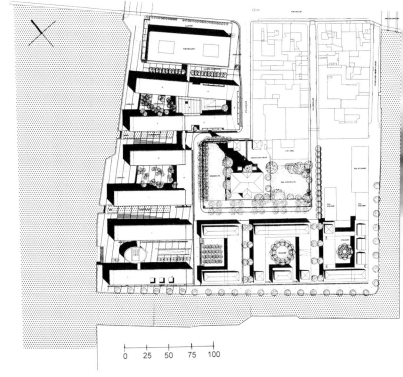

0 25 50 75 100

necessary to incorporate gentle depressions between them to drain the flat ground. The intended horizontal effect can thus be perceived along the strips and across them.

To return to the buildings, the glass facades and the gables between the wings open invitingly towards the harbour, the quay promenade and the afternoon sun, but these appearances belie the reality of the situation. To ensure security, the building more or less consists of a fortress with very few entrances, and while the quay promenade is public, benches are not allowed. The two spaces enclosed on three sides and laid out like gardens resemble quiet patios, but do not have any connection to the interiors. Indeed, they were never intended to be recreation areas for the employees, but can nevertheless be seen from the computer workplaces and thus fulfil an important visual function. Since the occupants of the building look out onto an opposite wing, where they see other employees dressed in similar black and white clothes sitting at similar desks, something was needed to interrupt their gaze. This has been provided for in the form of willows whose boughs move in a constant slowly, undulating rhythm, thus providing stressed eyes with a soft, soothing sight.

Each of the two gardens features some 25 willows, which will soon become too large if they are not limited in their growth. Accordingly, all their branches will be removed every third year, leaving behind stems that will be covered with thousands of green shoots a few months later on. Seen from above, the gardens also present a carpet pattern of box hedges reminiscent of telephone doodlings, swirls on ice, or anything else that comes to mind. Three of the spaces between the wings are public,

wie quer zu den Granitbändern wahrgenommen werden. Kehren wir zu den Gebäuden zurück: Die Glasfassaden und die Giebel zwischen den Gebäudeflügeln öffnen sich einladend zu Hafen, Uferpromenade und Nachmittagssonne hin. Diese etwas malerische Erscheinung täuscht jedoch über die Wirklichkeit hinweg. Das Bankgebäude ähnelt eher einer Festung, nur wenige Eingänge öffnen sich nach außen hin. Die Gewährleistung der Sicherheit der Bank macht diese Bauweise erforderlich. So finden sich auf der Uferpromenade keinerlei Bänke, obwohl sie doch öffentlicher Raum und für jedermann zugänglich ist. Die beiden Freiräume, die jeweils von drei Seiten durch die Bankgebäude geschlossen sind, ähneln ruhigen

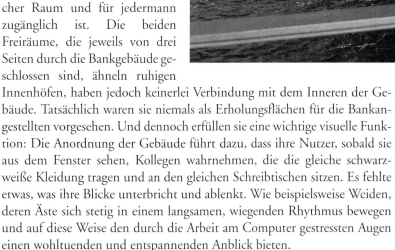

Innenhöfen, haben jedoch keinerlei Verbindung mit dem Inneren der Gebäude. Tatsächlich waren sie niemals als Erholungsflächen für die Bankangestellten vorgesehen. Und dennoch erfüllen sie eine wichtige visuelle Funktion: Die Anordnung der Gebäude führt dazu, dass ihre Nutzer, sobald sie aus dem Fenster sehen, Kollegen wahrnehmen, die die gleiche schwarzweiße Kleidung tragen und an den gleichen Schreibtischen sitzen. Es fehlte etwas, was ihre Blicke unterbricht und ablenkt. Wie beispielsweise Weiden, deren Äste sich stetig in einem langsamen, wiegenden Rhythmus bewegen und auf diese Weise den durch die Arbeit am Computer gestressten Augen einen wohltuenden und entspannenden Anblick bieten.

Wir haben jeder der beiden Flächen etwa 25 Weiden zugeordnet, die ihnen einen ganz eigenen Charakter verleihen. Die Bäume werden stark wachsen. Folglich werden sie alle drei Jahre so weit zurückgeschnitten, dass nur noch kahle Stümpfe übrigbleiben, die einige Monate später allerdings

Strengen Sicherheitsauflagen ist es zu verdanken, dass die Höfe zwar öffentlich zugänglich sind, jedoch keinen Zugang zu den Bankgebäuden besitzen. Um den computergestressten Angestellten einen harmonischen Ausblick zu bieten, bilden in jedem Hof Buchshecken, die sich undiszipliniert durch die Höfe schlängeln mit 25 Weiden ein Teppichmuster.

Although the courts are publicly accessible, they have no connection to the interior of the buildings due to stringent security requirements, yet are seen from the computer workplaces and thus fulfil an important visual function. In order to make them a pleasant sight for the employees and provide stressed eyes with a soft, soothing sight, the landscape architects installed willows and box hedges in carpet patterns.

wieder von abertausenden von grünen Trieben überdeckt sein werden. Betrachtet man die Gärten von oben, wirken sie wie ein Teppichmuster aus Buchsbaum und erinnern an ein während eines Telefongesprächs angefertigtes Gekritzel, an Schlittschuhspuren auf dem Eis oder an so manches, was einem in den Sinn kommen mag.

Drei der Flächen, die sich zwischen den Gebäudekomplexen herauskristallisieren, sind öffentlich. Eine von ihnen wurde als befahrbarer Bereich gestaltet, der Parkplätze für VIP-Bankkunden bietet. Eine Reihe aus norwegischen Ahornbäumen gliedert nicht nur die Parkflächen, sondern bildet den Übergang zwischen dem ehemaligen Bürogebäude und dem ersten Bürokomplex der Uni-Bank. Die Gestaltung der beiden verbleibenden Flächen war hingegen weitaus schwieriger. Sie sollten nach den Vorstellungen der Architekten den Eindruck vermitteln, als ob sich die Gebäude rechts und links von ihnen unmittelbar aus dem Wasser erheben. Sie sollten also eine Fortführung des Hafens darstellen. Eigentlich eine sehr gute Idee, die aber vor allem in Hinblick auf die darunter liegende Tiefgarage schwierig umzusetzen war. So schufen wir eine Wasserfläche, die zum Hafen hin abfällt und aus einer Vielzahl von Treppen besteht. Die Stufen

one of them being a street offering private parking spaces for VIP bank visitors. A row of Norway maples along this street forms the transition between an earlier office building and the closest wing, and helps organise the parking spaces.

As for the remaining two open spaces, the architects wanted the buildings at their sides to create the impression of rising directly from the water, meaning that the spaces had to seem like a continuation of the harbour. A good idea, but difficult to implement in view of the underground parking garage. Our solution has been to create a sheet of water that slopes towards the harbour, running towards it in steps placed at the same intervals as the granite strips while also corresponding to adjacent ground terraced in a lateral direction. I am not sure whether we would have had this idea had we not seen the cascades at Chatsworth many years ago. The level sections of

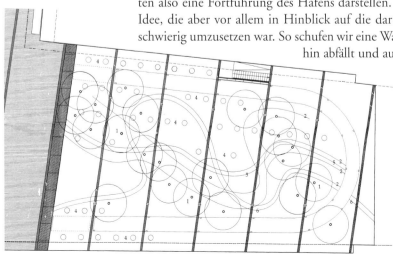

the steps are tilted slightly backwards to keep the water at an even level whenever the circulation system is out of function. A forty-metre-wide space was considerately left by Henning Larsen alongside the road next to the church. We provided the road with a linden avenue and a lawn sixty metres in length, and a coffee-house in the shape of a conservatory is also to be built. The lawn is the only green public space for local inhabitants, and makes it possible to see the church from a distance. In fact, the only other thing I would need for perfect contentment would be the possibility to linger in a café on the ground floor of one of these buildings, watching the sunset with a friend at the heart of Copenhagen's port. In the Norwegian town Bergen there is a wonderfully lofty coffee restaurant arranged in a former bank palace. Dare I reveal the name of the restaurant? It is Banco Rotto.

entsprechen der Breite der Granitbänder und sind in den gleichen Abständen angeordnet. Ihre Höhenentwicklung orientiert sich an der des umliegenden Geländes, das im Gegensatz zu den Wassertreppen allerdings in die andere Richtung, also nach oben hin, abgestuft ist. Ich bin mir nicht sicher, ob wir auf diese Idee gekommen wären, wenn wir nicht vor vielen Jahren die Kaskaden in Chatsworth gesehen hätten. Die Wassertreppen sind leicht rückwärts geneigt, damit sie das Wasser auf einem gleichmäßigen Niveau halten können, wenn das Zirkulationssystem außer Betrieb ist. Im Südosten der Uni-Bank, zwischen der Kirche und der angrenzenden Straße ließ Henning Larsen eine etwa vierzig Meter breite Fläche unbebaut – eine sehr gute und umsichtige Maßnahme, stellt sie doch den einzigen grünen öffentlichen Freiraum für die umliegenden Anwohner dar. Wir ergänzen diesen Ort durch eine Allee aus Linden und eine offene Rasenfläche. Ein Kaffeehaus in der Form eines Wintergartens ist geplant. Ganz zufrieden wäre ich gewesen, wenn ich hier, zentral am Kopenhagener Hafen, im Erdgeschoss eines der Gebäude gemütlich mit einem Freund bei einer Tasse Tee den Sonnenuntergang genießen hätte können. Im norwegischen Bergen kenne ich ein schönes Restaurant, das in einem ehemaligen Bankgebäude untergebracht wurde. Es trägt den schönen Namen »Banco rotto«.

Für die Raumwirkung sind die Weiden noch wichtiger als die Buchshecken, die durch Rosen, Scilla und Krokus ergänzt werde. Das Ausmaß der Pflanzung war durch die Platzanforderungen der Fensterputzer leider limitiert.

The willows play a more important role in spatial terms than the box hedges, which are supplemented with roses, scilla and crocus. Space had to be left for the window cleaners, which limited the extent of the plantings.

Open spaces at Uni-Bank, Christiansbro, Copenhagen, Denmark
Client: ATP
Architect: Henning Larsens Tegnestue
Landscape architect: Sven-Ingvar Andersson Landskabsarkitekt Aps –
Sven-Ingvar Andersson, Lise Schou
Size: 24,000 square metres
Construction: 2000

Erasmus Garten, Arboretum Trompenburg, Rotterdam

Erasmian Garden, Arboretum Trompenburg, Rotterdam

In der Vergangenheit sprach der Park für sich selbst, er war die Antithese der Stadt. In jeder bedeutenden Stadt gab es einen reichlich ausgestatteten städtischen Park. Heute ist dieser reichhaltige Ort verschwunden. Die zeitgenössische Stadt mit ihrer komplexen Infrastruktur, Fragmenten archäologischer Landschaft und ausufernden Stadträndern braucht keinen autonomen Park. Ein Park braucht eine dichte urbane Kultur. Parkgestaltung muss sich in eine neue Richtung bewegen. Momentan konzentriert sich Parkgestaltung auf einen mittleren Maßstab, sie sollte aber auf einen großen Maßstab fokussieren, verbunden mit der dazu erforderlichen Gartenkunst. In einer chaotischen städtischen Umgebung wird eine neue expansive Natur benötigt, die Ruhe, Dunkelheit, Stille, ökologischen Ausgleich erzeugt und den Wechsel der Jahreszeiten zeigt. Bereiche von mehr als 160 Quadratkilometern sind für die heutige Stadt relevant, damit sie nicht nur Fragment sind. Im urbanen Holland können Campingplätze und militärische Übungsgelände »Yellowstone Parks« sein. Andererseits gibt es einen dringenden Bedarf an neuen Gartentypen – Gärten, die nur als Gärten dienen, abgeschieden, umschlossen und versteckt in der Großstadt. Gartenkunst ist eine äußerst wichtige Disziplin, um Selbstreflexion anzuregen und Illusionen zu schaffen. Gärten sind klein, gepflegt, geschätzt und wachsen unaufhörlich.

Der Entwurf für den Erasmus Garten ist ein Teil der Erweiterung des Arboretum Trompenburg in Rotterdam. Pergolen über bestehenden Kanälen sollen eine Reise entlang eines Tunnels aus Blauregen ermöglichen. Nach einer Bootsfahrt in der Morgendämmerung zwischen Wasserlilien und azurblauen Blüten gelangen Besucher in den Garten, eingebettet zwischen den grünen Hängen des Arboretum. Der Pavillon und der Garten behandeln das Thema »Werden, Leben und Niedergang«. Der Garten ist als Stillleben gestaltet: eine Komposition aus Texturen, geknickten versteinerten Bäumen neben lebenden Mammutbäumen mit welligen Stämmen, vertikalen Steinen mit Krähenexkrementen und schnell wachsendem Schachtelhalm in seichtem Wasser, der sich in gedruckter Form auf einer Glaswand wiederholt. Diese Glaswand umgrenzt den Pavillon und den Garten und erzeugt verschwommene Reflexionen. Vom Pavillon kann man einen ausgezeichneten Blick zum Garten genießen. Die Glasplat-

Adriaan Geuze

Durch einen Tunnel aus Blauregen sollen Besucher in den Erasmus Garten gelangen, einer Oase der Stille in der Stadt.

Visitors can reach Erasmian Garten, an oasis of peace in the hectic city, by punting through a pergola tunnel of wisteria.

In the past, public parks were self-explanatory, the antithesis of the city. Each city of any significance had a park rich in landscape elements and facilities, but today such parks are less in demand. There is no need for autonomous parks in contemporary cities, with their complex infrastructure, fragments of archeological landscape and sprawling fringes, nor do they provide the dense urban culture that such parks need.

Park design must thus take a new direction. At the moment, it is based on the middle scale but should focus on the grand scale and also incorporate garden art – an ambition that is currently lacking. The chaotic environment of modern cities requires large swathes of nature where quietness, darkness, ecological regeneration and the changing of the seasons can be experienced. Such areas have to be over 40,000 acres in size if they are to be more than just a fragment, or of any relevance to modern-day cities. In urban Holland, even tiny camp sites and military ranges have the potential to be 'Yellowstone Parks'.

On the other hand, cities also need gardens that serve exclusively as gardens, small, cherished and forever evolving to maturity while also being isolated, enclosed and hidden from the metropolis. And they should include garden art, as it is an important discipline for self-reflection and the creation of illusion.

Erasmian Garden is the latest extension to Arboretum Trompenburg in Rotterdam. The designers, West8, have covered an existing system of canals with wisteria pergolas, creating a long continuous boating tunnel. A nice way of experiencing Erasmian Garden it is to take a quiet boat trip at dawn through the water lilies, surrounded by azure blue flowers and the lush greenery of the

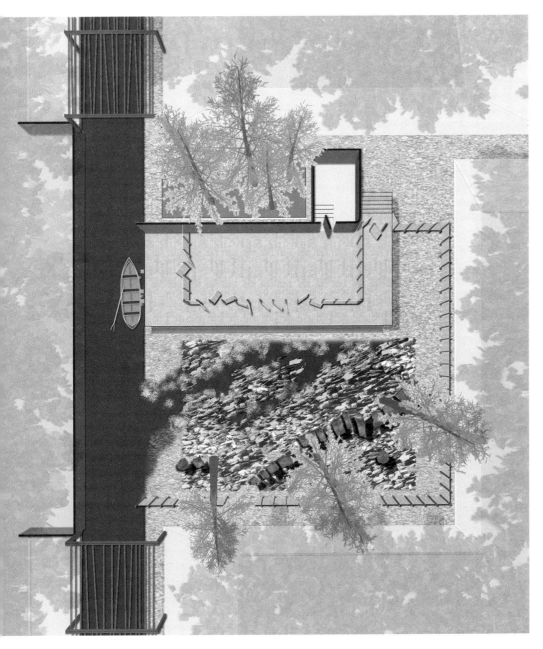

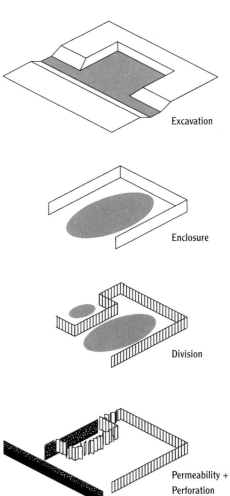

Excavation

Enclosure

Division

Permeability +
Perforation

Der Erasmus Garten, Teil einer
Erweiterung des Arboretum
Trompenburg in Rotterdam,
soll ein klar umgrenzter, ruhi-
ger Ort zur Erholung werden,
den man mit dem Boot erreichen kann. Ein Pavillon bietet
Rückzugsmöglichkeit an einem
seichten Wasserbecken.

Erasmian Garden, the latest
extension to Arboretum
Trompenburg in Rotterdam,
will be created as a clearly
defined space conducive to
rest and recreation. A pavilion
set up next to a shallow pool
of water is a particular place
of seclusion.

Erasmian Garden at Trompenburg Arboretum, Rotterdam
Client: Breeze of AIR
Landscape architects: West 8 – Adriaan Geuze, Theo Reesink, Nigel Sampey,
Riëtte Bosch, Joyce van den Berg, Sabine Müller
Design: 2001

Arboretum, enclosed by sloping contours, red walls and ferns.

The Erasmian Garden includes a pavilion and garden that explore the theme of evolution, life and decay. The enclosed garden is a still life, a composition of textures: toppled and broken fossil trees; rough and angular blocks of upright slate; the fibrous, hairy trunks of living redwoods (Metasequoia); prehistoric horsetails (Equisetum), growing in shallow water and also projected like screen prints onto the transparent walls that surround the garden, creating dramatic and ambiguous reflections. The pavilion looks out onto the garden through panels of glass that can be pivoted in all directions, and the red walls surrounding the garden are freely perforated to enhance the sense of mystery. The result is a place sloping down to the water, where people can meditate and read, a place for the university and city alike.

The Erasmian Garden provides the Trompenburg Arboretum with a mature green icon while furnishing the city a secret within itself, an enclosed oasis.

Eine Bootsfahrt zwischen Wasserlilien und unter einem Baldachin aus Blauregen bringt Besucher zum Erasmus Garten. Die Glaswände des Pavillons können zur Seite gedreht werden. Auf den verdrehten Glaspaneelen ergeben sich interessante Spiegelungen und Reflexionen.

Visitors can reach Erasmian Garden by boat, floating past water lilies through a pergola tunnel hung with wisteria. The glass panels of the pavilion at the heart of the garden can be pivoted in all directions, creating interesting reflections.

ten können zum Garten gedreht werden. In der roten Mauer um den Garten finden sich Löcher, damit er noch geheimnisvoller erscheint. In diesem zum Wasser hin abschüssigen Raum können Besucher meditieren und lesen. Mit dem Erasmus Garten wird das Arboretum Trompenburg zum grünen Symbol. Die Stadt erhält einen geheimen Ort, eine umschlossene Oase.

Im abgesenkten Garten stehen Mammutbäume, im seichten Wasser wächst Schachtelhalm. Durch Gucklöcher in der roten Mauer können Neugierige ins Garteninnere spähen.

Redwoods grow in the sunken area, and horsetails thrive in the shallow water. The red enclosure walls are perforated to provide glimpses of the secluded garden.

Magisches Wasser in Ostwestfalen

Magical water in Westphalia

Henri Bava

Zur Landesgartenschau in Bad Oeynhausen und Löhne holten die Planer von Agence Ter das unterirdische Heilwasser der Kurregion ans Licht. For the regional garden show in Bad Oeynhausen und Löhne, the Agence Ter planners brought subterranean water out into the open.

Statt üppige Blumenbilder nach dem Geschmack der meisten Besucher einer Landesgartenschau zu komponieren, haben wir uns entschieden, wie bei all unseren Projekten vor allem das Charakteristische des Grundstücks herauszuarbeiten, um dem Ort auf der Gemeindegrenze von Bad Oeynhausen und Löhne Identität zu verleihen. Was diesen Ort ausmacht, ist nicht sofort sichtbar, denn es befindet sich unter der Erdoberfläche: das Wasser. Wir nannten es »magisch«, da es heilend wirkt. Auf diesem Wasser gründet die Wirtschaft der Region, seinetwegen sind hier Thermen und Kliniken entstanden. Gleichzeitig verbannen Thermen und Kliniken das Wasser aber auch in die Welt der Heilanstalten. Uns lag deshalb daran, das Wasser aus dem klammen Halbdunkel dieser Anstalten ans Licht und unter den freien Himmel zu holen.

Selbst wenn das Wasser in der Erde verborgen bleibt, ist es nicht weniger wirklich. Hydrogeologen haben seine Ströme kartiert – entlang unterirdischer Verwerfungslinien, die erstaunlich parallel verlaufen. Das Wasser an sich ist nichts weiter als eine Abstraktion des Materials, in dem es fließt, sich entwickelt und von dem es sich lenken lässt: der Erde. Wenn wir also für das vergängliche Schauspiel einer Gartenschau das omnipräsente, aber kaum sichtbare Wasser in Szene setzen, dann nur im Zusammenspiel mit seinem Grund, der Erde, die schließlich unser aller Grund ist. Wir arbeiteten deshalb in der dritten Dimension, in der Tiefe der Boden-

Instead of luxuriant beds of flowers that appeal to the taste of most regional garden show visitors, we decided - as in all our projects - to concentrate on the characteristic element of the site and thus underscore its identity. Water, the element of the site in question, located between the towns of Bad Oeynhausen and Löhne in Westphalia, northern Germany, was not immediately apparent, since it exists below the surface of the

earth. We called it "magical" as it is healing in effect. It forms the basis of the regional economy and has led to the establishment of thermal baths and clinics. At the same time, thermal baths and clinics keep the water concealed within their walls, and it thus became our intention to bring the water out into the open. Hydrogeologists have mapped its flow along subterranean faults that run in astonishingly parallel lines. As such, the water is nothing other than an abstract version of the earth, the material in which it flows, builds up and allows itself to be guided. In other words, if we wanted to stage the omnipresent but scarcely visible element of water as the focus of the very temporary spectacle of a garden show, we had to do this in interaction with the earth, the basis and foundation not only of water but of all life on this planet. For this reason, we worked in the third dimension, plunging down into the depths of the earth's strata and reaching upwards towards the sky. For this reason, all the resulting water gardens are dug into the earth. This excavation work involved scratching the surface in some places, and gouging out great holes in others, as for the Water Crater, and came to stand for the search for the 'truth' of the site. At other places we piled earth onto earth, thus creating 'artificial' places to underscore the artificiality of the event. The World Climate Avenue, the main axis of the garden show park, therefore rises out of the

fields like an elongated platform, viewing terrace and stage all in one, and features embankment walls faced in Cor-Ten steel to emphasise the man-made character of the avenue. Flower gardens, nursery gardens, cemetery gardens and other classical garden show elements are located on level ground, between the two extremes of the downward-looking and upward-striving landscape interventions. This gives the various gardens on the fertile earth a 'normal' touch, an ele-

schichten und in der Höhe der Aufbauten. So sind die Wassergärten allesamt in die Erde eingegraben – dazu mussten wir Boden abtragen, manchmal nur oberflächlich, manchmal metertief, wie beim Wasserkrater. Das Graben und Ausschneiden steht für die Suche nach der »Wahrheit« des Ortes. An anderer Stelle hingegen fügten wir Erde hinzu, schütteten Boden auf und setzten der Landschaft »künstliche« Orte auf, um die Künstlichkeit der Gartenschau zu betonen. Die Hauptachse des Gartenschauparks, die Allee des Weltklimas, hebt sich deshalb als langgestreckter Podest aus den Feldern heraus, Aussichtsterrasse und riesige Bühne für die Gärten zugleich. Ihre Stützmauern aus Corten-Stahl unterstreichen das Menschengemachte der Anlage. Zwischen den beiden Extremen, der nach innen gekehrten und der ausgestellten Landschaft, befinden sich auf ebener Erde Blumengärten, Baumschulgärten, Friedhofsgärten – die klassische Palette der Gartenschau. Ihr kommt der Status des »Normalen« zu, schlicht auf dem fruchtbaren Grund angelegt, wie die Äcker nebenan.

Das sprudelnde, lebendige, launenhafte und beinahe gefährliche Wasser lässt sich besonders im Hohlraum des Wasserkraters erleben. Das Spektakel eröffnet sich einem nicht auf den ersten Blick. Da das Wasser in der Erde verborgen ist, muss man an einen Ort hinabsteigen, der beim Betreten im Ungewissen liegt. Ankommende sehen zunächst nur eine wogende Fläche, nämlich die Baumkronen einer Gruppe Felsenbirnen, die in einem Senkgarten rund um den Krater ge-

pflanzt sind. Die Baumkronen verlängern die Ebene der Wiese, über die man sich nähert. Eine Rampe und eine Treppe führen fünf Meter hinab in den Senkgarten, man gleitet unter die Bäume

Auf der Suche nach dem Wasser steigen die Besucher im Krater 18 Meter tief unter die Erdoberfläche. Wände aus Gabionen und Treppen aus galvanisiertem Stahl vermitteln das Rohe des Untergrundes. Aus dem Bassin schießt eine Fontäne durch die Öffnung des Eingangsplateaus, zur Einweihung bewundert von Bauherr, Politikern und zwei der Planer (standesgemäß in Schwarz).

In search of the water, visitors descend 18 metres below ground level inside the crater. Walls covered with gabions and stairs of galvanised steel express underground roughness. A fountain shoots up from the pool through the opening in the entrance platform. Onlookers at the inauguration include the client, politicians and two of the planners (up to standard in black).

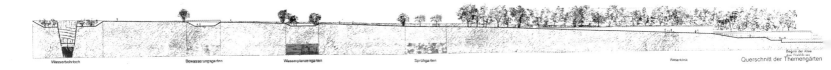

Schnitt durch das Gartenschaugelände mit Bodenaufbauten und Vertiefungen (ganz oben), Schnitt durch den Wasserkrater.

ment of simplicity like the neighbouring fields. At the garden show, the lively, moody and almost threatening character of water can be experienced most closely within the deep cavity of the Water Crater. The spectacle involved does not reveal itself at a first glance. Since the water is hidden in the earth, visitors have to descend down into unknown places. At first all they see is the swaying canopy made up of the tops of amelanchiers planted into a sunken garden around the inside the crater, their tops acting as a continuation of the fields across which the crater is approached. A ramp and a stairway lead five metres down into the sunken garden. From here visitors continue along beneath the trees to the centre of the garden. This features the tops of gigantic walls made of Cor-Ten steel that line a tapered hole, an enormous well, that plunges 18 metres into the earth. The insides of the walls are faced with gabions, down which the water trickles.

The materials deep down inside this crater have been left in a deliberately rough-hewn shape, as if at a construction site. Simple and unadorned stairs made of galvanised steel spiral their way to the bottom of the drill-hole. Making the descent between the rough-hewn walls and close to the gurgling water is a little eerie, and a look up to the surface reveals a circle of sky, with the light shining down like the beams of a spotlight. Such places have long existed in the history of garden design, and thus the Oeynhausen Water Crater can be regarded as a modern version if the Roman nymphaeum.

One can immerse oneself in this closed space, this *hortus conclusus,* to experience that astonishing and vital element of water with the whole of one's body and all of one's senses.

Schnitt durch das Gartenschaugelände mit Bodenaufbauten und Vertiefungen (ganz oben), Schnitt durch den Wasserkrater.

Cross-section of the garden exhibition grounds shows the raised and sunken elements (top above); cross-section of the Water Crater.

und läuft auf das Zentrum des Gartens zu. Riesige Corten-Stahl-Mauern umschließen es – sie sind nur der obere Rand eines in die Erde versenkten Kegels, die Wände eines enormen Brunnen-Bohrlochs. Auf der Innenseite sind diese Wände mit Gabionen verkleidet, über die das Wasser bis zum 18 Meter tief gelegenen Grund hinabrieselt.

Formen und Materialien im Inneren sind bewusst roh gehalten, wie auf der Baustelle. Einfache, schmucklose Treppen aus galvanisiertem Stahl winden sich spiralförmig in die Tiefe. Ein wenig unheimlich ist einem beim Abstieg zumute – zwischen den rohen Mauern, in der Nähe des gurgelnden Wassers, beim Zurückblicken nach oben zu dem kreisrunden Ausschnitt, der das Tageslicht in die Tiefe schickt wie ein Spot einen Lichtstrahl. In der Geschichte der Gartenkunst hat es solche Orte schon früh gegeben – der Oeynhauser Wasserkrater lässt sich auch als zeitgenössische Variante des römischen Nymphäums lesen. Man kann sich versenken in diesen geschlossenen Raum, einen Hortus conclusus, um mit dem ganzen Körper und mit allen Sinnen jenes erstaunliche Element Wasser zu erleben.

Water Crater at the regional garden show 2000 in Bad Oeynhausen and Löhne, Germany
Client: Landesgartenschaugesellschaft Bad Oeynhausen und Löhne
Landscape architects: Agence Ter, Paris (Henri Bava, Olivier Philippe, Michel Hoessler)
with Alexander Bölk (project head)
Competition: 1998
Planning: 1998 – 2000
Construction: 1999 – 2000
Costs: DEM 5 million (Water Crater), DEM 55 million (park in total)

La Dehesa del Saler – die Küstenzone La Albufera, Valencia

La Dehesa del Saler, the coastal zone of La Albufera, Valencia

La Albufera is a 3,000-hectare lagoon south of El Saler, near Valencia. Its shores form a vast wetland zone threaded with canals. A narrow peninsula with dunes covered with pines, which is a wetlands conservation area under the Ramsar Convention, separates the lagoon from the sea: La Dehesa del Saler.

Two kinds of boundaries divide the land from the sea: dunes and dikes. While dunes are created by deposits of sediment from rivers and by waves and wind, and are thus subject to natural processes, dikes are used as technical barriers to control and conquer nature.

Plans to develop this stretch of coastline for the tourist trade began in the 60s. The result was that ecosystem consisting of pine forests, moors, dunes, counter-dunes and water-filled sinkholes was eventually destroyed and a massive dike built. Wide paved roads provided access to large housing developments. The dunes and wetlands were crowded out; the pine forest and the beach eventually receded due to the lack of natural protection. After the change of government in 1975 the new democratic government made the area into a natural park that is now one of the most important wetland sites in Europe. But getting to that stage was very difficult. On the one hand the ecosystem had to be regenerated, and on the other the requirements of the population of Valencia and the tourists had to be considered.

Restoring ecological balance became the primary objective. To begin with, the existing infrastructure and the road along the dike were demolished and replaced by a natural barrier to the coast. Now there are alternating rows of the first dune, the counter-dune and the second dune. The dunes are aligned with the wind from the sea

La Albufera ist eine 3000 Hektar große Lagune südlich von El Saler, nahe Valencia. Sie liegt inmitten einer riesigen, von Kanälen durchzogenen Feuchtzone. Ein schmaler Landstreifen mit pinienbewachsenen Dünen, eine nach der Ramsar-Konvention geschütze Naturlandschaft, scheidet die Lagune vom Meer: La Dehesa del Saler.

Zwei Arten von Begrenzung trennen das Festland vom Meer: Dünen und Deiche. Während die Dünen, entstanden aus abgelagerten Flusssedimenten, Seegang und Wind, natürlichen Prozessen unterliegen, werden die Deiche als technische Barriere eingesetzt, um die Natur zu kontrollieren und zu beherrschen.

Die touristischen Entwicklungspläne in diesem Küstenstrich begannen in den 60er Jahren. In der Folge wurde das Ökosystem, bestehend aus Pinienwäldern, Mooren, Dünen, Gegendü-

Alfred Fernández de la Reguera
Ignacio Salvans
Jordi Solé

Die Grundlagen der Geometrie halfen dabei, das ökologische Gleichgewicht eines empfindlichen Küstenabschnitts wiederherzustellen.

The fundamentals of geometry helped regenerate ecological balance along a sensitive stretch of coastline.

Das ökologische Gleichgewicht der sensiblen Feuchtgebiets- und Dünenlandschaft wiederherzustellen, galt als vorrangige Aufgabe. Die Zugänge zum Strand wurden begrenzt. Ein Weg mit Pergolen aus Holz verläuft nun parallel zur Küste.

Restoring the ecological balance in the sensitive landscape of wetlands and dunes was the top priority. Access to the beach was restricted. A new path featuring wooden pergolas now runs parallel to the coast.

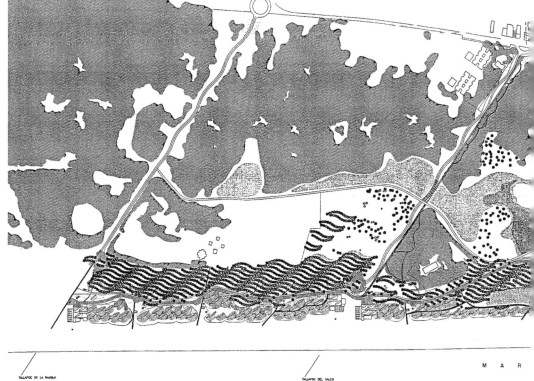

Eine natürliche Küstensperre
schützt heute das Feuchtgebiet, gestaltet als eine Abfolge
von Hügeln und Tälern.
A natural barrier to the coast
now protects the wetlands. It
was designed as a series of
hills and valleys.

nen und Wassersenken, zerstört und ein mächti-
ger Deich errichtet. Breite Asphaltstraßen führten damals zu großen Siedlungskomplexen. Die
Dünen und Feuchtgebiete wurden verdrängt, der
Pinienwald und der Strand bildeten sich schließlich mangels natürlichen Schutzes zurück. Nach
dem Regierungswechsel 1975 machte die neue demokratische Regierung
das Gelände zum Naturpark, heute eines der bedeutendsten Feuchtgebiete
Europas. Doch der Weg dahin gestaltete sich sehr schwierig. Einerseits sollte das Ökosystem wieder ins Gleichgewicht gebracht werden, andererseits
wollte man den Ansprüchen der Bevölkerung Valencias und der Touristen
gerecht werden.

Das ökologische Gleichgewicht dieses Gebietes wiederherzustellen, galt
schließlich als vorrangige Aufgabe. Zunächst wurden die bestehende Infrastruktur und die Deichstraße abgerissen und durch eine natürliche Küstensperre ersetzt. Abwechselnd reihen sich nun erste Düne, Gegendüne und
zweite Düne. Sie sind auf den Meereswind ausgerichtet und mit einer

and stabilised with autochthonous vegetation.
The extreme sensitivity of this dune system
makes it necessary to control passage and to lim-
it access to the beach. The roads and raised pathways were also removed. A new footpath now
runs behind the dunes parallel to the coast, with
a few additional trails. Pedestrians have intermit-
tent views of the sea between the dunes. The walk
along 'camí Vell dels Muntanyars' past pergolas
and lookout towers is particularly impressive.

All other asphalt-covered areas and service facilities were also torn down to allow the dunes
and forests to develop unhindered. A few new car
park bays and picnic spots were fit in. The areas
reserved for tourists are where the four access
roads begin. Here the row of dunes has a gap to
provide access to the beach and an extensive view

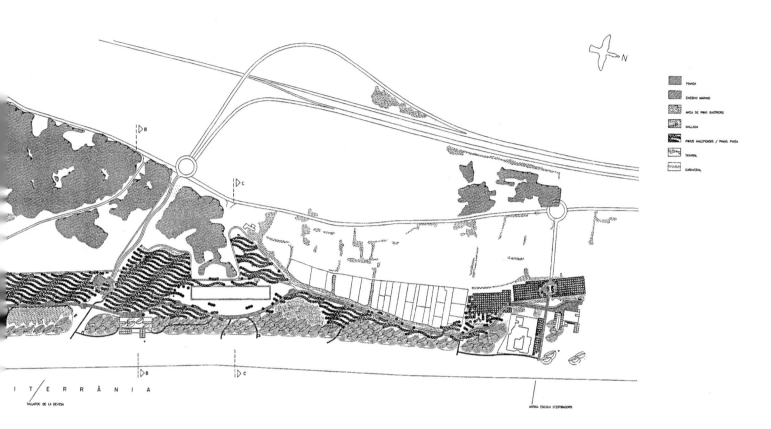

Ein ausgeklügeltes System aus erster Düne, Gegendüne und zweiter Düne schützt die Küste. Als Modell diente die Barchan-Düne, eine sichelförmige Einzeldüne, die zu Ketten verwächst. Die Dünen sind mit Schilfmatten befestigt.

An intricate system consisting of the first dune, the counter-dune and the second dune protects the coastline. Its structure is based on the Barchan type of dune, a sickle-shaped single dune that branches out into chains. The dunes are stabilised with reed mats.

of the sea. The floodplains that shelter breeding sites for the birds and aquatic animals were also regenerated. They also serve to block the access to the pine forests.

Our task was to design the landscape. We knew the ecosystem and its major components, but what form should we give the landscape? Should we imitate natural formations and copy picturesque landscapes? In terms of form our design approach was already contained in the microcosm of the surroundings. After all, the movements of the waves sketched by the wind, the impressions on the ground, the moving water, the colours, textures and rhythms were all to be found on site. All we had to do was transpose them into a larger scale. In order to do so, we called to mind the fundamentals of geometry.

autochthonen Vegetation befestigt. Die extreme Sensibilität dieses Dünensystems erfordert es, die Durchgänge zu kontrollieren und die Zugänge zum Strand zu begrenzen. Des weiteren wurden auch die Verkehrsstraßen und die erhöhten Wege aufgelassen. Ein neuer Fußweg verläuft jetzt hinter den Dünen parallel zur Küste, ergänzt durch einige Pfade. Immer wieder hat man zwischen den Dünen hindurch Aussicht aufs Meer. Besonders eindrucksvoll ist der Weg »camí Vell dels Muntanyars«, der an Pergolen und Aussichtstürmen vorbeiführt.

Abgerissen wurden auch alle sonstigen Asphaltflächen und Versorgungseinrichtungen, so dass Dünen und Wälder unbehindert neu entstehen können. Hier fügen sich einige Parkbuchten und Picknickplätze ein. Die für Touristen ausgewiesenen Gebiete befinden sich am Anfang der vier Zugangsstraßen. Dort ist die Dünenkette unterbrochen, um eine entsprechende Verbindung zum Strand und einen weiten Blick aufs Meer zu bieten. Wieder eingerichtet wurden auch Überschwemmungsgebiete, die Vögeln und Wassertieren Brutplätze bieten. Darüber hinaus versperren sie den Weg in die Pinienwälder.

La Dehesa del Saler, La Albufera, Valencia, Spain
Site: El Saler, Valencia
Client: Spanish Ministry of the Environment, Department of Public Works,
Urbanism and Transport of the Valencia Government, Valencia City Council,
European Union Cohesion Fund
Planning: 1995
Completion: 1999
Architects: Alfred Fernández de la Reguera (head), Ignacio Salvans, Jordi Solé
Collaborators: Ignacio Gil, Francisco Solves

Unsere Aufgabe bestand darin, eine Landschaft zu gestalten, von der wir zwar das Ökosystem und seine Hauptbestandteile kannten. Aber welche Gestalt sollten wir der Landschaft geben? Sollten wir ähnliche Formationen nachahmen, pittoreske Landschaften kopieren? Formal war unser Gestaltungsansatz bereits im Mikrokosmos der Umgebung enthalten. Denn die Wellenbewegungen, die der Wind skizziert, die Abdrücke im Boden, das bewegte Wasser, die Farben, Texturen und Rhythmen sind alle vor Ort zu

We oriented ourselves on a dune type known as Barchan, a sickle-shaped single dune that can branch out into long chains perpendicular to the direction of the wind. Barchans develop when the wind pushes the sides around faster than the centre. We used them to organise the vast coastal area. Set up like a mountain range, the dunes form a series of hills and valleys. We stabilised the dunes with reed mats. Between them, depending on the height and direction of the dune in question, we seeded innumerable autochthonous plants. Pines, *Pinus pinea* and *Pinus halepensis,* are going to spread down to the coast again in fu-

finden und brauchten nur auf einen größeren Maßstab übertragen zu werden. Um das zu erreichen, besannen wir uns auf die Grundlagen der Geometrie. Wir orientierten uns an der sogenannten Barchan-Düne, einer sichelförmigen Einzeldüne, die zu langen, quer zur Windrichtung verlaufenden Ketten verwachsen kann. Barchane entstehen dadurch, dass die Seiten vom Wind schneller bewegt werden als die Mitte. So gliederten wir das rie-

ture. They are to protect the coast from the effects of the 'Llevant.' This wind and the rain and the tides will gradually soften and change the severe geometry of the design. Nature is a living process determined by many factors and functioning according to its own laws. Humans must restrain themselves in order to prevent irreversible damage. The regeneration of El Saler could not have come about any other way. The project is incomplete, as is any activity in the landscape, for time and minimal maintenance and mature plants are still needed. An intervention of this kind has no foreseeable end. These are the insights of a city-dweller who respects the environment.

sige Küstengebiet. Wie ein Gebirge angelegt, besteht es aus einer Abfolge von Hügeln und Tälern. Die Dünen befestigten wir mit Hilfe von Schilfmatten. Zwischen diese setzten wir, je nach Höhe und Ausrichtung der Düne, unzählige Samen autochthoner Pflanzen. Kiefern, Pinus pinea und Pinus halepensis, sollen sich künftig wieder bis zum Ufer erstrecken. Sie sollen vor den Auswirkungen des »Llevant« schützen. Dieser Wind, der Regen und die Gezeiten werden die strenge Geometrie allmählich aufheben und verändern.

Die Natur ist ein lebendiger Prozess, der von vielen Faktoren bestimmt ist und nach eigenen Gesetzen funktioniert. Der Mensch muss sich beschränken, so dass keine irreversiblen Schäden entstehen. Nur so konnte sich die Regeneration von El Saler vollziehen. Es ist ein unvollendetes Werk, wie jede Aktion in der Landschaft, da Zeit und minimale Pflege und Reife der Pflanzen nötig ist. Es sind Arbeiten, deren Ende nicht vorhersehbar ist, eine Erkenntnis eines Städters, der seine Umwelt respektiert.

Neue Fußwege erschließen das Gebiet, Überschwemmungszonen wurden eingerichtet, Dünen und Pinienwälder können neu entstehen.
New footpaths provide access to the area, floodplains were set up, and the dunes and pine forests allowed to re-develop.

Göteborg: Neues Leben im Hafen

Göteborg: New uses for the shipyards

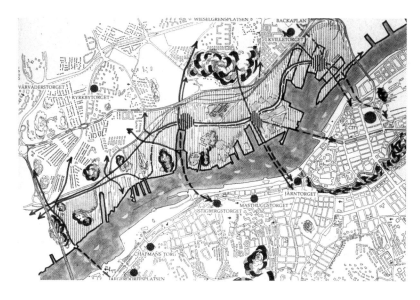

Kolbjörn Wærn
Rasmus Wærn

Wasser ist ein irrationales, ein unproduktives Element in der schwedischen Landschaft. Es behindert die Planung und erzwingt oft aufwendige Brücken- oder Straßenbauten. Und doch lieben wir Schweden das Wasser. Stolz präsentieren wir Stockholm als das Venedig des Nordens. Was aber macht das Wasser so anziehend? Wahrscheinlich seine unkontrollierbare Natur. Es sträubt sich weitgehend gegen Planung und Management. Was immer sich im Dunkel unter seiner Oberfläche verbirgt, kann nicht vollständig manipuliert und beherrscht werden.

Land dagegen hat einen Wert als Immobilie, die man optimal verwalten kann. Selbst der tiefe schwedische Wald mit seinen Gnomen und Trollen ist vor allem Produktionsstandort. Aber auch hier ist überall Wasser, in Seen, Flüssen und entlang der Küste – ohne erkennbaren Nutzen. Das gefällt uns. Ist die schwedische Wasserliebe ein Erbe der Wikinger? Alle ihre Siedlungen lagen dicht am Wasser, und auf Wasserstraßen drangen sie tief ins Landesinnere. Runensteine an Seeufern zeugen von ihren Expeditionen in ferne Länder. Das Leben am Wasser erlaubte ihnen, dem Alltag zu entfliehen und das Abenteuer zu suchen. Gilt das auch heute noch?

Göteborg gewann mit dem Ende der Werft-Industrie ein neues Stadtviertel – nah an der City, nah am Fluß. Ein Traum schwedischer Planer. Göteborg gained a new waterside district with the demise of the shipyards – a dream opportunity for Swedish town planners.

Water is an irrational and unproductive element in the Swedish landscape. Waterways are seen as posing obstacles to physical planning, forcing the country's engineers to construct costly bridges and build long detours. Yet the Swedes love water, and they proudly present Stockholm as the Venice of the North.

Why do Swedes find water so attractive? Because it is uncontrollable and defies planning and management. Water is simply there, and cannot be put to any major profitable use. Perhaps the Swedish love of water is a remnant of the Viking heritage. All Viking settlements were located close to water and their waterways penetrated deep into the country. Rune-inscribed stones near inland lakes tell of expeditions to remote countries. Living by the water made it possible for the Vikings to leave the drudgery of everyday life and set off on adventurous travels. Does water still represent the possibility to escape from it all in our society?

The ideal of most Swedes is to buy or rent a red country cottage by the water. A pond or a little lake will do, a larger body of water is better, but a river or chain of water bodies is best.

Several decades ago, the overwhelming desire to live by the water had reached such proportions that laws had to be drawn up prohibiting the erection of buildings within 300 metres of any shoreline, including that of the smallest pond. This, of course, only made water even more attractive. Closeness to water even increases the value of one's home, and in Göteborg, for example, a view of the estuary is worth approximately 200,000 Swedish crowns. Even the sound of a foghorn or a ship increases the value of a property. Consequently real estate is taxed in relation to

he proximity of water. This might make sense in
 desert state but must, to the uninitiated, seem
ery strange in a country of abundant rain.

   Returning to Göteborg, the city was not
ounded on the mouth of the river Göta because
7th-century Swedes were enamoured of the view,
ut in order to control Sweden's only direct outlet
o the North Sea. The city and harbour were orig-
nally established on the south bank of the Göta,
vith industry and major shipyards settling on the
orthern bank later on. During the 20th century,
nore and more harbour activities moved from the
ncreasingly cramped quarters on the south bank
o the north, where there was still space available
or handling goods. As a result, the harbour atmos-
here of the south bank slowly faded away; canals
vere turned into streets, docks were filled in and

   Jedenfalls muß das rote Sommerhäuschen, der Traum der meisten
Schweden, an einem großen Gewässer liegen, zumindest an einem kleinen
See oder einem Teich. Schon vor Jahrzehnten wurde der Traum so über-
mächtig, daß gesetzliche Regelungen nötig wurden. Seither darf niemand
am Ufer bauen, dreihundert Meter Abstand ist das Minimum, selbst bei
einem kleinen Teich. Natürlich hat dies die Begehrlichkeit noch verstärkt:
Viele Bürger scheuen keine Mühe, Ausnahmegenehmigungen zu erwirken.
Zumal sich die Nähe zum Wasser deutlich in den Immobilienpreisen nie-
derschlägt. Der Blick aufs Wasser ist in Göteborg rund 200 000 schwedische Kronen wert. Selbst wenn nur Nebelhörner zu hören sind, ist das noch
wertsteigernd. Entsprechend bewerten auch die Steuerbehörden Immobili-
enbesitz nach Wassernähe. Ein Prinzip, das vielleicht für einen Wüstenstaat
sinnvoll erscheint, dem Uneingeweihten aber dort merkwürdig vorkommt,
wo Regen nur allzu häufig ist.

   Göteborg jedoch wurde im sechzehnten Jahrhundert nicht etwa wegen
der Sicht aufs Wasser an der Mündung des Flusses Göta errichtet; vielmehr
ging es darum, den einzigen Zugang zum Meer im Westen des Landes zu

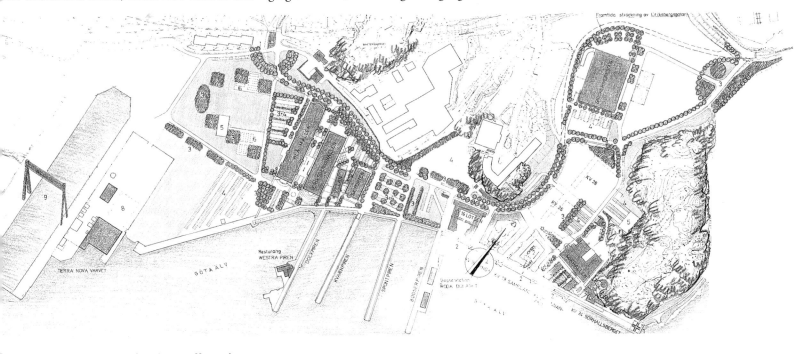

Gegenüber: Masterplan für das
Nordufer des Göta-Flusses,
das sich zwischen den beiden
Hauptbrücken erstreckt. Her-
vorgehoben sind die geplanten
zusätzlichen Verbindungen
zwischen der Innenstadt und
der Insel Hisingen. Oben: Stand
der Entwicklung im Bereich der
Eriksberg-Werft 1994.
Plan: Bruno Richter

Opposite page: Master plan
for a section of land between
the two main bridges on the
northern bank of the Göta
river, emphasizing the planned
additional links between the
old part of Göteborg and the
island of Hisingen. Above: The
state of development at the
former Eriksberg Shipyard in
1994. Plan: Bruno Richter.

»Dock-Walks« als neue Spa-
ziererfahrung im Bereich der
Eriksberg-Werft in Göteborg –
auch mit künstlerischen
Designideen und Details
nimmt das Gestaltungskonzept
Bezug auf die verlorenen
Hafenfunktionen. Das Nordufer
des Göta erfüllt so den in der
City am Südufer unerfüllbaren
Traum einer Stadtentwicklung
am und mit dem Fluß.

"Dock walking" is a new pas-
time at Eriksberg Shipyard in
Göteborg. Design ideas and
artistic details refer to the
area's shipbuilding past.
The northern bank of the
Göta river fulfils the longing
felt by the crowded opposite
shore of the city centre for
waterfront life.

»Man vermißt die Kuh erst,
wenn der Stall leer ist« –
dieses schwedische Sprichwort
trifft gut den scheibchenweisen
Verlust des Wassers als Motiv
für die Stadtplanung Göteborgs. Heute bieten nur noch
die umgenutzten Werftareale
Spielraum für romantische
Uferszenen: die Wohnhäuser
von Eriksberg, direkt am
Schleppboot-Hafen.

"You don't miss your cow till
the stall is empty" – a Swedish
proverb that describes the way
Göteborg feels about the loss
of water as an urban development element. Only the transformed shipyards are still
available for romantic waterfront scenes, as typified by
housing at the Eriksberg
trawler basin.

kontrollieren. Die Stadt und der Hafen wurden zunächst am Südufer des Flusses gebaut. Am Nordufer siedelte sich Industrie an, es entstanden die großen Werften. Im 20. Jahrhundert verlagerten sich dann mehr und mehr Hafenfunktionen auf das Nordufer, wo es noch genügend Raum für die Frachtabfertigung gab. Gleichzeitig verlor die City auf dem Südufer ihre Hafenatmosphäre und den Kontakt zum Wasser. Kanäle wurden zu Straßen, Docks zugeschüttet und eine Stadtautobahn gebaut.

Als der innere Hafen praktisch seine Bedeutung verloren hatte, erwachte das Interesse der Stadtplaner am Fluß. Doch es erwies sich als ungeheure Aufgabe, die City am Südufer wieder mit dem Fluß zu verbinden. Pläne für Tunnelbauten und für die Freilegung zugeschütteter Docks liegen zwar vor, sind aber kaum bezahlbar. Die Stadtautobahn ist kaum zu überwinden. Ein Versuch war auch der Bau der Neuen Oper. Ihre Fassade weist in Richtung Fluß. Ironischerweise wäre das vor zwanzig Jahren undenkbar gewesen, als der Fluß noch das lebendige Bild bot, das wir uns heute so wünschen. Wie sagt doch ein schwedisches Sprichwort: Man vermißt die Kuh erst, wenn der Stall leer ist.

Eine andere Entwicklung nahm das Nordufer. Dessen industrielle Ära endete in den siebziger Jahren abrupt. 1972 war Göteborg noch weltweit führend im Schiffbau, 1979 war alles vorbei. Die großen Trockendocks, in denen berühmte Schiffe wie die Japan oder Bergemaster gebaut wurden, liegen heute verlassen da. Unschwer erkannte man während des Baubooms der achtziger Jahre die Chancen für die Siedlungsentwicklung. Anders als das Südufer, das längst von Verkehrsachsen blockiert war, zeigte sich das Nordufer nun als ruhige, verlassene Gegend, citynah, mit Südexposition und Blick zum Fluß. Die rohe Architektur der Schiffsbau-Ära wurde Zug um Zug abgebaut oder in eine kultiviertere architektonische Form gebracht. Der erste Neubau auf dem Nordufer war ein Luxusrestaurant, das zum einen Standards für die folgende Entwicklung setzen und zum anderen die Aufmerksamkeit auf brachliegende Flächen lenken sollte. Göteborgs erstes Guide-Michelin-Restaurant in der industriellen Wildnis des Nordufers – das wäre noch vor zehn Jahren unvorstellbar gewesen.

Stadtplanerisch gesehen ist das Nordufer ein viereinhalb Kilometer langer Streifen zwischen den beiden großen Brücken, der drei ehemalige Werften beherbergt. Zusammen mit allen Becken und Docks nimmt die Uferlinie zehn Kilometer in Anspruch. Das Gebiet hat eine Fläche von rund 2,5 Quadratkilometern und bietet Raum für schätzungsweise je eine Mil-

Client: Eriksbergs Förvaltnings AB
Landscape architect: Bruno Richter Arkitektkontor
Architects: Arkitektlaget AB und Arkitekturkompaniet; White Arkitekter AB
Artists: Claes Hake, Pål Svensson, Per Kirkeby, Bengt Lundin, Görel Steg, Torsten Jurell
Construction period: 1990 to 1993

replaced by an expressway. The southern section o the city of Göteborg had lost touch with the ver water that led to its foundation.

By the time interest began to arise in the riv er as an element of city planning. However, resto ration of the lost connection to the river prove to be a gigantic undertaking. The expressway i an almost insuperable barrier and while magnifi cent tunnel projects have been drawn up, thei realization is a costly business.

Meanwhile, on the north bank the industria era had come to an abrupt end. In 1972, Götebor was still the largest shipbuilding city in the world by 1979, everything was gone. Shortly after, how ever, Sweden went through a construction boon and it did not take long to recognize the area's po tential for housing, particularly with its view of th river and the city on the opposite bank. Thus th scars of the shipbuilding era were either decon structed piece by piece or rebuilt as cultivated ver sions of the raw shipyard architecture. The firs new building to be completed in the vast industri al wastes of the north bank was a luxurious restau rant that sought not only to establish standards fo coming construction but also to attract attentio to the empty lots. Ten years ago, it would have in deed been inconceivable that Göteborg's firs Guide Michelin restaurant would be located in th industrial wilderness of the north.

In urban planning terms, the north bank con sists of a four-and-a-half-kilometre stretch o land between two major bridges, including thre former shipyards. With all the docks and basin the shoreline measures ten kilometres. It has bee estimated that the two-and-a-half square kilome tre area has room for two million square metres o housing and office floor space, corresponding t

bout 20,000 inhabitants and the same number of ob opportunities. The north bank development is hus the largest planning project experienced by he city since the suburban expansion of the sixties. ndeed, no development of comparable impact has aken place this close to the city since the realization of the city grid in the 19th century.

Apart from housing, industries and offices, he northern bank is to house parks, boulevards, lock walks, marinas, hotels, restaurants, exhibition halls, theatres and sports grounds, and new bridges and ferry lines will link it to the opposite hore. The main prerequisites for construction re proximity to the river and a marine profile. ndeed, without the water, the urban development nent project would be of little interest.

Private developers have been invited to contruct housing, while the infrastructure is being upplied by the main landowner, Eriksbergs Förvaltnings AB, a company belonging to the ormerly state-owned Celsius Corporation. The levelopment plans are laid down by the City Planning Authority in a master plan, the objective being to obtain extensive local variation and high level of exploitation on the basis of a basically square but somewhat irregular layout. Further objectives include creation of an integrated mix of functions; preservation of valuable buildings and environmental features; construction on moderate scale in adaptation to local conditions; the establishment of good links to the rest of the city, and public transportation.

A grid of streets and plantings has been developed in accordance with these guidelines, and the master plan outlines public space details to guarantee a homogeneous character. Varieties of paving and lighting are limited, as they were in the

lion Quadratmeter Büro- und Wohnfläche, was einer Zunahme von rund 20 000 Einwohnern und ebensovielen Arbeitsplätzen entspricht. Die Entwicklung des Nordufers ist damit das größte stadtplanerische Projekt seit dem Bau der Trabantenstädte in den sechziger Jahren, für die Innenstadt sogar seit der Anlage des Grundrasters im 19. Jahrhundert. Geplant sind neben ausgedehnten Wohn- und Gewerbegebieten Parks, Boulevards und Dock-Promenaden, Yachthäfen und Hotels, Ausstellungshallen, Theater sowie Sportplätze. Neue Fähren und Brücken sollen die Verbindung mit der City herstellen. Die Nähe zum Wasser und ein maritimes Profil sind bei allen Bauwerken die entscheidenden Gestaltungskriterien. Ohne das Wasser wäre das Projekt bei weitem nicht so interessant.

Private Entwicklungsgesellschaften waren aufgerufen, sich zu engagieren; die Infrastruktur steuert der Haupteigentümer bei, die Eriksbergs Förvaltnings AB. Die Entwicklungspläne werden in ihren Grundzügen von der Stadtplanungsbehörde entworfen. Ziel ist eine hohe Bebauungsdichte mit hohem Nutzungsgrad und stellenweise großen Variationsmöglichkeiten. Man will dies durch ein rechteckiges aber in gewisser Weise unregelmäßi-

Wohnbebauung entlang eines ehemaligen Trockendocks der Eriksberg-Werft nach den Vorstellungen des dänischen Architekturbüro Arkos. Das Büro hatte 1992 den skandinavienweiten Wettbewerb zur Umgestaltung des westlichen Teils des Nordufers gewonnen.

Housing development along a former dry dock at the Eriksberg Shipyard, as designed by the Danish architecture office Arkos. The practice won the Scandinavian competition for the conversion of the western section of the northern bank.

Nach dem Niedergang der
Schiffbau-Industrie in Göteborg boten sich Mitte der
achtziger Jahre ungeahnte
Möglichkeiten für eine city-
nahe Stadtentwicklung mit
Hafenambiente. Die ehe-
maligen Werfthallen werden
zu Hotels, Theatern, Aus-
stellungshallen und Büros
umfunktioniert.

The demise of the shipbuilding
industry in Göteborg made
way for undreamed-of development possibilities, close to
the city centre but with a
docklands atmosphere.
Former shipyard buildings
are now being turned into
hotels, theatres, exhibition
halls and offices.

Was vor zehn Jahren undenkbar gewesen wäre: Göteborgs erstes Guide-Michelin-Restaurant mitten in der »industriellen Wildnis« am Nordufer des Götaflusses. Das Luxusrestaurant war der erste Neubau im Bereich der Eriksberg-Werft. Mit seiner preisgekrönten Architektur setzte es Maßstäbe für die künftige Entwicklung des Gebiets.

A restaurant located in the industrial wilderness of Göteborg has been included in the Guide Michelin – something that would have been inconceivable ten years ago. The prize-winning architecture of the luxurious eating-place, the first new building to be completed in the Eriksberg Shipyard area, set standards for all future construction.

ges Straßen- und Grünflächenraster erreichen. Der Masterplan fordert unter anderem eine starke Mischung der Funktionen, den Erhalt wertvoller Gebäude und Landschaftsteile, zurückhaltende angepaßte Bebauung, sowie eine gute Anbindung an die City. Die Hauptstraße im Gebiet wird für Privatautos gesperrt sein.

Um dem Gebiet einen einheitlichen Charakter zu verleihen, wurde die Detailplanung für die öffentlichen Freiräume in den Masterplan aufgenommen. Beispielsweise ist die Auswahl etwa bei den Bodenbelägen oder der Beleuchtung wie im alten Hafen ziemlich beschränkt. Ein durchgehendes Thema ist die Qualität, sowohl beim Design als auch beim Material: Granitpflaster und die Arbeit von Künstlern machen die Dock-Promenaden zugleich robust und einladend. In jedem Detail ist die Handschrift des Architekten und Landschaftsarchitekten erkennbar. Die öffentlichen Freiflächen des Nordufers bestechen nicht durch Extravaganz, sondern durch lebendige Zeitlosigkeit und Funktionalität. Das Design ist gefällig und schlicht, es folgt wenigen, aber guten Regeln. Eine davon ist die Einbindung in den übergeordneten Kontext, was allerdings die Gefahr birgt, daß die Landschaftsarchitektur die Formen des Masterplans und das Design der Gebäude lediglich widerspiegelt.

Als Anfang der neunziger Jahre der Immobilienmarkt kollabierte, stellten die privaten Wohnbaugesellschaften ihr Engagement fast vollständig ein. Die Entwicklung der Infrastruktur konnte jedoch dank der wirtschaftlichen Stabilität des Hauptbauträgers mit ungebrochenem Glauben an die Zukunft des Areals weitergehen. Trotz der dürftigen wirtschaftlichen Aussichten für die kommenden Jahre blieben die Qualitätskriterien unberührt.

Auch wenn die derzeitige Bevölkerung nur einen Bruchteil der geplanten 20 000 Personen ausmacht – die hübschen Straßenzüge, Boulevards und Promenaden und die vielfältigen Einrichtungen des öffentlichen Lebens sind bereits da. Kunst ziert die Freiräume in einem für Göteborg bislang unerreichten Ausmaß.

Hartnäckig negiert das neue Viertel am Nordufer die Tatsache, daß der Boom vorüber ist. Der Traum von einem neuen, citynahen Stadtteil entstand zu einer Zeit, als das Leben im Zentrum für gutes Leben stand. Wie beim Traum des Ikarus war das eine erhabene Idee, deren Flügel schmolzen. Allein, sie weigert sich abzustürzen. Die wirtschaftlichen Schwierigkeiten haben die Entwicklung lediglich gebremst, was sich vielleicht als Vorteil erweist. So kann das Nordufer langsam wachsen, wie die Bäume und Menschen.

old shipyards, and quality is a consistent theme with regard to both design and material. There is an abundance of artistic participation, the dock walks are robust and inviting and the presence of the architect and landscape architect is obvious in every detail. The public spaces are generally designed along simple lines in accordance with the principle of subordination to the larger context. When the Swedish real estate market collapsed in the early nineties, the private housing companies cut down construction of new apartment buildings to practically nil. Despite this, development of the infrastructure has continued, thanks to the economic stability of Eriksbergs Förvaltnings AB, and bears witness to an unshakable belief in the future of the area. And despite the meagre economic outlook for the coming years, quality has never been tampered with.

Although the current inhabitation levels are just a fraction of the 20,000 planned, the nicely laid-out streets, boulevards and promenades have already been completed, along with other features of public life. Sculptures and other artistic embellishments of public space are also present to an extent earlier unknown in Göteborg.

The north bank stubbornly refuses to accept that the real estate boom of the eighties is over. The idea of creating a new city district three kilometres away from the city's heart was born in the days when downtown living was regarded as part of the good life. As in the case of Icarus, the ambition was majestic, but now the wax melted from the wings – but the north bank refuses to fall. Admittedly, the economic problems have slowed things down, but this may prove to be a blessing in disguise in that the north bank will now have time to grow together at the pace of the trees and the people.

Links: Das Werftgelände Lindholmen wurde zu einem Ausbildungszentrum umgestaltet. Granit stellt Verbindungen zur umgebenden Landschaft her und knüpft an Handwerkstraditionen an. Mitte: Hoffläche zwischen Wohnhäusern von Eriksberg. Rechts: Lundby Strand, früher Fabrikgelände, heute Büroviertel mit Granitskulpturen.

Left: Granite, which is used for the links to the surrounding landscape, recolects old craft traditions and also plays the main role at Lindholmen training centre, a former shipyard. Centre: A court between residential blocks in Eriksberg. Right: The former factory site of Lundby Shore is now an office quarter embellished with granite sculptures.

Im Mittelpunkt: die Themse

The Thames as nucleus

Eva Henze

London is pioneering an imaginative new approach to planning. The landscape is now recognized as the main organizing principle, integrating the meaning, function and structure of the city through its architecture, open space, recreation and nature conservation. This process has been initiated by the British landscape architect Kim Wilkie, who developed "The Thames Landscape Strategy", for the stretch of the river as it enters London between Hampton and Kew. Putting the Thames where it belongs – at the centre of landscape – Wilkie primarily revealed in his comprehensive consideration that landscape is the main factor in local and regional development.

Stimulated by the request to contribute to the Royal Fine Art Commission's "Thames Connections Exhibition" in 1991, Wilkie primarily showed the network of vistas in this historically important stretch of the Thames.

Auf zu neuen Ufern: Die Landschaft steht seit kurzem im Mittelpunkt der räumlichen Planung Greater Londons. Initiiert wurde diese Entwicklung durch die »Thames Landscape Strategy« des britischen Landschaftsarchitekten Kim Wilkie, der den abwechslungsreichen Themseabschnitt zwischen Hampton und Kew am Südwestrand Londons in den Mittelpunkt seiner Entwürfe stellte und so erstmals verdeutlichte, daß die Landschaft der zentrale Faktor der Gebietsentwicklung ist. Angeregt durch den kurzfristigen Auftrag, zur »Thames Connections Exhibition« (1991) der Royal Fine Art Commission beizutragen, beschäftigte Wilkie sich vorerst mit den Blickbeziehungen in diesem kulturhistorisch sehr bedeutsamen Themse-Abschnitt, der nicht nur als administrative Grenze fungiert, sondern auch als verbindendes Element.

Wollte man die Region in ihrem Charakter erhalten, das wurde deutlich, reichten die bestehenden Planungen auf der Ebene des Landes und der der einzelnen Boroughs nicht aus. Das Fehlen einer regionalen Zwischenstufe entpuppte sich in diesem Fall jedoch als positiv: Unterstützt durch die vier betroffenen Boroughs, sechs nationale Körperschaften öf-

Die Themse quert Greater London von West nach Ost. Auf 11 Meilen Länge zwischen Hampton und Kew wurde sie Gegenstand der Thames Landscape Strategy. Hier bildet sie die Grenze verschiedener Boroughs, obwohl sie eigentlich als Mittelpunkt der Landschaft zu sehen ist.

An eleven-mile stretch of the River Thames between Hampton and Kew was the subject of the Thames Landscape Strategy. As a dominant landscape element that crosses the Greater London area from west to east, the Thames needs to be seen as a connecting corridor rather than as an administrative boundary.

Die kulturhistorisch bedeutende Themse-Landschaft zwischen Hampton und Kew bildet den Kern der räumlichen Planung Greater Londons. New spatial planning for Greater London focuses on the historic and culturally rich Thames landscape between Hampton and Kew.

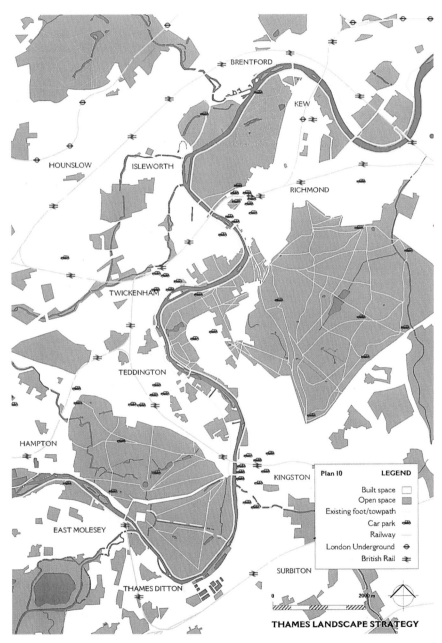

BRENTFORD

KEW

HOUNSLOW   ISLEWORTH

RICHMOND

TWICKENHAM

TEDDINGTON

HAMPTON

KINGSTON

EAST MOLESEY

SURBITON

THAMES DITTON

Plan 10   LEGEND

Built space
Open space
Existing foot/towpath
Car park
Railway
London Underground
British Rail

2000 m

THAMES LANDSCAPE STRATEGY

Revealing the considerable network of links, many of which still exist, helped demonstrate that the river is the dominant element, and that it needs to be seen as a connecting corridor rather than as an administrative boundary.

Supported by the four Boroughs involved, six national bodies and several local interest groups working together for the first time, Wilkie managed not only to cross administrative borders but also to combine all the different aspects that contribute to the character of this stretch. For these reasons the Strategy is also a very good example of the catalyst function of landscape architecture.

The strategic and transport advantages and rich natural resources of the area have attracted royalty and the patronage of architects and artists since the time of Henry V.

Several impressive maps in the Strategy show not only how many architects, painters and other artists have been connected with the area but also the number of famous people who have worked or lived there. Names like Christopher Wren, Lancelot Brown, Alexander Pope, Horace Walpole, J. M. W. Turner, Oskar Kokoschka and Mick Jagger appear.

In terms of cultural landscape this stretch of the river is unique. Not only is it the cradle of the English landscape movement, but there are also, due to the aristocratic nature of its architecture, more Grade I listed buildings and parks clustered together than anywhere else in Great Britain.

Kim Wilkie's career has influenced his perspective on the cultural landscape. Before studying landscape architecture at the University of California, Berkeley, he studied history for his M. A. degree at New College, Oxford. The central part of Wilkie's Strategy, complementing the

Weiträumige Kulturlandschaft und dicht besiedelte Arbeits- und Wohngebiete prägen den vielfältigen Charakter des Themseabschnittes westlich von Kew. Jeder Stadtteil, durch den die Themse fließt, hat sein eigenes Gesicht. Zum linearen Themsepark, der die Uferbereiche umfaßt, kommen weitere ausgedehnte Freiflächen.

Stretches of cultivated land and densely-populated tracts of living and working landscape mark the section of the Thames upstream from Kew. Each suburb through which the river flows has its own particular identity and is complemented by a "linear park" made up of the river banks and other large parks.

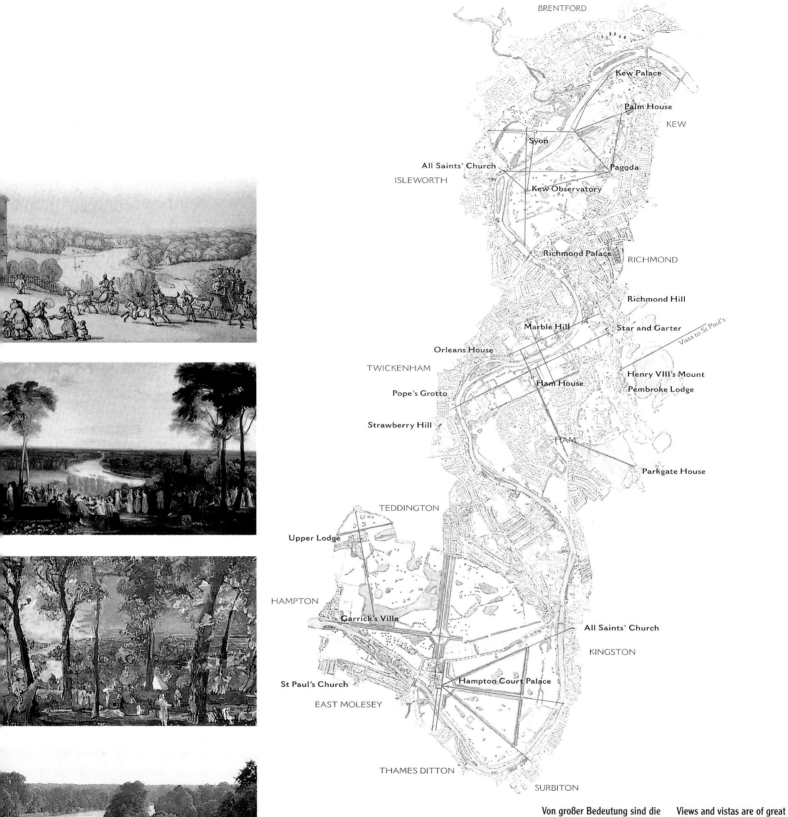

BRENTFORD

Kew Palace

Palm House

KEW

Syon

All Saints' Church

Pagoda

ISLEWORTH

Kew Observatory

Richmond Palace

RICHMOND

Richmond Hill

Marble Hill

Star and Garter

Vista to St Paul's

Orleans House

TWICKENHAM

Henry VIII's Mount

Pembroke Lodge

Ham House

Pope's Grotto

Strawberry Hill

HAM

Parkgate House

TEDDINGTON

Upper Lodge

HAMPTON

Garrick's Villa

All Saints' Church

KINGSTON

St Paul's Church

Hampton Court Palace

EAST MOLESEY

THAMES DITTON

SURBITON

Von großer Bedeutung sind die Ausblicke und Blickbeziehungen in der Themselandschaft. Einige der historischen Vista lines sind noch gut erhalten, so jene vom Henry VIII's Mound im Richmond Park zur St. Paul's Cathedral. Der Ausblick vom Richmond Hill beeindruckte etliche Maler. Von oben: Rowlandson 1803, Turner 1819, Kokoschka 1962.

Views and vistas are of great significance in the Thames landscape. Some of the historic sightlines are still in existence, such as the view from Henry VIII's Hill in Richmond Park onto St. Paul's Cathedral. The view afforded by Richmond Hill has long been a favourite with painters. From the top down: Rowlandson, 1803; Turner, 1819; Kokoschka, 1962.

fentlichen Rechts und einige Verbände, die hier erstmals zusammenarbeiteten, wurde nicht nur ein Überschreiten administrativer Grenzen, sondern auch eine ressortübergreifende Planung ermöglicht. Hierdurch konnte den Wechselbeziehungen Rechnung getragen und die Arbeit zu einem Paradebeispiel für die »Katalysatorfunktion« der Landschaftsplanung werden.

Dort, wo die Themse nach Norden schwenkt, um den massiven, tonigen Richmond Hill und seine Ausläufer zu umgehen, trugen die Lage am Verkehrsweg Themse, die strategische Funktion des Flusses, aber auch die natürliche Ausstattung der Landschaft zur großen Attraktivität des Raumes bei. Vor allem seit der Regierungszeit Heinrichs V. zog die Begeisterung der Aristokratie für diese Landschaft eine überwältigende kulturelle und künstlerische Entwicklung nach sich.

Die Anzahl der vor Ort tätigen oder dort lebenden Architekten, Maler und anderer Künstler war und ist beachtlich. Man trifft auf Namen wie Christopher Wren, Lancelot Brown, Alexander Pope, Horace Walpole, J. M. W. Turner, Oskar Kokoschka und Mick Jagger. Aber auch die Jahrhunderte während Konzentration der unterschiedlichsten Künstler auf bestimmte Regionen ist erstaunlich.

Darüber hinaus liegt in dem betroffenen Gebiet nicht nur die Wiege des englischen Landschaftsgartens, sondern es befinden sich hier, als Folge der herrschaftlich-architektonischen Aktivitäten, mehr denkmalgeschützte Gebäude als irgendwo sonst in Großbritannien. Die gründliche Berücksichtigung der letztgenannten Aspekte bei der »Thames Landscape Strategy« ist sicher nicht ganz unbeeinflußt vom Werdegang des Planers, der vor seinem Studium der Landschaftsarchitektur an der Universität von Berkeley/Kalifornien in Oxford Geschichte studiert hat.

Bemerkenswert an der Auseinandersetzung Wilkies mit den landschaftsprägenden Faktoren ist aber nicht nur die umfassende Bestandsaufnahme der vielfältigen kulturhistorischen Einflüsse im Raum, sondern auch die behutsame Einarbeitung der heutigen »Wohn- und Arbeitslandschaft Themse«. Denn der Planer ist nicht nur für die Ästhetik der Landschaft, sondern auch für ihre »Funktionstüchtigkeit« verantwortlich.

Dementsprechend geht es Wilkie nicht um die museale Konservierung einer zweifelsohne kulturhistorisch bedeutsamen Landschaft, denn das würde Stagnation bedeuten. Vielmehr geht es ihm darum, den Charakter einer Landschaft zu verstehen, um ihn auf heutige Verhältnisse übertragen

extensive analysis of historical influences on the landscape, is the integration with today's "living and working landscape". His way of thinking makes it clear that the landscape is not merely created by its visual appearance but also by its use. Wilkie's intention is not simply to conserve or restore historically important landscape. That could lead to stagnation. His purpose is to understand all the factors which contribute to the character of a special landscape and allow that character to continue to inspire new design.

Recognizing both the invaluable role of the boat building industry in the life and character of this stretch and its present economic crisis, Wilkie for example suggested the encouragement of further economic development which compliments the landscape.

With regard to a possible revival of river transport (in times of crowded roads), his proposal of mixed uses – boatyards and riverrelated businesses – seems to be a constructive solution to the problem. It keeps the main structures viable and leaves space for further development.

This stretch of the Thames also plays an important role as a "linear park" especially for Londoners and visitors. The opening of the royal parks at Hampton Court and Bushy Park already attracted thousands of visitors in the late 1830s. The growing metropolis has still left many open spaces as relics of an aristocratic landscape. These open spaces work as green divisions between different towns with specific identities as well as green links for recreation. In connection with recreation Wilkie's main concern is to explain "how the landscape works" and to contribute towards a general understanding of this as the main basis for the acceptance and support of

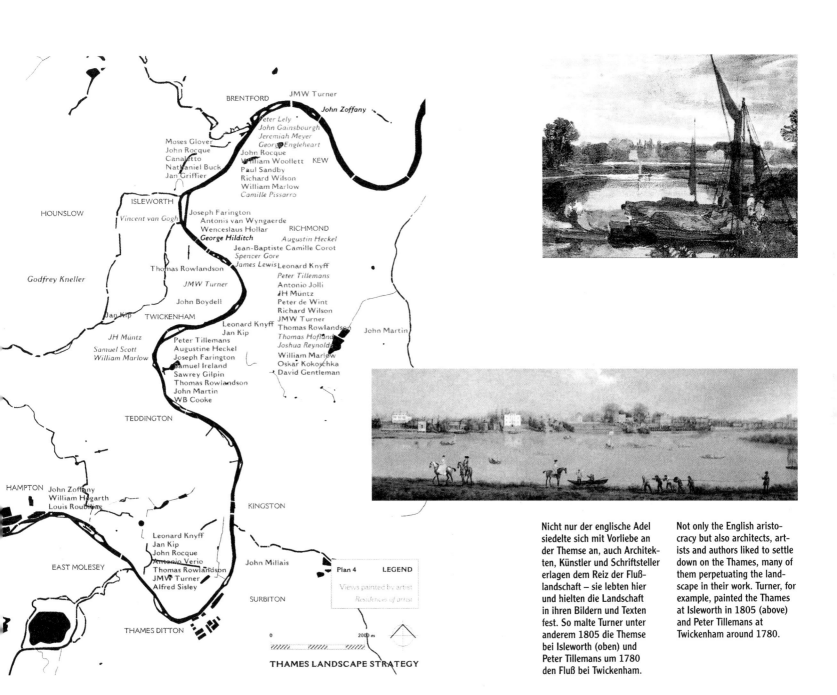

BRENTFORD
JMW Turner
John Zoffany

Peter Lely
John Gainsbourgh
Jeremiah Meyer
George Engleheart
Moses Glover
John Rocque
John Rocque
Canaletto
William Woollett
KEW
Nathaniel Buck
Paul Sandby
Jan Griffier
Richard Wilson
William Marlow
Camille Pissarro

ISLEWORTH
HOUNSLOW
Joseph Farington
Vincent van Gogh
Antonis van Wyngaerde
Wenceslaus Hollar
RICHMOND
George Hilditch
Augustin Heckel
Jean-Baptiste Camille Corot
Spencer Gore
Thomas Rowlandson
James Lewis
Leonard Knyff
Peter Tillemans
JMW Turner
Antonio Jolli
JH Müntz
John Boydell
Peter de Wint
Richard Wilson
JMW Turner
Leonard Knyff
Thomas Rowlandson
John Martin
Jan Kip
Thomas Hofland
TWICKENHAM
Joshua Reynolds
JH Müntz
Peter Tillemans
William Marlow
Samuel Scott
Augustine Heckel
Oskar Kokoschka
William Marlow
Joseph Farington
David Gentleman
Samuel Ireland
Sawrey Gilpin
Thomas Rowlandson
John Martin
WB Cooke
Godfrey Kneller
Jan Kip

TEDDINGTON

HAMPTON
John Zoffany
William Hogarth
Louis Roubiliac
KINGSTON

Leonard Knyff
Jan Kip
John Rocque
EAST MOLESEY
Antonio Verio
Thomas Rowlandson
John Millais
JMW Turner
Alfred Sisley
SURBITON

Plan 4   LEGEND
Views painted by artist
Residences of artist

THAMES DITTON

0   2000 m

THAMES LANDSCAPE STRATEGY

Nicht nur der englische Adel siedelte sich mit Vorliebe an der Themse an, auch Architekten, Künstler und Schriftsteller erlagen dem Reiz der Fluß-landschaft – sie lebten hier und hielten die Landschaft in ihren Bildern und Texten fest. So malte Turner unter anderem 1805 die Themse bei Isleworth (oben) und Peter Tillemans um 1780 den Fluß bei Twickenham.

Not only the English aristo-cracy but also architects, artists and authors liked to settle down on the Thames, many of them perpetuating the land-scape in their work. Turner, for example, painted the Thames at Isleworth in 1805 (above) and Peter Tillemans at Twickenham around 1780.

Auch wenn der Verfasser erkennt, daß die Werften zu einer unschätzbaren Bereicherung dieses Themse-Abschnitts beitragen, muß – angesichts der Krise in der Schiffsindustrie – nach Auswegen gesucht werden, die große Eingriffe in den Charakter der Landschaft verhindern, ohne jedoch den wirtschaftlich desolaten Zustand zu zementieren. Insbesondere im Hinblick auf eine mögliche Wiederbelebung des Schiffsverkehrs (in Zeiten überlasteter Straßen) erscheint der Vorschlag, kleinere Betriebe und Büros mit in die Werftgebäude aufzunehmen und so den Charakter des Gebietes weitgehend zu erhalten, als adäquater Lösungsansatz.

Eine weitere wichtige Funktion dieses Themse-Abschnitts ist die eines »linearen Parks« für die Londoner Bevölkerung. Wo schon 1838 die Öffnung der königlichen Ländereien in Hampton Court und Bushy Park für die Bevölkerung zu vierstelligen Besucherzahlen führte, sind nach dem Heranrücken der Großstadt immer noch zahlreiche Parks als erfreuliches Relikt herrschaftlicher Strukturen erhalten geblieben. Sie stellen wichtige Grünzonen zwischen den einzelnen Siedlungskernen dar und unterteilen diesen Teil Londons in überschaubare Stadtteile mit eigener Identität. Im Zusammenhang mit der Erholungsnutzung geht es Wilkie darum, die landschaftsbedeutsamen Faktoren herauszuarbeiten und sie in das allgemeine Bewußtsein zu bringen. Dies ist eine Grundvoraussetzung für die Akzeptanz und Unterstützung der Planungen. Auf diese Weise bietet sich die Chance, daß auch großangelegte Entwicklungsmaßnahmen, wie die Umgestaltung von einem guten Drittel der Uferrandbebauung in Kingston, von allen getragen, wenn nicht gar mit Engagement mitverfolgt wird.

Auch für den Arten- und Biotopschutz ist die Flußlandschaft bedeutend, worauf in der Strategy näher eingegangen wird. Dieser Themenbereich soll hier jedoch nicht weiter vertieft werden. Vielmehr möchte ich an einem Beispiel näher auf die zweite Maßstabsebene der Strategy eingehen. Nach den bisherigen Untersuchungen und der Entwicklung von Zielvorstellun-

these proposals. This leads to the opportunity where even major new projects could enhance rather than destroy the river landscape and be greeted with excitement, as in the case of Kingston, where nearly 40 percent of the waterfront is to be redeveloped.

After analysis of the eleven-mile stretch as a whole and developing general policies on a small scale (ca. 1 : 50.000), Wilkie divided the landscape into twelve different Landscape Character Reaches. These parts have been analysed and proposals drawn up on a larger scale (ca. 1 : 5.000). Corresponding to the scale detailed designs still need to be worked up, but there are written proposals for the enhancement, development and management of every reach. In the Landscape Character Reach 2 "Hampton Court" for example the planting of trees is suggested to reduce the impact of new buildings and enhance the nature conservation value of the river edge. Another proposal concerns the Banqueting House of Hampton Court Palace where trees should be thinned to reveal the view. In both cases the final choice of which trees are to be removed or planted is left to the relevant bodies.

To promote nature conservation it is for example suggested the area of closemown grass be reduced, without limiting the specific areas or defining all other management strategies.

These proposals all follow the general policies for the whole stretch without restricting the landowner's own individuality or responsibility.

When it was published in 1994, the Thames Landscape Strategy was something of a landmark in integrated planning and community involvement. The approach has won international awards and has been much copied since. Achie-

Am Fluß lassen alte Bootshäuser, wenn auch umgebaut oder vom Verfall gekennzeichnet, den Charme der Gegend erahnen. Obwohl die Werftindustrie zum Erliegen kam, siedeln sich neue Betriebe an.

Dilapidated or renovated boathouses provide an idea of the area's charm. Although the boatbuilding industry has died out on upper reaches of the Thames, new kinds of businesses have moved into the sheds.

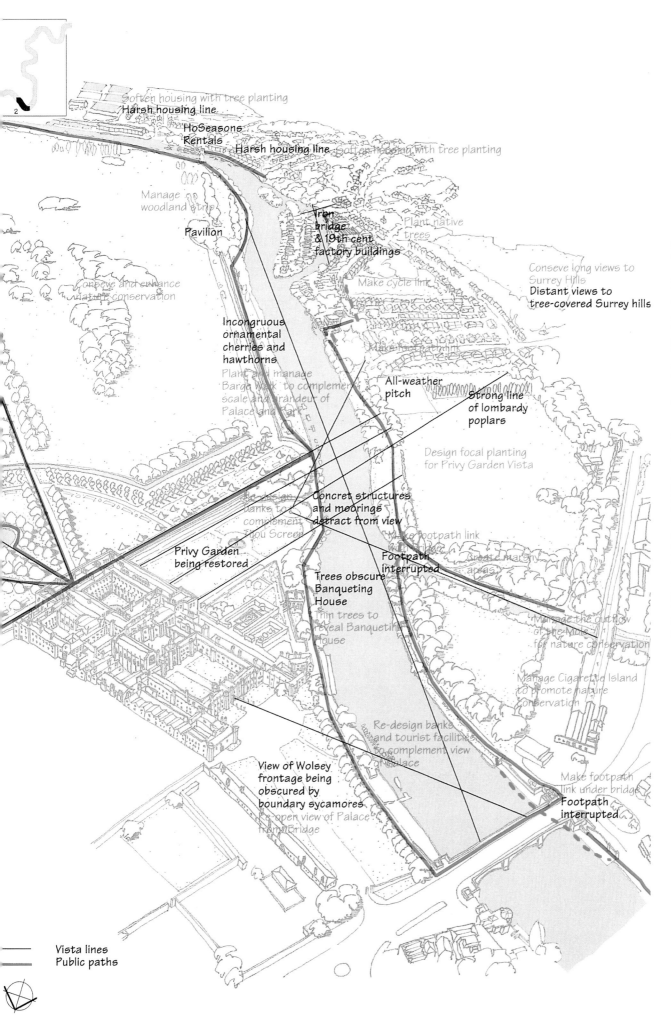

Soften housing with tree planting
Harsh housing line
HoSeasons Rentals
Harsh housing line
Soften housing with tree planting

Manage woodland strip

Pavilion

Iron bridge & 19th cent factory buildings

Plant native trees

Conseve long views to Surrey Hills
Distant views to tree-covered Surrey hills

Make cycle link

Conseve and enhance nature conservation

Incongruous ornamental cherries and hawthorns

Plant and manage Barge Walk to complement scale and grandeur of Palace and Gdn

All-weather pitch

Make footpath link

Strong line of lombardy poplars

Design focal planting for Privy Garden Vista

Re-design banks to complement Tijou Screen

Concret structures and moorings detract from view

Make footpath link

Create marsh areas

Privy Garden being restored

Footpath interrupted

Trees obscure Banqueting House

Thin trees to reveal Banqueting House

Manage the outflow of the Mole for nature conservation

Manage Cigarette Island to promote nature conservation

Re-design banks and tourist facilities to complement view of Palace

View of Wolsey frontage being obscured by boundary sycamores
Re-open view of Palace from Bridge

Make footpath link under bridge

Footpath interrupted

Vista lines
Public paths

In der Thames Landscape Strategy werden 12 Teilbereiche gesondert bearbeitet. Hier Analyse und Planungsvorschläge für den Bereich 2 bei Hampton Court, dominiert vom Palast und von mehreren großen Parks. Der Bewertungsplan mit den Anmerkungen (schwarze Schrift) wurde mit einem Deckblatt versehen, der die schriftlichen Vorschläge enthält (hier grün wiedergegeben). Diese Darstellung erlaubt den verschiedenen Trägern der Planung noch einen gewissen Gestaltungsspielraum.

The Thames Landscape Strategy differentiates between twelve sections of the river. Analysis and planning proposals are illustrated here for Landscape Character Reach 2, which is dominated by Hampton Court Palace and several extensive parks. The evaluation plan, which bears remarks in black, was accompanied by a cover sheet that puts forward solutions, reproduced here in green type – a procedure that provides other authorities with greater scope in making suggestions.

gen im ungefähren Maßstab 1:50000 wurde der insgesamt elf Meilen lange Themse-Abschnitt in zwölf landschaftliche Untereinheiten geteilt. Diese Teilbereiche wurden im Maßstab 1:5000 näher überplant. Allerdings sind auch hier, dem Maßstab entsprechend, keine exakt lokalisierten Forderungen aufgestellt, sondern die Vorschläge für Änderungs- und Unterhaltungsmaßnahmen verbal eingebracht worden. Dies soll im Abschnitt 2 »Hampton Court« gezeigt werden. Hier wird unter anderem die Einbindung von Neubaugebieten durch Baumpflanzungen gefordert, ohne daß der genaue Standort oder Pflanzenarten vorgegeben würden. Auch sollen die Blickbeziehungen zum sogenannten Banqueting House des Palastes wiederhergestellt werden, wobei die Auswahl der zu entfernenden Gehölze den zuständigen Körperschaften überlassen bleibt.

Mit diesen etwas stärker konkretisierten Zielvorstellungen ist den lokalen Handlungsträgern beziehungsweise den Grundeigentümern eine Richtung gewiesen, aber nicht jeglicher Handlungsspielraum oder das Verantwortungsbewußtsein genommen worden. Sie können (je nach Budget) tätig werden und somit auch ihr Engagement bekunden.

Als die Thames Landscape Strategy 1994 veröffentlicht wurde, war sie ein Paradebeispiel für integrative Planung und Bürgerbeteiligung. Die vorbildliche Herangehensweise führte dazu, dass der Arbeit internationale Preise zuteil wurden und sie häufig kopiert wurde.

Die Strategy hat bereits jetzt zahlreiche Planungs- und Richtlinienentscheidungen beeinflusst sowie mit ausgeführten Projekten Zeichen gesetzt. So wurde zum Beispiel aufgrund von Planungsentscheidungen die Bebauung im Uferbereich von Seething Wells und Brentford verhindert. Bereits ausgeführt sind unter anderem die Restauration von Abschnitten des Grand Union Kanals, der Uferbereiche in Hampton Court und Kingston, Garricks Tempel, die Neupflanzung der Alleen am Ham House und die Wiederherstellung der Flutwiesen um Syon House. Weitere detaillierte Studien werden in Abschnitten in Auftrag gegeben.

Der jüngste Erfolg war die Zuteilung von 2.1 Millionen Englische Pfund aus Lotteriemitteln, und die Wiederherstellung der Flutwiesen, womit einer Unterstützung von weiteren 2 Millionen Pfund aus europäischen Fördermitteln gerechnet werden kann.

Der Londoner Bürgermeister hat sich nun für eine Ausdehnung des Konzepts stromabwärts durch die Hauptstadt und weiter bis zur Themsemündung ausgesprochen.

vements of the Strategy so far include planning and policy decisions as well as projects on the ground. Major planning decisions to prevent development include the Seething Wells and Brentford Waterfront decisions. Specific projects include the restoration of stretches of the Grand Union Canal the Hampton Court and Kingston riverbanks and the replanting of the Ham House avenues.

The last big leap has been the award of £2.1 million to the project by the Heritage Lottery Fund and the reinstatement of the tidal meadows which should be supported by a further £2 million of European environmental funds. The Mayor of London is now supporting an expansion of the Strategy through the centre of the capital.

Die Stadtteile entlang der Themse präsentieren sich am Fluß recht unterschiedlich. Oben neue Bebauung neben Richmond Bridge, eine von Geschäfts- und Wohnhäusern umgebene Terrassenlandschaft. Der Gebäudekomplex bei Kingston Bridge bezieht sich auf die Geschichte dieses Stadtteils als größter Marktplatz des Boroughs.

The waterfront of towns on the Thames differ greatly. Above: New development at Richmond Bridge – a terraced slope surrounded by business and residential buildings. The complex at Kingston Bridge reflects the community's past as the largest market town in the borough.

Place des Terreaux, Lyon

Place des Terreaux, Lyon

Christian Drevet

On an aerial photograph Place des Terreaux seems to interrupt the urban web of Lyon. It is a kind of gap connecting the Rhône with the Saône. Here the buildings stand close together, as if lined up. It is surprising how little planning was done in this area, and how it developed from the 17th to the 19th century all by itself on the grounds of the former fortifications. It is the beginning of the whole city, determining its two main axes: the east-west axis of urban growth and the north-south axis of the rivers. Located at the crossroads of both, the Place des Terreaux seems the city's major articulation. On a symbolic level it connects four powers: the city (city hall), the Church (Palais Saint-Pierre), the bourgeoisie (Massif des Terreaux) and the people (frontage of

Wenn man die Place des Terreaux auf einem Luftbild betrachtet, erscheint sie als Loch im Stadtgewebe von Lyon. Sie ist eine Art Durchschlupf, der die Rhône mit der Saône verbindet. Hier stehen die Gebäude eng aneinandergereiht. Mit Erstaunen stellt man fest, wie die Stadt vom 17. bis zum 19. Jahrhundert auf dem Terrain der ehemaligen Festungsanlagen gewachsen ist. Hier liegt der Ursprung der Stadt, der ihre Entwicklungsrichtungen vorgab: die Ost-West-Achse, entlang der die Stadt gewachsen ist, und die Nord-Süd-Achse, gebildet durch die Flüsse. Auf dem Kreuzungspunkt der zwei Achsen gelegen, erscheint die Place des Terreaux als wichtigstes Gelenk der Stadt. Auf symbolischer Ebene vereint sie vier Mächte: die Stadt (Rathaus), die Kirche (Palais Saint-Pierre), die Bourgeoisie (Massif des Terreaux) und das Volk (die Front des Croix-Rousse-Viertels). Diese vier Elemente umfassen den Bartholdibrunnen, also ein Kunstwerk.

Daß die Place des Terreaux das Zentrum der Stadt ist, wollten Daniel Buren und ich in unserem Entwurf deutlich machen. Deshalb leiteten wir ihn aus den vier Seiten des Platzes ab. Erfinden mußten wir zu seiner Ge-

Daniel Buren und Christian Drevet gestalteten einen Platz im Schnittpunkt zweier Achsen und vier Mächte – der Ursprung der Stadt Lyon.
Daniel Buren and Christian Drevet designed a square at the intersection of two axes and four powers where the city of Lyon began.

Nord-Süd- und Ost-West-Linien bilden ein Raster, in Daniel Burens Entwurf sogar auf der Nordfassade. Fontänen steigen aus den Rasterquadraten des Platzes empor.
Lines running north-south and east-west form a grid on the square in Daniel Buren's design, where they even appear on the north elevation. Fountains rise from each rectangle.

he Croix-Rousse quarter). These four elements
e grouped around the Berthold fountain, that
, around a work of art.

In our design Daniel Buren and I wanted to
ake it clear that Place des Terreaux is the hub of
he city. We therefore based our design on the
our sides of the square. Nothing needed to be in-
ented for it. First we moved the Berthold foun-
ain, turning it by 90 degrees, in front of the
orth side of the square. The construction of an
nderground car park gave the impetus for this.
'he fountain had to get out of the way of the pit,
nd we proposed giving it a new location right
way and not to move anything back – an eco-
omical solution in any case. The new position
f the fountain exposes the beautiful facade of the
Massif des Terreaux, which had disappeared be-
ind it. The three impressive facades, city hall,
'alais Saint-Pierre and Massif des Terreaux, are
ow set off from the common north side of the
quare. The architecture of the plain residential
uildings recedes more into the background.
Having the king, the priest and the bourgeois on
hree of its sides and the people on the fourth, the
quare recounts the social history of our country.
One could even say that the fountain now ex-
resses the idea of democracy: the sculpture of
he victorious quadriga virtually proceeds from
he hill of the Lyon silk weavers and heads south.
The fountain hereby corresponds to the geogra-
hy, because the Rhône and the Saône flow from
he mountains in the north towards the sea in the
outh. The base of the fountain seems to have
een chipped off the hill of the Croix-Rousse
uarter rising between the two rivers. The horses,
training in all directions, also address the city
all and the buildings in the Terreaux quarter.

Gestreifte Säulen und kubische Bänke erheben sich aus dem Raster der Place des Terreaux in Lyon. Die Säulen bilden den Hintergrund für den mächtigen Bartholdibrunnen, den Christian Drevet und Daniel Buren von der Stirnseite des Platzes an die Längsseite rückten. Hinter den Säulen verstecken sich zahlreiche Durchgänge in das Croix-Rousse-Viertel.

Striped columns and cubic benches stand out from the grid of Place des Terreaux in Lyon. The columns form a stage set for the massive Berthold fountain, which Christian Drevet and Daniel Buren moved from the square's facade to the longitudinal side. Numerous passages into the Croix-Rousse quarter are concealed behind the columns.

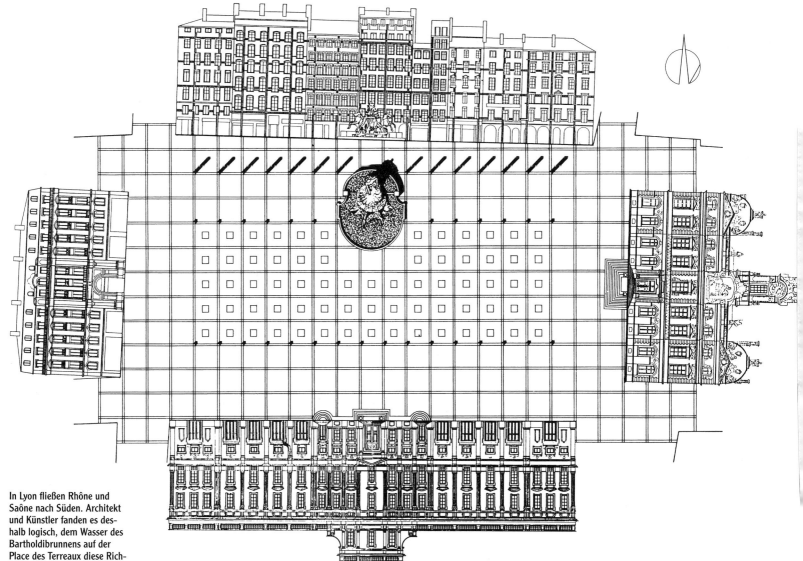

In Lyon fließen Rhône und Saône nach Süden. Architekt und Künstler fanden es deshalb logisch, dem Wasser des Bartholdibrunnens auf der Place des Terreaux diese Richtung zu geben. Das Platzraster leitet sich aus dem Pilastermaß der Südfassade ab.

The Rhône and the Saône run south in Lyon. The architect and the artist therefore found it consequential to give the waters of the Berthold fountain the same direction on the Place des Terreaux. The square's grid is based on the dimensions of the pilasters on the south elevation.

staltung nichts. Zunächst rückten wir den Bartholdibrunnen vor die Nordfassade des Platzes, um 90 Grad gedreht. Der Bau einer Tiefgarage gab den Anlaß dazu. Der Brunnen mußte der Baugrube weichen, und wir schlugen vor, ihn gleich neu zu plazieren und nicht mehr zurückzuschieben – allemal eine ökonomische Lösung. Durch die neue Position des Brunnens kommt die schöne Fassade des Massif des Terreaux wieder zum Vorschein. Die drei noblen Fassaden – Rathaus, Palais Saint-Pierre und Massif des Terreaux – setzen sich nun von der populären Nordfassade des Platzes ab, und die Architektur der einfachen Wohnhäuser rückt stärker in den Vordergrund. Mit König, Priester und Bürger auf drei Seiten, dem Volk auf der vierten, erzählt der Platz die Sozialgeschichte unseres Landes. Man kann sogar sagen, daß der Brunnen nun die Idee der Demokratie übersetzt: die Skulptur des siegreichen Vierspänners fährt geradezu aus dem Hügel der Lyoner Sei-

They have more room along the length of th• square than they had earlier on the width. Th• square's grid is derived from the facade of th• Palais Saint-Pierre. The 5.90-metre distance between the columns became the fundamenta• unit of the quadratic grid we extended over th• square. The square thus appears considerabl• larger than it was. We traced the lines of the gri• in granite. Lengthwise the grid runs along th• axis of the line extending from the entrance of th• city hall to the Galerie des Terreaux. Following it• extension leads to both rivers. Cars drive only o• the periphery of the square.

The new waterworks are movable three-dimensional elements. The force of the Berthold fountain and the position of the Place des Terreaux between the Rhône and the Saône made installing waterworks appropriate. In the centre of every rectangle in the grid we set a small water jet; there are 69 in all. Roads, café terraces and the area in front of the city hall were excluded. A shallow basin of black granite surrounds each jet. It can become a fountain, its basin a reflecting surface of water. When it dries it disappears completely, leaving room for other uses. The impression of walking through a forest of water or even of walking on water lends charm to the square. Traffic noises are muffled by the fountains, which is an advantage for the outdoor cafés. The facades are reflected in the 69 water surfaces, their lines superimposed on the grid on the ground. In the summer, visitors to the stone square appreciate the coolness radiated by the fountains.

Three major static elements stand out from the grid: the Berthold fountain, the row of columns behind it in the rhythm of the grid, and the cubic benches on the edge of the grid in the area between the fountain and the columns. The row of columns reinforces the stage-like base of the Berthold fountain. The columns create a space connecting the square and the frontage of the Croix-Rousse quarter, yet without narrowing the width of the square. This space became an open gallery. The columns counter the colossal pilasters of the Palais Saint-Pierre. At the same time they stand for the numerous entrances to the Croix-Rousse quarter, contrasting with the small number of entrances on the square's other three sides. The edge of the square is a refuge where cubic benches invite taking a meditative break.

denweber heraus, in Richtung Süden. Damit fügt sich der Brunnen auch logisch in die Geographie, denn Rhône und Saône fließen nach Süden. Der Sockel des Brunnens scheint gleichsam aus dem Hügel des Croix-Rousse-Viertels gebrochen, der sich zwischen beiden Flüssen erhebt.

Das Raster des Platzes leitet sich aus der Fassade des Palais Saint-Pierre ab. Der Säulenabstand von 5,90 Meter wurde zur Grundeinheit des Quadratrasters, das wir über den Platz spannten. So erscheint der Platz beträchtlich größer als vorher. Die Rasterlinien gestalteten wir in Granit. Die Längsrichtung des Rasters liegt auf der Achse, die sich vom Eingang des Rathauses zur Galerie des Terreaux ziehen läßt. In ihrer Verlängerung erreicht man die beiden Flüsse. Autos fahren nur am Rande des Platzes, der größere Teil bleibt den Fußgängern vorbehalten.

Die neuen Wasserspiele sind bewegliche, dreidimensionale Elemente. Die Kraft des Bartholdibrunnens und die Lage der Place des Terreaux zwischen Rhône und Saône legten es nahe, Wasserspiele zu installieren. Im Mittelpunkt jedes Rasterfeldes installierten wir eine kleine Wasserdüse, insgesamt 69. Fahrwege, Caféterrassen und Rathausvorplatz blieben ausgespart. Eine flaches Becken aus schwarzem Granit umfaßt jede Düse. Sie kann zum Springbrunnen werden, das Becken aber auch zur spiegelnden Wasserfläche. Trocknet es ab, verschwindet es vollständig und läßt Platz für andere Nutzungen. Der Eindruck, durch einen Wasserwald zu schreiten oder sogar auf dem Wasser zu laufen, verleiht dem Platz seinen Reiz. Verkehrsgeräusche werden durch die Springbrunnen gemildert – ein Gewinn für die Caféterrassen auf der Place des Terreaux. Die Fassaden spiegeln sich in den 69 Wasserspielen, ihre Konturen überlagern sich mit dem Bodenraster. Im Sommer schätzen die Besucher des steinernen Platzes die von den Springbrunnen verbreitete Frische.

Drei statische Hauptelemente erheben sich aus dem Raster: der Bartholdibrunnen, hinter ihm eine Säulenreihe im Rasterrhythmus und kubische Bänke auf den Schnittstellen des Rasters im Bereich zwischen Brunnen und Säulen. Die Säulenreihe verstärkt den Bühnengrund des Bartholdibrunnens. Die Säulen vermitteln zwischen dem Platz und der Fassade des Croix-Rousse-Viertels, ohne jedoch die Breite des Platzes zu schmälern. Dieser Raum ist zur offenen Galerie geworden. Die Säulen antworten auf die kolossalen Pilaster des Palais Saint-Pierre und stehen gleichzeitig für die zahlreichen Eingänge ins Croix-Rousse-Viertel – ein Gegensatz zu den wenigen Eingängen in den drei anderen Häuserfronten am Platz.

Place des Terreaux, Lyon
Client: Grand Lyon and City of Lyon
Architect: Christian Drevet, Lyon
Sculptor: Daniel Buren, Paris
Assistants: Bruno Bossard, Catalin Badea; architects
Art and architecture coordinator: Sylvaine van den Esch (Art/Entreprise)
Size: 8000 square metres
Construction: April – December 1994
Costs: FF 20 million

Platz der Menschenrechte in Evry

The Square of Human Rights at Evry

Kathryn Gustafson

Ein Platz als Gemeindezentrum – angelegt für Aufführungen aller Art und bereichert von drei ganz verschiedenen Wasserspielen.
Various kinds of water features characterize a public open space at the centre of the new town of Evry, near Paris.

Der Platz der Menschenrechte liegt im Zentrum von Evry, einer neuen Gemeinde 20 Kilometer südlich von Paris. Er wurde als zentraler Raum konzipiert, prägnant und dynamisch, geeignet für Theater, Kunstperformances und andere kulturelle Aktivitäten. Ursprünglich fiel das Gelände nach Norden zum Boulevard Coquibus hin ab und lag somit mit dem Rücken zur Südsonne.

Die neue Gestaltung mit einer vertieften Mitte ermöglicht es, die umliegenden Flächen, die wie eine flache Schale leicht ansteigen, als Zuschauerbereiche zu nutzen. Da bei der Planung des Platzes und des Boulevards die Fußgänger be-

Human Rights Square is located in the centre
f Evry, a new town located some 20 kilometres
outh of Paris, and consists of a plaza bordered to
ne north by Boulevard Coquibus and the train
ation, and by the new town hall and Mario
otta's cathedral to the south. It is set off from the
hamber of Industry and Commerce to the east
y a walkway and from the cathedral cloister to
ne west by the principal vehicle access road.

The square was conceived as a central area
here free expression, both concise and dynamic,
as to be possible, and is therefore suitable for
laying, performances and cultural activities. In
s original design, the plaza sloped down north-
ards to the Boulevard Coquibus, but has now
een given a new geometry featuring a shallow-
owl like depression in the middle. The treat-
ent of the square and boulevard gives priority
o pedestrians while reducing the impact of traf-
c. Light gray granite from Brittany was chosen
or the paving in order to show off the surround-
ng buildings, while a grid of white crystal gran-
e paving introduces an element of articulation.

All in all, the plaza has three water features,
ach with a different feel. The "Dragon Basin",
n organically-shaped water pool made of Brazil-
an green granite, forms a horizontal line at the
ase of the Town Hall and cathedral, thus an-
horing them in a spatial sense and dividing them
ff from the sloping movement that leads down
o the centre of the plaza.

The second water feature, titled "Fences and
Grasses", consists of a field of water jets. The
urved movements of the water were inspired by
ne way wind moves through fields of wheat, re-
alling the agricultural character of the site before
ne new town was built. At the same time, by

vorzugt wurden, sind
die Störungen durch
den Straßenverkehr ge-
ring. Für den Belag
wurde ein hellgrauer
Granit aus der Breta-
gne gewählt; ein Raster
aus weißem Kristall-
granit strukturiert die
Oberfläche des Platzes.
Darauf befinden sich
drei Springbrunnen,
die ganz unterschied-
lich gestaltet sind. Das
Spiegelwasserbecken,
»Drachenbrunnen« ge-
nannt, ist ein organisch
geformtes Becken aus
grünem brasilianischem
Granit. Es bildet eine
horizontale Linie an
der Basis von Rathaus
und Kathedrale, veran-
kert sie im Raum und
trennt sie von der zum
Platzzentrum abfallenden Ebene. Das Wasserspiel »Zäune und Gräser« ist
ein Feld mit Wasserdüsen. Die Kurven und Bewegungen dieser Düsen
wurden von großen, im Wind wogenden Kornfeldern inspiriert. Sie
symbolisieren die landwirtschaftliche Vergangenheit der Region. Die
Aufgabe dieses Wasserspiels ist es, das Amphitheater zu beleben, wenn es
gerade nicht bespielt wird. Es bringt dem Platz Licht und Bewegung, kann
aber bei Aufführungen abgeschaltet werden. Es ist eine verspielte Anlage,
die über neun getrennte Kreisläufe geregelt wird, wobei die Höhe der
Wasserstrahlen bis zu drei Metern betragen kann. Das dritte Element des
zentralen Platzes in Evry ist ein turbulente Becken, ein sich beständig
bewegender Wasserstreifen, der an den kochenden Kern der Erde erinnern
soll. Das Becken wird von drei kleinen Fußgängerbrücken aus weißem

Zäune und Gräser« nennt die
andschaftsarchitektin Kathryn
ustafson eins ihrer Wasser-
piele auf dem zentralen Platz
er neuen Stadt Evry bei Paris.
ie Bewegung des aus Düsen
rojizierten Wassers erinnert
n die wogenden Kornfelder,
e sich hier erstreckten. Oben
chts zwei weitere Wasser-
stallationen, der »Drachen-
runnen« und das »turbulente
ecken«.

"Fences and Grasses" is the
name that Kathryn Gustafson
gave a field of water jets at the
central square in the new town
of Evry, near Paris. The curved
movements of the jets were inspired by the way that wind
moves through fields of wheat
and recall the site's agricultural past. Above right: The
two other water features:
the "Dragon Basin" and the
"Turbulent Pool".

Das organisch geformte Becken des »Drachenbrunnen« auf dem Platz der Menschenrechte in Evry ist aus grünem brasilianischem Granit gefertigt. Die Wasserprojektionen auf einer schiefen Ebene des Platzes leiten über zu einem Bassin, dessen Wasser sich ständig bewegt und aus dem kochenden Kern des Erdinneren zu entspringen scheint.

The organically-shaped "Dragon Basin" at the Place des Droits de l'Homme in Evry is made of Brazilian green granite. The water produced by the jets in the "Fences and Grasses" water feature runs down the sloping square and gathers in a pool of turbulent water that seems to emerge from the fiery mantle beneath the earth's surface.

Granit überquert, wobei das bewegte Wasser von unten durch Scheinwerfer angestrahlt wird.

Der Platz bietet vielerlei Blickbeziehungen und Verbindungen zwischen den Niveaus, die gleichzeitig die verschiedenen Gebäude verbinden. Der leicht geneigte Boden verbindet das Rathaus mit dem Boulevard und dem Bahnhof. Die fast überwältigende Präsenz des Wassers ist das Element, das am besten zur mineralischen Welt paßt.

Ein Teil des Platzes liegt über einer Tiefgarage, deren Eingänge und Zufahrt in die Platzgestaltung integriert werden mußten. Auch die Garage selbst hat den Entwurf beeinflußt. Eine Reihe von Elementen dient dazu, den Übergang in die Tiefgarage angenehmer zu gestalten. Die beiden Eingänge sind zur besseren Orientierung unterschiedlich gestaltet. Der östliche, die »Signalwand«, führt in eine Zwischenebene hinab. In der Wand befindet sich auf Augenhöhe ein langer Schlitz, der den Blick auf das Wasserfeld und das bewegte Becken freigibt. Der Klang des Wassers und das Sonnenlicht fließen in den Raum und begleiten den Übergang zum Parkhaus. Der westliche, die »Große Treppe«, entspricht in ihrem Maßstab und Stil der Kathedrale von Mario Botta. Eine Reihe von schlanken Bäumen begleitet diesen Eingang und verbindet die Kathedrale mit dem Boulevard Coquibus.

Lichteffekte schaffen zudem eine theatralische Atmosphäre. Indirektes, reflektiertes Licht beleuchtet die verschiedenen Kompositionselemente. Die Ränder und Fußwege erhielten eigens für den Platz entworfene Laternen, die mittlerweile im Handel erhältlich sind.

adding light and animation, the water featur[e] combats the problem of emptiness and non[-]fulfilment that amphitheatres tend to have whe[n] not in use, but can be turned off when a pe[r]formance is in progress on the square.

The third water feature consists of a turbulen[t] pool, a strip of water in permanent motion, in[-]spired by the boiling of rock inside the earth. [It] is crossed by three small footbridges in whi[te] granite, with submerged lights illuminating th[e] movement of the water from below.

The square provides many viewpoints, an[d] the differences in level are connected in all direc[-]tions, forming links between the buildings, whil[e] the slight inclination of the site establishes [a] visual relationship between the town hall and th[e] railway station. Water, which is almost over[-]whelming in its presence at the square, is the ele[-]ment that best combines with the mineral world.

Part of the square is built over an under[-]ground public car park, meaning that pedestria[n] and vehicle access had to be incorporated into th[e] design. A series of elements serve to make th[e] transition to the subterranean garage more agree[-]able. The two pedestrian entrances are marke[dly] different; the eastern one, known as the "Mu[r] Signal" (Signal Wall), leads down to the interme[-]diate level area and features a long, eye-level sl[it] in the wall that furnishes a view of the jet fiel[d] and the turbulent pool. Sunlight and the sound of the water flow into this space, guiding th[e] transition down into the car park. The wester[n] entrance, the "Grand Escalier" (Grand Flight [of] Steps), is dimensioned in response to the scal[e] and style of Mario Botta's cathedral and is accom[-]panied by a line of columnar trees that link th[e] cathedral to Boulevard Coquibus.

Client: City of Evry
Landscape architect: Kathryn Gustafson
Collaborator: Gérard Pras
Size: 1.5 hectares
Completion date: October 1991

Barceloneta: ein neuer Horizont

A new horizon for Barceloneta

Maria Cristina Tullio

As the French land-scape architect Michel Corajoud puts it, all the tension of a land-scape concentrates on the horizon, and it was in keeping with this tenet that the Catalonian architects Artigues–Henrich–Roig–Carraso–Castañeda recently designed a seaside promenade in the Barceloneta district of Barcelona. The district itself was originally erected in the 17th century, but the ground plan and buildings had undergone frequent changes over time, with the streets soon being extended to an area of reclaimed bottom land, and factories and port facilities being built along the shoreline. They were joined in this century by a lido, which soon attracted bars and eating places erected without building permission. These, however, were recently torn down at the instruction of the Spanish Ministry of Construction and the Environment in keeping with the Coasts Act, returning the shoreline with its views of the sea and the horizon to the public domain.

The architects do not only believe in the power of the horizon but also in simple forms and undorned elegance. In order to mark the border between the city and the shore, they continued the alignment of the streets and pathways, which

Für den französischen Landschaftsarchitekten Michel Corajoud konzentrieren sich die Spannungen einer Landschaft stets an ihrer langen Horizontlinie. Das Meer und seinen Horizont erfahrbar zu machen, war das Ziel der kürzlich fertiggestellten neuen Uferpromenade im Barceloneta-Viertel in Barcelona. Allerlei zusammengebastelte und zum Teil baufällige Buden bildeten hier zuvor eine undurchlässige Barriere zwischen der Stadt und dem Meer. Als Fischersiedlung erbaute der Ingenieur Cenneño das Barceloneta-Viertel im siebzehnten Jahrhundert. Seitdem sind Stadtgrundriß und Gebäude immer wieder verändert worden: Das Straßennetz dehnte sich bald auf das neugewonnene Schwemmland aus, zu den ursprünglichen Bauten kamen zahlreiche Fabriken und Hafeneinrichtungen am Ufer hinzu. In unserem Jahrhundert schließlich entstand eine Badeanstalt, und nach und nach siedelten sich illegale Gaststätten auf der schma-

Zugang zum Meer statt Nostalgie – eine schlichte Uferpromenade hat die Buden am Strand des Barceloneta-Viertels abgelöst.

A simple seaside promenade has replaced the ramshackle collection of bars and shacks that once lined a Barcelona beach.

Im 17. Jahrhundert als kleine Fischersiedlung erbaut, wuchs das Barceloneta-Viertel bis heute zur dichten Stadt mit einer Mischung aus Wohnen und Produzieren in Hafennähe. Berühmt und berüchtigt waren seine Bars und Fischrestaurants am Strand. Ihr Abriß bedeutete Platz für neue öffentliche Räume zwischen Stadt und Meer.

Originally built in the 17th century as a small fishing settlement, Barceloneta has since grown into a dense residential and commercial port district, famous and infamous alike for the dives and fish restaurants that lined the beach. These were torn down recently, making way for the creation of new public space between the city and the sea.

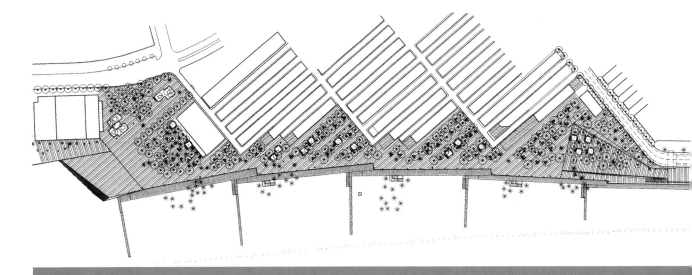

Die klaren Linien und einfachen Formen der neuen Uferpromenade verleihen der
bunten Meeresfront des Barceloneta-Viertels ein einheit-
liches Aussehen. Die Architekten ergänzten willkürlich
abbrechende Straßen mit
einem Steinpflaster, das die
strenge Geometrie der
Häuserparzellen aufnimmt.

The clear lines and simple
forms of the new promenade
lend a sense of coherence to
the colourful seaside front of
Barceloneta. The architects
continued the outlines of
streets that come to an abrupt
stop by using stone paving
laid in the strict geometry of
the building plots.

Geschickt eingefügte schräge Ebenen und Treppen überwinden die Höhensprünge zwischen den alten Straßen des Viertels und der neuen Uferpromenade. In Streifen gepflanzte Känguruhbäume, Tipuana tipu und weiße Maulbeerbäume leiten von der Stadt zum Strand über. Dort bieten Phoenix dactilyfera und Washingtonia-Palmen den Besuchern schattige Inseln.

Differences in elevation between the old streets of Barceloneta and the new seaside promenade are overcome with skillfully inserted slopes and stepways. Strips of she-oak, Tipuana tipu and white mulberry lead from the city to the beach, where Phoenix dactylifera and Washingtonia palms provide welcome shade.

Promenade at Barceloneta, Barcelona
Client: Ajuntament de Barcelona; Ministeri d'Obras Públiques i Medi Ambient
Architects: Jaume Artigues, Jordi Henrich, Miquel Roig, Olga Tarraso,
Anna M. Castañeda
Size: 25,000 square metres
Planning: 1993
Construction: 1994–1995
Costs: Pts 1,131, 813,715

len Uferzone an. Daß diese kürzlich abgerissen wurden, veranlaßte das spa nische Bau- und Umwelt-Ministerium unter Berufung auf die Küstenge setze. Das Ufer ist somit wieder zum öffentlichen Raum geworden.

Die neue Uferpromenade ist das Werk der katalanischen Architekte Artigues–Henrich–Roig–Tarraso–Castañeda. Ihr Motto: einfache Forme und schlichte Eleganz. Um eine klare Grenzlinie zwischen Stadt und Küst zu schaffen, ergänzten sie die willkürlich abbrechenden Straßen und Weg mit einem Steinpflaster, das die strenge Geometrie der Häuserparzellen auf nimmt. Höhensprünge zwischen neuen und alten Wegen überwanden si durch geschickt eingefügte schräge Ebenen und Treppen, deren Spiel vo Licht und Schatten das Gelände beleben. Mit rhythmisch auf der Ufer promenade gepflanzten Baumgruppen (Känguruhbaum, Tipuana tipu weißer Maulbeerbaum) gaben sie dem Viertel eine unverwechselbare Mee resfassade. Am Strand wachsen verschiedene Palmenarten (Phoenix dacty lifera, Washingtonia) und bieten den Besuchern schattige Orte zum Ver weilen.

Das Thema der Grenze zwischen Stadt und Meer taucht immer wiede in der Gestaltung der Architekten auf. So schaffen zum Beispiel hölzern Stege den Übergang vom Steinpflaster der Promenade zum Sandstrand de Meeres. Das Holz fügt sich als natürliches, warmes Material harmonisch i die Umgebung und trennt gleichzeitig die Bereiche voneinander. Ein Lichtinszenierung unterstreicht des Nachts den Strand.

Der wiedergewonnene Meereshorizont tröstet über das Verschwinde des Barceloneta von früher hinweg – jenes heruntergekommenen, aber le bendigen Viertels mit seinen Buden und Tischen auf dem Sand. Und es is sicher eine Frage der Zeit, bis auch das neue Viertel sich mit alltäglichen Leben füllt, mit Geschichten und mit Spaziergängern, die den Horizont su chen. Dann wird der Ort für die Bewohner wirklich zu ihrem Ort und be siegt die Nostalgie, die unweigerlich aufkommt, wenn gewohnte Stätter verändert werden, und sei das neu Entstehende noch so gut.

Wenn Italo Calvino von seiner »unsichtbaren Stadt« Zenobia spricht gibt er zu bedenken, daß sich Städte in zwei Kategorien einteilen lassen »diejenigen, die im Laufe der Jahre und der Veränderungen immer wiede Wünschen zu Form verhelfen, und diejenigen, in denen die Wünsche ent weder dazu beitragen, die Stadt auszulöschen, oder aber selber aus der Stad ausgelöscht werden.« Barcelona gehört sicherlich auch heute zu der erster Gruppe von Städten.

Als schmale Trennlinie verläuft ein Holzsteg zwischen dem Steinpflaster der Stadt und dem Sandstrand. Weitere Holzstege führen zum Meer (Belagsplan gegenüber). Das Holz fügt sich als warmes, natürliches Material harmonisch in die Umgebung und trennt den Stein der Stadt vom Sand des Meeres.

A wooden boardwalk divides off the city from the beach; others lead down to the sea (opposite: paving plan). The warm natural material of the boardwalk merges in harmoniously with the surroundings and creates a clear distinction between the stone paving of the shoreline and the sand of the beach.

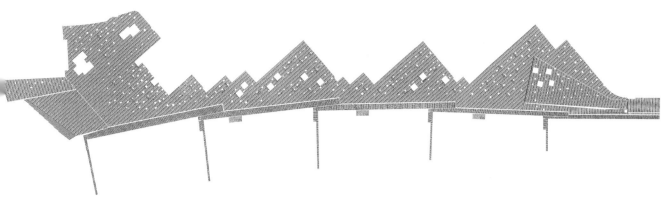

low come to an abrupt stop, with stone paving that traces the angular geometry of the former buildings. Differences in elevation between the new and old paths are overcome with skillfully inserted slopes and stepways that create an interesting play of light and shade, thus contributing to the liveliness of the links. Moreover, they have given the district an unmistakable maritime backdrop with rhythmic plantings of groups of trees (she-oak, *Tipuana tipu,* white mulberry), while various kinds of palms, such as *Phoenix dactylifera* and *Washingtonia* grow on the beach.

The theme of the boundary between city and sea is ever-present in the architects' work. At Barceloneta, for example, wooden boardwalks link the promenade to the beach; the wood, a warm natural material, merges in with the paving and the sand while marking a clear distinction between the two. At night, the clear lines of the beach are underscored by lighting. The reclaimed view of the sea and the horizon help reconcile one to the loss of the old Barceloneta beach front, with its dilapidated but lively shacks and the tables set out on the sand. With time, the district will refill with life, and with people who enjoy gazing out at the horizon. The beach and the waterfront will gain the feeling of home again, and help overcome the nostalgia that inevitably arises when changes are abruptly made to a familiar place, no matter how much improvements the changes mean. In his book "Invisible Cities", the Italian novelist Italo Calvino points out that there are two categories of city: "those that give form to wishes over the course of years and the changes of time, and those in which wishes help destroy the city, or are destroyed by the city." Barcelona surely belongs to the first category.

Wenn Industrie und Hafen Stück für Stück zurückweichen, gewinnt der öffentliche Raum. Die Barceloneta-Promenade ist einer der Bausteine der neuen Waterfront Barcelonas.

In Barcelona, industrial development and port facilities have been replaced step by step by public open spaces. The Barceloneta promenade is one of the component in Barcelona's new waterfront.

Malmö rückt näher ans Meer

Malmö moves closer to the sea

Agneta Persson

Schon seit langem gibt es Diskussionen darüber, wie die Grenze der Stadt Malmö zum Meer aussehen soll. Bis weit ins 19. Jahrhundert bildeten die Häuserblocks den Abschluss zum Wasser. Langsam rückte die Strandlinie weiter hinaus, als die Eisenbahn ein Stück in den Sund verlegt wurde und Aufschüttungen neues Land für Industrie und Hafenanlagen brachten. Die lang gestreckte Halbinsel Västra Hamnen entstand zwischen 1947 und 1987 aus unterschiedlichem Aufschüttungsmaterial. In den 1980er Jahren sollte das Areal für Industrieansiedlungen genutzt werden. Nach vielen Diskussionen schuf das Amt für öffentliche Bauvorhaben von Malmö den Scaniapark als Grünstreifen am Wasser – nicht sehr aufwändig, aber interessant durch seine Lage als Verlängerung des Ribersborgstrandes.

Zum Jahreswechsel 1997/98 beschloss die Stadt, die internationale Bauausstellung Bo01, Stadt der Zukunft, nach Västra Hamnen zu verlegen. Denn die Stadtverantwortlichen wollten Malmö in der Zwischenzeit als Technologie- und Forschungsstandort etablieren und am Hafen ein durchmischtes Quartier schaffen. Västra Hamnen, bis dahin trostloses, windexponiertes Ödland, änderte so Status und Identität. Die Bo01-Arbeitsgruppe unter der Leitung von Professor Klas Tham legte im Frühjahr 1998 den endgültigen Standort im Westen von Västra Hamnen fest und betonte so die Exponiertheit und Einzigartigkeit des Ortes: das Meer, den Himmel, den Wind, den Sonnenuntergang und den Horizont.

Bo01 hatte eine klare Vision zur Frage, wie nahe am Meer gebaut werden sollte: Die Bewohner von Malmö würden eine neue urbane Promenade am Meer lieben, einen Ort, an dem man dem Wasser nahe sein, die Sonne genießen, die Kräfte des Wetters auf sich wirken lassen und die großartige Aussicht genießen kann. Das Amt für öffentliche Bauvorhaben vertrat die Linie, die sie in den 1980ern so engagiert verfolgt hatte: Entweder ein Park oder ungestaltete Natur sollten direkt ans Meer grenzen. Das Resultat der Diskussionen mit der Stadt ergab einen Kompromiss: Die südliche Hälfte des Parks sollte eine einladende Strandpromenade werden, mit Sitzgelegenheiten in der Abendsonne. Die nördliche Hälfte sollte als Daniapark in ihrer ursprünglichen Breite erhalten bleiben.

Zehn Landschaftsarchitekturbüros wurden geladen, nach klaren Vorgaben von Bo01 Entwürfe für den öffentlichen Freiraum zu erarbei-

Die Einwohner von Malmö genießen das urbane Leben auf der neuen Strandpromenade im Bo01-Viertel Västra Hamnen.

The inhabitants of Malmö enjoy urban life on the new seafront promenade in the Bo01 district at Västra Hamnen.

For a long time, there have been discussion about how the border between the city of Malm and the sea should look. Far into the 19th century, blocks of houses made the border to the sea Slowly, the shoreline moved outward, as the railway was shifted partially into the water and land fills created new land for industrial plants an docks. The elongated peninsula Västra Hamnen was developed between 1947 and 1987 out of deposits from various fill materials. In the 1980 industrial plants were to be established at thi site. After many discussions, the Departement c Public Works of Malmö created Scaniapark, linear green space on the waterfront – not ver elaborate, but yet still interesting, its location be ing an extension of the Ribersborgstrand.

At the turn of 1997/98, the city decided t move the international housing exhibitio Bo01 City of Tomorrow to Västra Hamner City officials now wanted to establish Malmö a a technology and research location and in thi spirit create a diverse quarter. With this deci sion Västra Hamnen, a desolate windswep wasteland changed both status and identity The Bo01 project team under Professor Kla Tham, determined the final location in th west of Västra Hamnen and thus emphasise the exposed position and uniqueness of the lo cation: the ocean, the sky, the wind, the sunset and the horizon.

Bo01 had a clear vision on just how close t the ocean buildings should be erected: The in habitants of Malmö would love a new urba promenade at the sea – a place, where the could be close to the water, enjoy the sun, fee the powers of the weather and enjoy the grea view. But the Departement of Public Work

Auf der Sundspromenade können Spaziergänger auf einem
dreihundert Meter langen
Holzdeck direkt am Öresund
schlendern. Holztreppen führen
Passanten ans Wasser. An son-
nigen Tagen lädt das Meer ein
zum Schwimmen, an stürmi-
schen Tagen ist die Uferlinie
Wind und Wetter ausgesetzt.

On Sundspromenade strollers
can take a walk on a three
hundred metre wooden boardwalk directly along the Öresund. Wooden steps lead down
to the water's edge. On sunny
days the calm ocean invites
people to take a swim, on
stormy days the beach is exposed to wind and weather.

Sitzstufen sind ins Holzdeck integriert. An den Gebäuden findet sich Straßenpflaster mit einem Band aus schräg verlegten Glasplatten. Die raue Steinschüttung war bereits Teil der alten Ufersicherung.

Steps to sit on are integrated into the wooden deck. Alongside the buildings the street is paved with a stretch of diagonally laid glass plates. The rough rock fill was already a part of the old shore protection.

took the same stand it had so avidly pursued in the 1980s: a park or unspoiled nature should form the border to the sea, not an industrial or urban district. The result of the discussion with the city's officials was a compromise: The southern part of the park should be turned into an inviting promenade, Sundspromenade, with seating facilities in the evening sun. The northern part of the park should be kept in its original width – as Daniapark.

Ten landscape architecture offices were invited to design plans for the public open space, following clear instructions by Bo01. The outcome of the competition was that four different offices were commissioned to design the public open space: FFNS, Sweden, represented by Thorbjörn Andersson and PeGe Hillinge, planned Daniapark. Jeppe Aagaard Andersen Landscape Architects, Denmark, designed Sundspromenade, Stig L. Andersson Landscape Architects, Denmark, were responsible for Ankarpark and 13.3 Landscape Architects from Norway, represented by Tormod Sikkeland and Eivind Saxhaug, concentrated on the inner section including the lowered square Scaniaplatsen between Sundspromenade and Daniapark.

Sundspromenade. Today, the vision of an urban promenade, filled with pulsating life is reality. Jeppe Aagaard Andersen's magnificent three hundred metre long wooden deck with spacious steps leading to the sea invites visitors to use the location in various ways. Old couples sit here and drink coffee from their thermos, children jump up and down on the steps, playing, skimpily dressed teenagers stretch out in the sun, others sit right at the waterfront, with their feet in the water, reading. Fashion photo shoots are taken on

Sundspromenade, Malmö, Sweden
Client: City of Malmö
Landscape architect: Jeppe Aagaard Andersen
Engineer: Jens Abildgaard
Size: 10,300 square metres
Construction 2000 – 2001
Costs: 2,7 million Euro

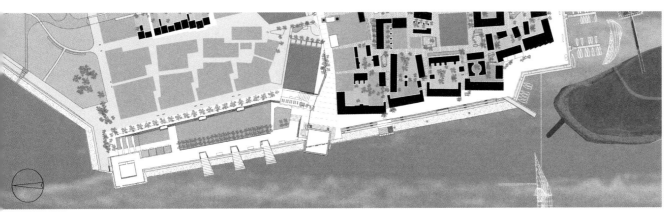

he deck, which thus turns into a catwalk – the dramatic sky serving as a backdrop. Inline skaters and cyclists glide by on the way to Daniapark and Scaniapark.

When the sun sets into the sea behind the Öresund Bridge and darkness falls, you can enjoy the clear, starry sky. On the paved section of the promenade thousands of little sparkling lights line the deck. Here and there, glass panes are lowered into the ground and are illuminated from underneath in different shades of blue. Jeppe Aagaard Andersen successfully created a poetic site that emphasises the ocean and the sky. The deck itself is on the verge of non-design, yet the details are carefully thought through. The rest of the floor consists of paved stone with playful inlays of glass and wood. Sitting against the outside of the pier wall, one can enjoy the ocean view, slightly hidden but protected from the wind.

The rough boulder line already existed – without it the fill material would be washed out into the sea. The art work "Diamonds are everywhere" from Sigmundur Gudmundsson makes the grey stones look like sparkling diamonds.

ten. Ergebnis des Wettbewerbs war, dass vier verschiedene Büros mit der Gestaltung des öffentlichen Raumes beauftragt wurden: FFNS Schweden, vertreten durch Thorbjörn Andersson und PeGe Hillinge, planten den Daniapark, Jeppe Aagaard Andersen Landschaftsarchitekten, Dänemark, gestalteten die Sundspromenade, Stig L. Andersson Landschaftsarchitekten, Dänemark, projektierten den Ankarpark und 13.3 Landschaftsarchitekten, Norwegen, vertreten durch Tormod Sikkeland und Eivind Saxhaug, konzentrierten sich auf den inneren Bereich mitsamt dem abgesenkten Platz Scaniaplatsen zwischen Sundspromenade und Daniapark.

Sundspromenade. Heute ist die Vision einer urbanen Strandpromenade mit pulsierendem Leben Realität. Jeppe Aagaard Andersens großartiges dreihundert Meter langes Holzdeck mit großzügig gestalteten Stufen zum Wasser lädt die Besucher ein, den Ort auf unterschiedliche Weise zu nutzen. Älter Paare sitzen da und trinken mitgebrachten Kaffee, Kinder hüpfen auf den Stufen herum und spielen, leichtbekleidete Teenies liegen ausgestreckt in der Sonne, einige sitzen am Ufer mit den Füßen im Wasser und lesen. Models werden auf dem Steg fotografiert, der so zum Catwalk wird, mit einem dramatischem Himmel als Hintergrund. Inline-Skater und Radfahren gleiten vorbei auf dem Weg zum Daniapark und zum Scaniapark.

Wenn die Sonne im Meer hinter der Öresundbrücke versinkt und es dunkel wird, kann man den klaren Sternenhimmel sehen. Auf dem gepflasterten Teil der Promenade leuchten Tausende kleine Lichter in einer Linie mit dem Steg. Im Bodenbelag sind verstreut Glasplatten eingelegt, die von unten in Blautönen beleuchtet werden. Jeppe Aagaard Andersen

Insgesamt zeichnen vier Büros verantwortlich für die Gestaltung der Freiräume im Bo01-Viertel Västra Hamnen: für den Daniapark im nördlichen Teil der Uferkante Thorbjörn Andersson und PeGe Hillinge von FFNS, für die südlich anschließende Sundspromenade die Landschaftsarchitekten um Jeppe Aagaard Andersen. 13.3 Landschaftsarchitekten gestalteten den abgesenkten Scaniaplatsen dazwischen sowie die inneren Bereiche des Quartiers. Der Entwurf für den Ankarpark, der innerhalb des neuen Wohnviertels liegt, stammt von Stig L. Andersson (siehe Topos 40).

A total of four different offices are responsible for the design of the open spaces in the Bo01 district of Västra Hamnen: Thorbjörn Andersson and PeGe Hillinge from FFNS for the Daniapark in the northern part of the shore's edge, the landscape architects around Jeppe Aagaard Anders Andersen for the Sundspromenade adjoining on the southern side. 13.3 Landscape Architects designed the sunken Scaniaplatsen in between as well as the inner areas of the district. Stig L. Andersson contributed the plan for Ankarpark, which lies inside the new residential quarter (see Topos 40).

Daniapark, Malmö, Sweden
Client: City of Malmö
Landscape architects: Thorbjörn Andersson and PeGe Hillinge, FFNS Architects
Collaborators: Veronika Borg, Peter Ekroth, Clotte Frank, Sven Hedlund, Kenneth Hilldén, Anders Lidström
Lighting: Michael Hallbert
Size: 20,000 square metres
Construction: 2001
Costs: 5 million Euro

Die Wand der Bastion am nördlichen Ende des Daniaparks benutzen Teenager als Kletterwand. Die hölzernen Balkone bieten Ausblick auf die zentrale Rasenfläche, die sogenannten »Späher« Blicke aufs Meer. Im Schutz der hölzernen Palisaden stehen sechs Meter lange robuste Bänke.

Today, the wall of the bastion at the northern end of Daniapark is used by teenagers as a climbing wall. The wooden balconies offer a view onto the central meadows and the sea can be seen from the so-called scouts. Wooden palisades protect six metres of sturdy benches.

Den Steg, eine leichte Konstruktion, die von der Bastion hinaus ins Meer ragt, erkor die Malmöer Jugend innerhalb kürzester Zeit zu ihrem Lieblingsplatz. Wagemutig stürzen sie sich hinab ins Meer. Die Ängstlicheren können das herrliche Panorama mit der Öresund-Brücke im Hintergrund genießen.

Of light-weight construction and stretching from the bastion into the sea, the footbridge quickly became the favourite place for Malmö's youths. Audaciously they plunge down into the sea. The less daring can enjoy the magnificent panoramic view with the Öresund Bridge in the background.

gelang, einen poetischen Ort zu schaffen, der das Meer und den Himmel betont. Das Holzdeck selbst ist fast an der Grenze zum Nicht-Gestaltet-Sein, die Details jedoch sind wohl durchdacht. Der übrige Bodenbelag besteht aus Straßenpflaster mit verspielten Einlagen aus Glas und Holz. An der Mauer zum Pier kann man an der Außenseite etwas versteckt im Windschatten sitzen und aufs Meer schauen.

Die raue Steinschüttung existierte bereits – ohne sie würden die Aufschüttungen ins Meer hinaus treiben. Das Kunstwerk »Diamonds are everywhere« von Sigmundur Gudmundsson verwandelt die grauen Steine in glitzernde Diamanten.

Daniapark. Der Daniapark liegt noch dramatischer und exponierter am Meer. Teils grenzt er an die ruhige Ribersborgsbucht, teils an das stürmischere Meer im Norden. Die Bo01 wollte den Schnittpunkt der beiden Meeresteile betonen. Der Park sollte einerseits Raum für Aktivitäten wie auf der Sundspromenade bieten, andererseits für größere Veranstaltungen geeignet sein. Während die Sundspromenade an stürmischen Tagen Wind und Wetter total ausgesetzt ist, sollte es hier geschützte Bereiche und den sparsamen Einsatz von Vegetation geben.

Thorbjörn Andersson und PeGe Hillinge schufen einen formal strengen, klassischen Park mit starkem Bezug zum einzigartigen Ort. Die Grenze zum Meer und die Aussicht auf den Horizont dramatisieren sie auf geniale Weise. Geteerte, schützende Holzpalisaden betonen die bereits vorhandene Steinschüttung und erinnern an eine Festung. Aus den Palisaden brechen drei sogenannte Späher mit abschüssigen mauernumschlossenen Sitzstufen hinaus ins Meer. Während der Frühjahrs- und Herbststürme strömen kraftvolle Wellen herein. An ruhigen Tagen können Spaziergänger die stille, glatte Wasseroberfläche beobachten. Im Norden, beim Übergang der beiden Meeresteile, schufen die Landschaftsarchitekten eine Bastion. Eine

Scheinwerfer, montiert an drei 16 Meter hohen Masten, sorgen für Licht in der Parkanlage. Sie wirken, als würden sie sich gegen starken Wind stemmen, der vom Meer kommt.

Floodlights mounted on three 16 metre high masts provide illumination for the park. They seem to brace themselves against the strong winds coming off the sea.

Daniapark. Daniapark lies in an even mor dramatic and exposed waterfront location. It par tially borders the calm Ribersborgsbucht, partial ly the stormy ocean in the north. Bo01 intendec to emphasise the point where these different char acteristics of the ocean meet. On the one hand the park was to offer space for activities like or Sundspromenade, on the other hand it shoulc also be able to host large events. While Sunds promenade is completely exposed to wind anc weather on stormy days of the year, the plan her called for protected areas and scattered vegetation

Thorbjörn Andersson and PeGe Hillinge cre ated a park, classical and rigid in its design, with strong relationship to its unique location. The dramatise the border to the sea and the view onto the horizon in a brilliant way. Tarred, protecting palisades made out of wood accent the existing boulder lining and resemble a fortress. From the palisades, three so-called scouts cut out into the se with sloping seat-steps, framed by a wall. During spring and autumn storms powerful waves roll in On calm days, pedestrians can watch the peaceful smooth surface of the sea. In the north, where the calm and the stormy sea merge, the landscape ar chitects created a bastion. A slanted plateau lead to an overwhelming vista. A light construction a the edge of the platform resembles a bow of a ship It didn't take long for the courageous youngsters o Malmö to declare this site their favourite spot With a daredevil attitude, they dive into the ocean At the ramp, inline skaters and skateboarders mee for an informal training session. Daniapark offer all kinds of options for its visitors. They can expose themselves to wind and water, or stay sheltered in side the park, where beautiful, rustic wooden bal conies that resemble cigar boxes offer protection from the wind as well as a great view from a distance. The large grass field offers space for big musical events as well as everyday activities. On the planned edge between buildings and park pin oak (quercus palustris) grows in a straight line; plantings of perennials can be found in areas which are more protected from the wind. The light creates an extraordinary experience. In the evening, the low light of the sun creates interesting effects on the rough surfaces, at night, Danipark seems almost continental with its lamp posts and bollards. Here, you can sit in one of the "cigar boxes", enjoy the ambience and listen to the ocean.

Sundspromenade and Daniapark complement one another in an harmonic way. Jeppe Aagaard Andersen's romantically and poetically playful approach stands opposite the classical and robust solution by Thorbjörn Andersson and PeGe Hillinge, who were inspired by the type of construction used for ancient fortresses. Both offices used beautiful natural materials like granite and wood. All detail work is carefully carried out.

The intensity of use of the new open space by the inhabitants of Malmö – even after Bo01 – surpassed everyone's expectations. The unusually warm and long summer attracted even more people to the Bo01 area. No one expected Malmö's new favourite bathing area to develop here, but during the summer, a steady stream of sun-worshippers besieged the wooden deck, steps, scouts and bastion. A café and restaurant have already established themselves. In June, the City of Malmö decided to hold a Västra-Hamnen-Festival in Daniapark, with music and activities, related to the sea – maybe the beginning of a tradition. In August, Sweden's largest daily newspaper stated: "...here, the urban planners hit a home run."

geneigte Ebene führt zu einem hervorragenden Aussichtsplatz. Eine leichte Konstruktion am Rande der Plattform lässt an einen Schiffsbug denken. Die mutige Malmöer Jugend erkor diesen Ort innerhalb kürzester Zeit zu ihrem Lieblingsplatz. Von hier aus springen sie voller Todesverachtung ins Meer. Bei der Rampe treffen sich auch Inliner und Skateboarder zum informellen Training. Der Daniapark lässt seinen Besuchern alle Wahlmöglichkeiten. Sie können sich Wind und Meer aussetzen oder mehr im Inneren des Parks aufhalten, wo schöne, rustikale hölzerne Balkone, die an Zigarrenkisten erinnern, sowohl Schutz vor dem Wind als auch Aussicht aus der Distanz bieten. Die offene Rasenfläche ermöglicht größere Musikveranstaltungen genauso wie alltägliche Aktivitäten. An der geplanten Bebauungskante zwischen Park und neuem Wohnviertel wachsen Sumpfeichen (Quercus palustris) in einer Reihe, Staudenpflanzungen finden sich in windgeschützteren Bereichen. Das Licht verschafft ein außergewöhnliches Erlebnis. Abends erzielt das flach einfallende Sonnenlicht entlang der rauen Flächen interessante Effekte, nachts wirkt der Daniapark kontinental mit seinen Laternenmasten und Pollern. Hier sitzt man gerne in einer der »Zigarrenkisten«, lässt die Stimmung auf sich wirken und lauscht dem Meer.

Sundspromenade und Daniapark ergänzen einander auf eine ungewöhnlich geglückte Weise. Jeppe Aagaard Andersens romantischer und poetisch verspielter Herangehensweise steht die klassisch robuste, vom Festungsbau inspirierte Lösung von Thorbjörn Andersson und PeGe Hillinge gegenüber. Beide Büros verwendeten schöne Naturmaterialien wie Granit oder Holz. Die Detailarbeiten sind durchgehend sehr gut gemacht.

Die Nutzung der neuen Freiflächen durch die Malmöer übertrifft die kühnsten Erwartungen, auch nach dem Ende der Bo01. Der extrem warme und lange Sommer lockte noch mehr Menschen hinaus in die Bo01-Gegend. Niemand rechnete damit, dass hier Malmös neuer Badeplatz entstehen würde, aber während der Sommermonate bevölkerte ein ständiger Strom von Sonnenhungrigen den Steg, die Treppen, die Späher und die Bastion. Ein Café und ein Restaurant konnten sich etablieren. Im Juni beschloss die Stadt Malmö ein Västra-Hamnen-Festival im Daniapark abzuhalten, ein Fest mit Musik und Aktivitäten, die mit dem Meer zu tun haben – vielleicht der Beginn einer Tradition. Im August stellte Schwedens größte Tageszeitung fest: »...dass hier die Stadtplaner einen Volltreffer gelandet haben«.

Der Ankar Park in Malmö

Ankar Park in Malmö

Stig L. Andersson

Wind und Wetter werden den Park am Meer mit seinen unterschiedlichen Materialien ebenso verändern wie die Pflege.

The wind and weather will change the park by the sea with its different materials just as much as maintenance will.

Die moderne Stadt braucht nicht nur qualitätvolle Freiräume, vor allem ist fachliche Unterstützung notwendig beim Artikulieren von Maßnahmen, wie man dieses Ziel erreichen kann. Kürzlich wurde ich in Dänemark von einer Behörde gebeten, einige Richtlinien aufzustellen, um Politikern zu helfen, die Anforderungen an den öffentlichen Raum in unserer Zeit zu verstehen. Das Ergebnis spricht für sich: Die Behördenvertreter erwarteten von mir, ich solle eine Formel vorlegen, in der der Prozentsatz von Granitflächen durch die Zahl der Bänke dividiert und anschließend mit Beleuchtungskörpern und Bäumen multipliziert wird. Dies beruhte zweifellos auf einer Furcht vor Entwurfsmethoden, die neue Wege aufzeigen, auf ein Programm und ein Gesamtbudget zu reagieren. Die beteiligten Politiker interessierte andererseits weniger der Entwurf, solange er die Liste jener zivilen Werte betonte und ausdrückte, die ich aufgestellt und denen ich Bedeutung für öffentliche Räume beigemessen hatte: Solidarität; unterschiedliches Erscheinungsbild im Rhythmus von Tageslicht und Jahreszeiten; Einfühlsamkeit; Rücksicht auf sowohl geistige als auch körperliche Unterschiede bei den Nutzern; das Vorhandensein von Natur; rationaler und logischer Aufbau; Erbauung.

Obwohl alle öffentlichen Räume einen Entwerfer und Nutzer haben, sollte man nicht vergessen: Das wesentliche Element besteht im Raum selbst, in seinem Anblick, der bleibt, wenn der Entwerfer und die Nutzer längst nicht mehr da sind. Diese Tatsache, die einen entscheidenden Einfluss auf die Art und Weise hat, wie ein Raum wahrgenommen wird, liegt jenseits der programmatischen Kontrolle des (Landschafts-)Architekten. Neue Nutzungen, die sich früher oder später einstellen, wirken sich auf den ursprünglichen Entwurf aus, gleich, ob sie diesem nun zuträglich sind oder nicht. Dies erklärt, wie wichtig es ist, dass sowohl das künstlerische Engagement des Architekten als auch die erwartete Erfahrung und Wahrnehmung von Nutzern im Entwurf ihren Platz finden, um sicherzustellen, dass persönliche Entwurfsvorstellungen zu einer allgemein gültigen Antwort führen. Der Raum muss in einer Weise entworfen und gebaut werden, die unterschiedliche Wege der Erfahrung und Interpretation ermöglicht.

Aus dieser Perspektive ist das Entwerfen öffentlicher Räume die Kunst, die grundlegenden

There is an urgent need not only for high quality environments in the modern city but also and all the more so, for qualified assistance in formulating measures to achieve them. In Denmark I was recently asked by a local authority to draw up a set of guidelines to help politicians understand the requirements that a contemporary public space should fulfil. The result tells its own story: the civil servants expected me to come up with a formula that expresses the percentage of granite surfaces divided by the number of benches and multiplied by lighting fixtures and trees. This, no doubt, was due to a fear of design approaches that indicate new ways of responding to a program of objectives and an overall budget. On the other hand, the politicians involved were less concerned with the possible form of the layout as long as it accentuated and expressed the list of civic values I had drawn up as being of importance for public spaces: solidarity; transformation of scenery in accordance with the rhythms of daylight and the seasons; sensitivity; consideration of both mental and physical differences among users; the presence of nature; rational logic; devotion.

Although all public spaces have a designer and users, it should not be forgotten that the essential constituent is the space, the component that remains when the designer and users are long gone. This fact, which has a profound influence on the way a space is perceived, is beyond the programmatic control of the (landscape) architect. The new uses that occur sooner or later also affect the original design, regardless of whether they are suitable or not. This explains the importance of incorporating both the artistic commitment of the architect and the expected experience and perception of users into the design to ensure that pri

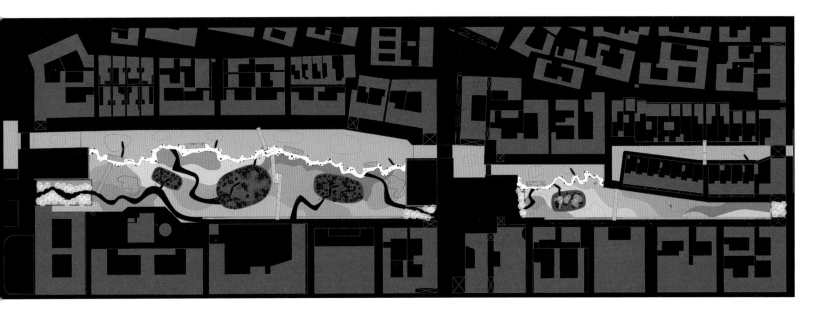

experience and perception of users into the design to ensure that private images evoke universal responses. The space has to be designed and built in a way that enables various kinds of experience and interpretation.

Seen from this perspective, designing public spaces is the art of synthesizing the fundamental conditions of modern existence into a composition of space, surfaces and textures to create a meaningful and accessible universe for people to use. These fundamental conditions include ethics, knowledge and beauty. They all need to be taken into account in a design.

It makes no sense today to play the classical tradition in landscape design off against the Romantic one. Both refer to historical conditions and perceptions that are reflected in the widest variety of styles. The design of Ankar Park is therefore not based on formal principles but de-

Bedingungen modernen Lebens in einer Komposition von Raum, Oberflächen und Strukturen zu synthetisieren, um bedeutsame und zugängliche Lebensumwelten zu schaffen. Diese grundlegenden Bedingungen schließen Ethik, Wissen und Schönheit mit ein, denen in einem Entwurf Rechnung zu tragen ist.

Es ist heute sinnlos, die klassische Tradition in der Landschaftsgestaltung gegen die romantische auszuspielen. Beide beziehen sich auf historische Bedingungen und Wahrnehmungsweisen, die sich in den unterschiedlichen Stilrichtungen widerspiegeln. Deshalb beruht auch die Gestalt des Ankar Parks nicht auf formalen Prinzipien, sondern sie ist durch Materie und Komposition bestimmt. Das drei Hektar große Ensemble am Rande von Malmö ist mittels einer Anzahl kleinerer Gartenbilder gegliedert, in denen Struktur, Masse, Präsenz, Materialien und Sinnlichkeit die Hauptrolle spielen, allesamt dem Wandel von Klima und Jahreszeiten unterworfen, der für diese Küstengegend in Schweden so typisch ist.

Der Park ist eine fließende Komposition von Räumen, Flächen und Strukturen, die in der Bewegung erfahren werden müssen. Hier ist die Szenerie nicht mehr als Bild mit frontaler, feststehender Perspektive ausgebildet. Stattdessen stellt sich der Park als ein Projekt dar, in dem Raumfolgen

Im Rahmen der Wohnbauausstellung Bo01 im Stadtteil Västra Hamnen entstand der Stadtteilpark Ankar Park nach Entwürfen des Landschaftsarchitekturbüros Stig L. Andersson. Räume, Wasser- und Vegetationsflächen sowie die Beschaffenheit der Materialien bewirken eine fließende Komposition.

Ankar Park was set up in the Västra Hamnen city district according to the design by Stig L. Andersson landscape architects within the framework of the Bo01 exhibition on residential architecture. Spaces, areas of water and vegetation, and different qualities of materials combine to create a flowing composition.

sich überlappen und offene Räume aufeinanderfolgen, die den Struktur-wechsel und die Qualitäten der verwendeten Materialien ins rechte Licht rücken sollen.

Bevor hier ein neuer Stadtteil wuchs, war die Gegend ein verlassenes Stück Hafen. So ist denn der Ankar Park ein Versuch, auszuloten, wie sich die Ma-terialien anfühlen, die mit diesem besonderen Ort verbunden sind. Beton, Asphalt, Gras, Holz und Eisen sind zeitgemäß und beziehen sich doch auf die Vergangenheit. Das Ergebnis ist ständig in Änderung begriffen, es fließt und entfaltet sich in einem überraschenden und unvorhergesehenen Zusammen-wirken von Materialien. Das gibt dem Parkerlebnis, bei jedem Besuch, eine neue didaktische Dimension.

Vor allem ist der Park auch als Abfolge eigenständiger, aber aufeinan-der bezogener Schauspiele gedacht – jedes mit eigenem Inhalt und Tem-po, von den sich langsam entwickelnden beständigen Biotopen bis hin zur schnellen und plötzlichen Reaktion auf das Wetter, die in der Bewegung des Windes im Gras und auf dem Wasser sichtbar wird. Das kann jeder fühlen, aber dennoch hat jede solche Wechselwirkung auch ein besonde-res visuelles Merkzeichen erhalten.

Die Ebene unterstützt den Raumeindruck. Der offene Blick von der Hafenkante in hellem Beton wird kontrastiert durch die dunklen Asphalt-wege, die sich durch die Wiesen schlängeln und neue Blickbeziehungen und eine Vielzahl von anregenden Erfahrungen mit den Materialien bieten. Heller Marmor bildet zusammen mit dunkelgrünen Kiefern und Beetein-fassungen aus rostigem Stahl eine Collage aus präzisen Kanten, Übergän-gen und Abfolgen von Ebenen und Materialien.

Die hölzernen Plattformen, die die Uferlinie verlängern, scheinen in ih-rer Art unauffällig und simpel. Aber dadurch, dass ihre Bretter in zwei Rich-tungen, nämlich senkrecht zu einander liegen, wird die Maserung, abhängig von der Sonneneinstrahlung, unterschiedlich wirken. Die Planken werden nie identisch aussehen, die strukturelle Qualität des Holzes wird bereichert.

Ähnlich verhält es sich mit dem Gras, von dem sieben verschiedene Ar-ten vorhanden sind: unter anderem Schilfgras, Blauschwingel und Bären-fellschwingel. Sie sind sehr unterschiedlich: Manche wachsen schnell, manche sind hoch und zart, andere sehr grün und saftig, aber alle reagie-ren auf Wind, so wie die kreisförmigen Stempel auf der Betonfläche auf das Klima reagiert. Jede Veränderung des Wetters kann an diesen Stempeln abgelesen werden: das allgegenwärtige Wasser wird sich unterschiedlich

in the outskirts of Malmö is orchestrated by number of minor narratives in which texture body, presence, materials and sensualism hold th major part, all conducted by the seasonal and cli matic changes that are so distinct for this coasta region of Southern Sweden.

The park is a floating composition of spaces surfaces and textures, which have to be experi enced in motion. The scenery here is no longer ar ticulated as a tableau with frontal and fixed per spectives. Instead the park presents itself as scheme of overlap-ping systems of sequences an open progressions put up to highlight the textur al variation and qualities of the given materials.

Before being transformed into a new urba district, the area used to be defunct harbour area Subsequently, the Anchor Park is an attempt t explore the full scope of tactility of the materials which are imbued by the specific local context Concrete, tarmac, grass, wood and iron brough together in a contemporary reference to the past The result is perpetually changing, floating an unfolding into a surprising and unforeseen in teraction of materials, adding a new didactic di mension to the experience of people every tim they visit the park.

Above all, the park has been conceived as a se ries of independent, yet correlated plays with eacl their modality and pulse, from the slow and tena cious pace of the biotopes to the quick and imme diate response to climate as it can be seen in th way the wind moves the grasses and the water. De spite the true sensation, each interaction is articu lated through a specific visual expression as well.

It is the plane, which supports the spatial ex pression. The open view from the coastline i bright concrete is counterpointed by the darl armac paths, which wind their way trough the meadow offering new sight lines and a multitude of textural stimulations. Bright marble brought together with dark green pine trees and rusted iron frames into a collage of precise edges, transitions, and changes in level and material.

The wooden platforms that prolong the laminated coastline may be plain and simple in their layout. Yet, by having the boards placed in two directions, perpendicular to each other, the grains will get different appearances depending on the direction of the sun-beams. The boards will never present themselves as identical but enrich the textural qualities of wood.

Similarly with the grass, of which there are even various kinds, sand reeds, blue grass and pear grass for instance. They come in all sorts: Some are fast growing, some tall and fragile, others very green and juicy, but they all respond to the wind on a constant basis, just like the circular stamps on the concrete slab react to the humidity. Whatever the weather, it can by read on its physical interaction with the stamps, because the omnipresent water will state itself differently whether in the form of ice, of dryness, of dust or of moisture.

Against these ever and fast changing appearances the Anchor Park presents another, and slower play, which is that of the co-existence between time and materials. If the climate stages an ongoing and uncontrollable interplay, the principles of maintenance decided and carried through by the public park authorities will provide the park with an unpredictable progression in terms of breaking down the state of the art.

The patterns of the various grasses that meet without a contour will get their shape and growth

Eine geschwungene Promenade aus Beton trennt die Wasserfläche von den Vegetationsflächen, bestehend aus unterschiedlichen Gräsern und Waldbiotopen. Im Lauf der Zeit werden sich die Materialien verändern: Grasflächen wachsen ineinander, Beton verwittert, Algen besiedeln die Flußkiesel.

A winding concrete promenade separates the water and vegetation areas. The latter consist of different grasses and forest biotopes. The materials will change in the course of time: grass species will intermingle, concrete will weather, and algae will cover pebbles in the riverbed.

Vielfalt in der Materialwahl machen Spaziergang und Aufenthalt im Ankar Park zu einem sinnlichen Erlebnis. In den betonierten Weg sind Holzpaneele, Felsen, Glas- und Betonmuster sowie stählerne Hocker eingelassen. Käferartige Gummi-Brücken führen sowohl in die Wasser- wie in die Vegetationsflächen hinein.

Variety in the choice of materials makes walking or lingering in Ankar Park into a sensual experience. Wooden panels, rocks, patterns in glass and concrete, and steel stools are set in the concrete path. Bug-shaped rubber footbridges lead into both water and vegetation areas.

darstellen – in Form von Eis, Trockenheit, Staub oder Feuchtigkeit. Diesen stets und schnell wechselnden Erscheinungen setzt der Ankar Park ein anderes, langsameres Schauspiel entgegen, nämlich das der Koexistenz von Zeit und Materialien. Während das Klima ein ständiges, unkontrollierbares Zusammenspiel inszeniert, wird die Pflege durch die zuständige Parkbehörde den Park unvorhersehbaren Veränderungen unterwerfen, das künstlerische Werk vergeht.

Die Muster der Gräser, die allmählich ineinander übergehen, werden in Form und Wachstum das jeweilige Pflegebudget spiegeln. Die Betonflächen werden über die Zeiten hinweg kaputtgehen, und das ist so beabsichtigt. Die 20 Tonnen Kiesel im Wasser werden allmählich von Algen durchsetzt oder überwuchert.

in a way which reflect any given operation budget. The concrete slabs will eventually fall into decay over a certain amount of time, and is intended to do so. The 20 tones of pebbles in the water may well gradually be invaded or covered by seaweeds.

Growth and material tolerances have always been a question of balance. However, adding to these permanent but incorporated uncertainties political decisions may alter the park with a new layer of physical additions like the ones, which have already taken place. The park is public, right therefore it has to have public dustbins all over despite the fact that people visiting the Anchor Park are most likely to behave in another way than when in other public spaces. Also, the Anchor Park is a park, therefore it must have benches, because if people cannot sit in a park, then it cannot be a park. Still, as this park has no fixed view points, it does not operate with a visual hierarchy. To a large extent, the conventional sitting facilities are therefore replaced by 137 rocks and a number of concrete stubbles spread all over the plane.

Such conditions, which have profound influence on how the landscape will actually be perceived, are beyond the programmatic control of the landscape architect but sooner or later, they will become part of his scheme, whether it is suitable or not.

The third continuous pulse is found in the biotopes. Here, the play is that of changes as they appear as the very slow and liquid weaving of materials over a long period of time. The biotopes are four well-defined landscape types, the alder marsh, the oak woods, the willow woods and the beech woods, which owe their existence to micro-organic processes. They do not require the slightest maintenance from the park

Während das westliche Ufer
entlang der Wohngebäude
geradlinig verläuft, schlängelt
sich der Uferweg im Osten den
Pflanzflächen entlang. Als Steg
dient die gummibezogene
käferartige Konstruktion, lockt
zum kleinen aber sicheren
Abenteuer; eine niedere Reling
bietet Halt.

While the western shore is a
straight line along the residential buildings, the shoreline
path in the east winds along
planted areas. A rubber-coated
bug-like structure serves as a
footbridge, attracting visitors
to a small but safe adventure;
a low railing provides stability.

Das Wachstum und die Belastbarkeit des Materials sind immer eine Fra-ge des Ausgewogenheit gewesen. Über diese ständigen, aber in der Natur der Sache liegenden Unsicherheiten hinaus können politische Entscheidungen den Park durch zusätzliche Ausstattung verändern, wie das bereits geschehen ist. Der Park ist öffentlich, also muss er überall öffentliche Abfallbehälter ha-ben, obwohl sich die Leute im Ankar Park wohl anders verhalten werden als in anderen öffentlichen Räumen. Außerdem ist der Ankar Park ein Park, deshalb muss er Bänke haben, denn wenn die Leute in einem Park nicht sit-zen können, ist es kein Park. Da er keine festen Blickpunkte hat, gibt es in ihm auch keine Hierarchie der Blickbeziehungen. So wurden die konven-tionellen Sitzmöglichkeiten großenteils durch 137 Felsen und eine Menge Betonstümpfe ersetzt, die übers Gelände verteilt wurden.

Solche Aspekte, die die Wahrnehmung der Landschaft stark prägen, entziehen sich der programmatischen Kontrolle des Landschaftsarchitek-ten. Früher oder später werden sie Teil der Planung, egal ob sie passend sind oder nicht.

Der dritte kontinuierliche Pulsschlag ist in den Biotopen zu finden. Hier entsteht das Schauspiel aus den Veränderungen, die im sehr langsa-men und fließenden Verweben der Materialien über lange Zeit hinweg be-stehen. Die Biotope sind vier sorgfältig definierte Landschaftstypen: der Er-lenbruch, der Eichenwald, das Weidengehölz und die Buchenwälder, die ihre Existenz mikroorganischen Prozessen verdanken. Sie brauchen nicht die geringste Pflege durch die Parkverwaltung – jedes Eingreifen läuft sogar den Absichten der Landschaftsarchitekten zuwider.

Während fließende und sich überlagernde Räume die Grundidee für den Ankar Park sind und sie die Aufmerksamkeit des Spaziergängers durch Ab-wechslung und viele reichhaltige Details auf sich ziehen, sind die Biotope als Zeitinseln gedacht, an denen man verweilen und sich ins wundersame Spiel der Natur vertiefen kann. Deshalb liegen sie in einer Wiese, die aus ver-schiedenen, durch Stahlkanten scharf unterteilte und gerahmte Monokultu-ren besteht, und die man nur durch kleine Gummi-Brücken (»Tritt-Käfer«) betreten kann. Alle vier Biotope sind in wissenschaftlicher Hinsicht eng an die Vorbilder von Mutter Natur angelehnt und werden so ihr eigenes Leben ohne menschliches Eingreifen leben können.

Verschiedene Materialien befinden sich im Zusammenspiel miteinan-der, und man muss jetzt einfach abwarten, was geschieht. Landschaftsar-chitektur wird zur Natur.

Ankar Park, Malmö, Sweden
Client: Municipality of Malmö
Landscape architect: Stig L. Andersson, landscape architects
Planning: 1999 first prize in competition by invitation
Construction: 2001

This article is based on publications in Topos 40 and Garten + Landschaft 4/02.

authorities; in fact any kind of intervention wil counteract the intentions of the architect.

Whereas the overall idea of the Anchor Park i that of floating and overlapping spaces, which ca for the attention of the wanderer with its diversi ty and rich details, the biotopes are conceived a pockets of time where one can dwell and becom absorbed by the miraculous play of nature.

Therefore, they stand in a horizontally divid ed grass meadow of different mono-cultures, tha are sharply separated and bordered by steel edg ings to which there is only access from the smal bridges (stepping bugs) of rubber.

All four biotopes are organised as scientificall close as Mother Nature would have done it hersel and as such it will go on living its own life beyonc human intervention. Various materials have been set into play with each other, now one just has tc wait and see what will happen. Landscape archi tecture becoming nature.

Parque de Catalunya, Sabadell

Parque de Catalunya is the result of a long struggle by the people of Sabadell, a city of 200,000 situated about 20 kilometres north of Barcelona, to finally gain a park in a city whose industrial past did not leave room for any other large public space. The park itself is situated on a vast natural space measuring more than 40 hectares, and lies in an area which is to become a new centre for Sabadell, itself an important service centre for the Barcelona area. It is one of the most important public open spaces to be created in Spain over the past few years.

Sabadell ist eine Stadt mit 200 000 Einwohnern, die nur 20 Kilometer von Barcelona entfernt liegt. Sie hat eine ruhmreiche industrielle Vergangenheit, aber auch ein ausgeprägtes Gründefizit. Ein Freiraum von 40 Hektar Fläche, der in einem zu entwickelnden Dienstleistungszentrum für Barcelona liegt, sollte zum *Parque de Catalunya* gestaltet werden. Die Größe und Funktion des Parks machen ihn zu einer der interessanteren Anlagen, die in den vergangenen Jahren in Spanien geschaffen wurden.

Von Anfang an wollten wir durch den Erhalt der vorhandenen Landschaftselemente wie Wälder und Wiesen und der typischen Topographie aus Hügeln und Mulden den *Parque de Catalunya* als Naturraum weiterentwickeln. Mehrere Pflanzaktionen mit der Bevölkerung haben dazu beigetragen, daß das Gelände reich bewaldet und damit zur Grundlage eines nutzbaren Parks wurde.

Zunächst galt es, die Randbereiche zu definieren und klar ablesbare Wege anzulegen. Die Randbereiche sollten die Verbindung zwischen Stadt und Park ermöglichen, und auf den Wegen sollte man den Park erkunden können. Das erlaubte uns zugleich, die vielen kleinen Trampelpfade zu verbessern, die durch die öffentliche Nutzung bereits entstanden waren.

Enric Battle
Joan Roig

Die Abgrenzungen des Parks wurden durch die neuen Umgehungsstraßen und die notwendigen Parkplätze bestimmt. Eine niedrige Mauer und die Service-Gebäude an den Eingängen setzen dem Park faßbare Grenzen. Durch seine Form und seine Lage wurde er zu einem linearen Raum gestaltet, der die Stadt mit der umgebenden Landschaft verbindet. So kann künftig das Wachstum der Stadt mit dem des Parks Hand in Hand einhergehen.

Der Länge nach verbindet ein Weg die verschiedenen Bereiche und Einrichtungen, die im Laufe der Zeit hinzukommen werden. Zugleich schafft er die erstrebte Naturnähe. Darüber hinaus wollte unser Konzept mögliche romantische Konnotationen verstärken, etwa den Gedanken

Der Parque de Catalunya zeichnet sich durch phantasievolle Details aus. Trittplatten dienen hier als Brücke über einen Wasserfall am künstlichen Teich.

Parque de Catalunya is full of imaginative details. Here concrete stepping stones cross the waterfall at the artificial pond.

Der Park verbindet die Stadt Sabadell mit der Landschaft. Seine Besucher finden hier nach Wunsch Ruhe oder Geselligkeit.

This park links the city of Sabadell and the countryside and provides visitors with areas of peace and activity.

Ein Verbindungsweg zwischen der Promenade am See und dem landschaftlichen Teil des Parkes verläuft hinter einem Wasserfall, der nachts beleuchtet ist.

A pathway that links the lakeside promenade with the rest of the park leads behind a waterfall; this is also floodlit at night.

der Verbesserung von Stadt und Natur oder die Vorstellung erwecken, daß der Pfad einer Flugbahn ins Unendliche folgt. Indem wir die Grenzen betonten, konnten wir die ebenfalls gewünschte visuelle Abgrenzung zwischen Park und Stadt herstellen. Der See liegt als teilendes und verbindendes Element an der Stelle, wo die gegensätzlichen Welten – Stadt und Natur, Platz und Park, die neue Avenue und der langgezogene Weg – am spannungsreichsten aufeinanderstoßen. Eine Brücke über den See ist Übergang und zugleich der Anfang des Weges, der aus der Stadt führt.

Der See löst den Widerspruch zwischen dem platzartigen Eingangsbereich und dem Park. Eines seiner Ufer wirkt landschaftlich, ist wie ein Damm gestaltet. Die andere Seite hat den Charakter einer Uferpromenade mit einem Bootssteg. Um den Wasserspiegel an die Höhenentwicklung der seitlichen Straßen anzupassen, wurde er in drei Becken auf verschiedenen Niveaus aufgeteilt, so daß zwei Wasserfälle entstanden. Der Scheitelpunkt und zugleich Quellpunkt des Wassers liegt an einem befestigten Platz. Es folgt ein großer Wasserfall, hinter dem ein Nebenweg zu den bewaldeten Bereichen des Parks führt. Das mittlere Wasserbecken ist ein von Booten befahrbarer Teich auf dem Niveau der Avenue, dem Symbol des neuen Stadtzentrums. Von dort aus durchbricht das Wasser eine Staumauer in einem weiteren Wasserfall. Das unterste Wasserbecken dient als Abfluß und macht das Wasser auf den dort angrenzenden Plätzen erlebbar.

Der Charakter des Parks wird bestimmt durch die Gestaltung der Grenzbereiche, den Eingangsplatz, den See und den Hauptweg. Zugleich sind die erhaltenen Waldbereiche und Wiesen und die Regenwasserkanäle, die zur Bewässerung der Pflanzungen am Fluß dienen, gestaltgebende Elemente. Durch seine lineare Form und seine Lage verbindet der *Parque de Catalunya* Stadt und Landschaft und wird mit dem Wachstum der Stadt Schritt halten können.

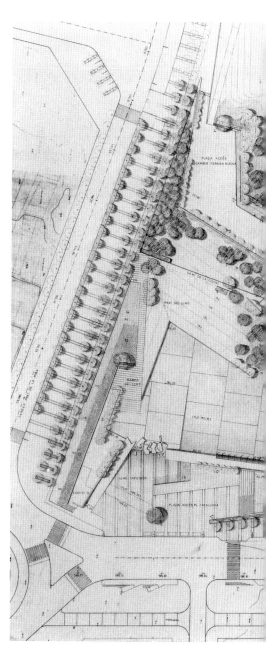

Der Schnitt durch einen Hangbereich im landschaftlich gestalteten Teil des Parks zeigt das Zusammenspiel von natürlichen und den von Menschenhand geschaffenen Elementen.

The cross-section of a slope in the landscape section of the park shows the interplay of natural and man-made elements.

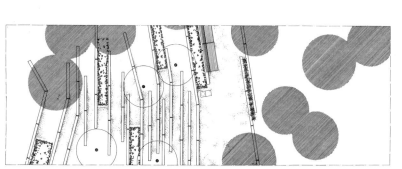

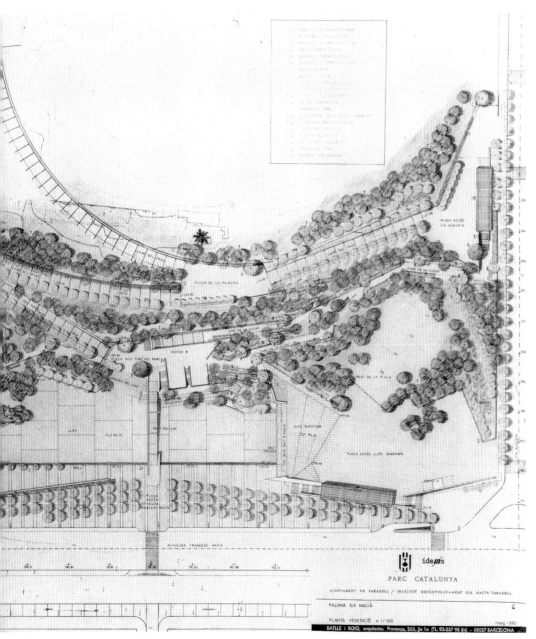

PARC CATALUNYA

AJUNTAMENT DE SABADELL / INSTITUT DESENVOLUPAMENT EIX MACIÀ SABADELL

FAÇANA EIX MACIÀ

PLANTA VEGETACIÓ e 1/500

BATLLE i ROIG, arquitectes. Provença, 355, 5a 1a (TL 93-257 98 84) · 08037 BARCELONA

An den Übergängen über die Hauptverkehrsstraßen wurden Promenaden und städtisch anmutende Plätze geschaffen. Von dort kann man an den See und in die Landschaft vorstoßen.

Promenades and open areas with an urban touch have been created at the main crossings and lead on to the lake and the countryside beyond the park.

From the very outset of the project, we sought to preserve the landscape elements that already existed at the site – woodland and meadows, hills and hollows – and thus retain its natural atmosphere. Repeated tree planting campaigns had reforested the area previously and helped contribute to its being regarded as a suitable site for a public park.

The lack of definition on the disfigured edges, and the need to establish clear pathways were the main matters requiring attention. Our solution has been to design the edges in such a way as to create a clear division between the city and the park, and to improve on the large number of minor paths created by random public use. The outer limits are now defined by new perimeter roads, including necessary parking spaces, thus establishing a relationship to the peripheral residential areas. The park itself is enclosed by a low wall and service buildings situated at the various entrances. A single path runs throughout the length of the park, creating a link between the individual areas and facilities and establishing the desired closeness to nature. At the same time, we also sought to awaken possible romantic interpretations, such as the idea of improving on not only the city but also existing nature, or that of the path following a trajectory to the infinite.

Another feature of significance is the lake, which is located at the place of greatest tension in that it unites and divides the two contradictory worlds of city and nature. A bridge over the lake forms a transition between the square and park, between the new avenue and the pathway, and is also the start of a path leading out of the city. The lake resolves the contradiction between the access

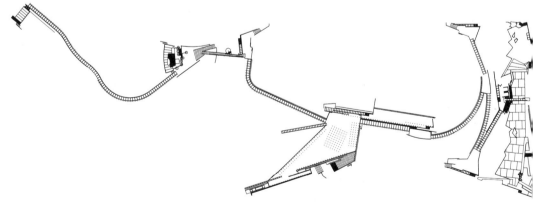

square and the park, one side of it delineating the boundaries of nature like a dam, the other, on the city side, being a kind of promenade or quay for mooring boats.

In order to adapt the lake to the topography of the adjacent streets, we divided it into three different levels. The highest level, where the water originates, is related to a paved square and leads to a large waterfall, behind which is the beginning of a secondary footpath leading into the park's woodland area. The intermediate level, which is on par with the avenue, the symbol of the new city centre, is used for boating; from here the water "breaks through" the retaining wall to drop down to the lowest outlet level, which is at the same niveau as the access square.

The general character of the park, whose main emphasis is placed on the definition of the perimeter limits, the design of the access square, the lake and the pathway, is determined by the preserved woodlands and meadows and the channels of rainwater created to irrigate riverside plantings. Due to its linear shape and location, the *Parque de Catalunya* successfully connects the city to the surrounding countryside and will be able to grow as the city expands.

Vom Detail zur großen Linie. Auch in den Grundformen der Stützmauern findet sich der gestalterische Schwung der Uferpartie wieder, der die Linienführung von Pergolen, Pflasterflächen und See prägt.

Basic forms are repeated throughout, as in the sweep of the retaining wall, which is reflected in the lines of the pergolas and paved areas and in the curved shore of the lake.

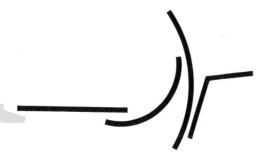

Am mittleren Becken, das mit Booten befahren werden kann, erstreckt sich eine viel benutzte Liegewiese. Ruhe und Aktivität, das Erlebnis von Stadt, Landschaft und Wasser in unmittelbarer Nachbarschaft machen den Parque de Catalunya attraktiv für die Bewohner.

A lawn at the middle boating lake is very popular with sunbathers.
The close proximity of peace and activity and urban, landscape and water elements makes Parque de Catalunya an attractive sport for local residents.

Plan: Enric Batlle and Joan Roig, with Lluis Gibert
Client: Sabadell Council / Idems (Institut de desenvolupament del Eix Macia, Sabadell)

Size: 40 hectares
Construction Period: 1985–1992

Gemeinschaftswerk Donaukraftwerk Wien

Pooling efforts on the Danube power plant in Vienna

Gottfried Hansjakob
Toni Hansjakob

Der Donauraum bei Wien ist einer der eindrucksvollsten Landschaftsräume, die wir in Europa kennen. Der Strom tritt hier, aus dem Hügelland kommend, in die Weite des Wiener Beckens ein, fächert sich breit in mehrere stark mäandrierende Arme auf und formt eine bewaldete Auenlandschaft von großer Schönheit, die Lobau und die Praterauen. Dieser breite, vom Fluß und seinen Überschwemmungen beherrschte Bereich, der die Stadt von Nordwesten nach Südosten durchzieht, bildete eine natürliche Barriere für bauliche Entwicklungen. Das Zentrum von Wien liegt am Rande dieser Flußlandschaft.

In der zweiten Hälfte des 19. Jahrhunderts erst verleibte sich die Stadt die Auenlandschaft der Donau ein, die Stadtoberen regulierten den Strom in den Jahren 1869 bis 1875, um den Hochwasserschutz zu verbessern und um die Entwicklung der Stadt auch jenseits der Donau fortsetzen zu können. Als starre geometrische Trasse durchschnitt von da ab das Strombett den ursprünglich lebendig figurierten Auenbereich. Das gewonnene Regulierungsland wurde fast vollständig der Industrie und dem Verkehr überlassen, die sich damit trennend zwischen Stadt und Strom schoben. Wien liegt eben nicht, wie Budapest, an der Donau.

Es stellte sich auch bald heraus, daß diese große Donauregulierung das Problem des Hochwasserschutzes nicht vollständig lösen konnte, da sie nur auf eine Abflußmenge von 11700 Kubikmeter pro Sekunde ausgelegt war, während im Katastrophenfall mit bis zu 14000 Kubikmeter pro Sekunde zu rechnen ist. So wurde im Laufe der Zeit eine Reihe von Projekten zur Verbesserung des Hochwasserschutzes ausgearbeitet. 1957 entstand der Plan, ein etwa 150 Meter breites Entlastungsgerinne als Neue Donau zu graben und mit dem Aushub zwischen Neuer Donau und Donaustrom eine etwa 200 Meter breite und 21 Kilometer lange Donauinsel aufzuschütten. Gleichzeitig sollten die Dämme am linken und rechten Donauufer erhöht werden, um so die erforderlichen Wassermengen bei Höchsthochwasser geregelt abzuführen. In einem zweistufigen Wettbewerb für die Gestaltung der Neuen Donau und der Donauinsel 1974 setzten die meisten Preisträger noch auf ein gigantisches Bauprogramm aus visionären Städten und Universitäten, um endlich den Traum von einem Wien bis an die Donau zu realisieren. Sie konstruierten dort,

The landscape formed by the Danube at Vienna is one of the most impressive pieces of European countryside that we know of. Flowing into the Viennese Basin from hilly country, opens up into several strongly meandering tributaries that form wooded bottom lands of great natural beauty. These broad floodplains accompany the river from the north-west to the south east of the capital, creating a natural barrier t construction. While the heart of Vienna lies clos to the western edge of this alluvial landscape, th channel was not engulfed by urban developmen until the second half of the 19th century, whe the city fathers began to regulate the river be tween 1869 and 1875 to improve flood contro and enable growth beyond the eastern bank Since that time, the river bed cuts through th meandering floodplains in a rigid geometric axis The land gained in the process has been almos completely devoted to the requirements of indus try and traffic, thus cutting off the city from th water. Unlike Budapest, Vienna does not reall lie on the Danube.

Be that as it may, it soon became apparen that the grand efforts to regulate the river had no solved the problem of flooding. Indeed, the re spective measures had been designed with a flo rate of 11,700 cubic metres a second in mind but did not take into account that a serious floo can produce up to 14,000 cubic metres a second As a consequence, a number of flood control pro jects were considered. In 1957 a plan was draw up to dig the Danube Canal, a bypass channe about 150 metres wide, and to use the resultin spoil to build an artificial island some 200 metre wide and 21 kilometres long while heightenin the banks on both sides of the river to enable

Das neue Donaukraftwerk Wien-Freudenau mit einem naturnah gestalteten Erholungsgebiet ist ein Entwurf für das Volk – bitte betreten!
The public are more than welcome at Vienna's new power plant at Freudenau, and can use the adjacent riverbanks for recreation purposes.

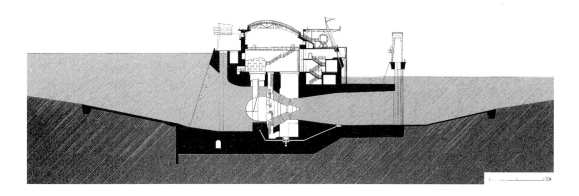

ontrolled discharge of the required water quanties in peak floods. In a two-stage competition eld in 1974 for the design of the Danube Canal nd the new Danube Island, most of the prize-inners proposed a visionary programme of ities and university buildings in an effort to realise the dream of continuing the city down to ne very banks of the Danube. In this they proosed erecting a new, artificial metropolis at the ery place where the historical city had ceased in s development, and in doing so displayed little egard for the existing landscape or the technical easibility of their plans. When the interdiscipliary jury examined the competition entries, it oon became apparent that the ecological aspects f the site were of greater value to Vienna than ne possibility of creating a further city district. n the seventies, Danube Island was consequenally designed as a leisure landscape, much to the atisfaction of the Viennese, namely by the landcape architect Wilfried Kirchner and ourselves.

Freudenau power plant. It was also at this time hat work began on planning a river dam to pow-r an electricity plant. The resulting two-stage ompetition, which was held by the city of Vien-a and the future operator of the plant under the tle "Opportunities for the Danubian Area", was nally decided on in 1988. Fortunately, the ients had learned a thing or two through the lanning of Danube Island, and accorded the ndscape architects the same status as the archi-cts and engineers, both at the competition stage nd henceforth. The competition itself was won y an interdisciplinary team made up of the ar-hitect Albert Wimmer, the engineer Herwig chwarz, and ourselves, and it was on this same asis that the team was commissioned to contin-

wo die historisch gewachsene Stadt ihre natürliche Zäsur, ihre grüne Mitte, hatte, ein neues, absolut synthetisches Metropolis, ohne Rücksicht auf die bestehende Landschaft und ohne die technischen und städtebaulichen Möglichkeiten vernünftig abzuwägen. Bei der Überarbeitung des Wettbewerbes in Zusammenarbeit mit einer interdisziplinär zusammengesetzten Jury zeigte sich schnell, daß der ökologische Nutzen der Stadt Wien mehr wert war als der Ausbau zur Stadt. In der Folge gestalteten wir zusammen mit dem Landschaftsarchitekten Wilfried Kirchner die Donauinsel in den siebziger Jahren als Freizeitlandschaft, zur großen Freude der Wiener.

Das Kraftwerk Freudenau. Gleichzeitig mit dem Hochwasserschutz wurde die Planung der Donaustaustufe für das Kraftwerk Freudenau begonnen. Der von der Stadt Wien und der Donaukraft (Österreichische Donaukraftwerke AG) interdisziplinär ausgeschriebene Wettbewerb »Chancen für den Donauraum« wurde schließlich 1988 nach zwei Bearbeitungsstufen entschieden. Aus den Erfahrungen der Donauinselplanungen hatten die Auftraggeber dazugelernt – sie standen den Landschaftsarchitekten schon beim Wettbewerb einen den Architekten und Ingenieuren gleichwertigen Rang zu. Ein interdisziplinäres Team, bestehend aus dem Architekten Albert Wimmer, dem Ingenieur Herwig Schwarz und uns Landschaftsarchitekten ging als Preisträger aus dem Wettbewerbsverfahren hervor – diese Gruppe bearbeitete im Auftrag der Donaukraft die Wettbewerbsausgabe weiterhin im Team.

Der Vorsitzende der Jury, Thomas Sieverts, Professor für Stadtplanung an der Universität Darmstadt, faßte seine Erfahrungen aus dem Wettbewerb wie folgt zusammen: »Die planenden Berufe wurden mit diesen Verfahren aufgefordert, sich zu interdisziplinären Teams zusammenzuschließen und neue Formen der Zusammenarbeit zu erproben. Die Ergebnisse des Wettbewerbes zeigen, daß hier zwar beachtliche Anfänge gemacht wurden, daß aber auch noch erhebliche Lücken in der interdisziplinären Zusammenarbeit bestehen. So hat sich etwa die Hoffnung, daß die Humanwissenschaften einen wesentlichen Beitrag leisten würden, nur sehr bedingt erfüllt. Auch die ökologische Fundierung der Landschaftsplanung hat nur in wenigen, freilich sehr guten Beiträgen ein tragfähiges Fundament für die Gestaltungsvorschläge geliefert. Die Ökologie hat die Chance, aus der kritisierenden Position in eine grundlegend konstruktive Rolle hineinzuwachsen, nur begrenzt wahrgenommen. In der interdisziplinären Zusammenarbeit liegt noch ein weiter Weg vor uns. Die Ergebnisse der Wettbe-

Der Schnitt durch das Krafthaus zeigt die minimale Ausdehnung des Kraftwerks Wien-Freudenau quer zur Flußrichtung. Voraussetzung dafür war, lediglich sechs leistungsstarke Turbinen einzusetzen. Der Fuß- und Radweg verläuft über dem Technikgebäude. Ein geschwungener Baldachin überspannt ihn. Flußabwärts eröffnen sich den Benutzern weite Ausblicke. Zeichnung aus Architektur aktuell 217/218.

The cross-section of the Freudenau power house in Vienna underscores the minimal transverse size. This was achieved in part by installing six turbines, albeit powerful ones. The combined footpath and cycleway, which is covered by a curving canopy, runs about the engineering building and provides sweeping downstream views. The drawing has been taken from Architektur aktuell, no. 217/218.

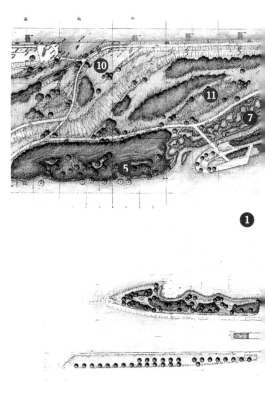

werbe waren hierfür ein wichtiges Indiz, das von den zuständigen Berufsverbänden und den Hochschulen aufmerksam zur Kenntnis genommen werden sollte. Die Hochschulen sollten hieraus Folgerungen für die Ausbildung ziehen. Für die Kammern bedeutet es, daß es dringend erforderlich ist, das enge berufsständische Denken zugunsten komplexer Denk- und Arbeitsweisen aufzugeben. Dies muß sich auch in den berufsständischen Ordnungen niederschlagen, zum Beispiel in der Zulassung von Landschaftsplanern und Ökologen.«

Nach positivem Abschluß einer Umweltverträglichkeitsprüfung und einer Volksbefragung in Wien im Januar 1991 fand im Mai und Juni 1991 die wasserrechtliche Hauptverhandlung über das Projekt in der Wiener Hofburg statt. Neben den Amtssachverständigen und Sondersachverständigen der Wasserrechtsbehörden wurde für die Überprüfung der projektkonformen Ausführung und Einhaltung der Bedingungen und Auflagen der Organe eine wasserrechtliche Bauaufsicht und eine ökologische Bauaufsicht bestellt. Am 28. November 1997 stauten die Verantwortlichen die Donau, was einem Aufstau bei Mittelwasser von 8,32 Meter entspricht. Offiziell in Betrieb genommen wurde das Kraftwerk Freudenau schließlich am 2. Juni 1998.

Zu den Hauptbestandteilen des Kraftwerks Freudenau zählen das Krafthaus, die Kraftwerksinsel mit Betriebsgebäude, die Wehranlage, die Schleuse, sowie der Umgehungsbach, den ein naturnah gestalteter Erholungsraum umgibt. Was unterscheidet nun Wien-Freudenau von bisherigen Kraftwerkskonzepten? Vor allem selbstverständlich dessen Lage im Stadtgebiet und somit die städtebauliche Einbindung: Gelegen zwischen den Landschaftsräumen Prater und Lobau schafft das Kraftwerk mit seinen im Strom neu errichteten Inseln (Kraftwerksinsel und Wehrinsel) ein gegliedertes und zugleich aufgelöstes Bauwerk. Architektur und Natur schaffen ein spannungsreiches Kräftespiel. Um die Ufer weitgehend öffentlich nutzen zu können, minimierte unser Planerteam die Ausdehnung des Kraftwerkes quer zur Flußrichtung. Dies gelang uns durch zwei entscheidende Maßnahmen: Wir beschränkten uns auf sechs leistungsstarke Turbinen, und wir schufen eine Kraftwerksinsel, auf

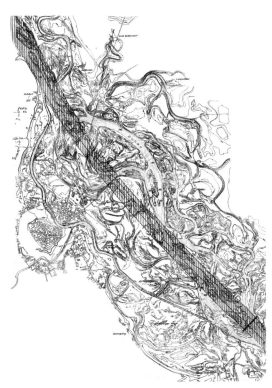

ue work on the project.

Thomas Sieverts, Professor of Urban Devel-opment at Darmstadt University and chairman of the jury, summed up his experience of the competition in the following words: "The planning professions were called on to form interdisciplinary teams and try out new forms of collaboration. The results show that although a remarkable start has been made in terms of interdisciplinary co-operation, much remains to be done. For example, the hopes that the humanities would make a substantial contribution have only been fulfilled to a certain extent, and it is only in a few, albeit very good contributions that the ecological foundation of landscape planning provided a solid basis for the design proposals. Ecology has made only limited use of the opportunity to abandon a purely critical role in favour of a fundamentally constructive one. As the results prove, we still have a long way to go in terms of interdisciplinary co-operation. This is something that the professional associations should be careful to note, and that universities ought to take into consideration in the contents of their courses. It also

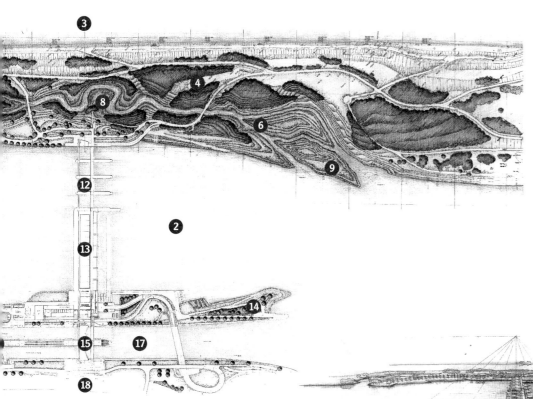

Die Donauinsel (4) ist das beliebteste Ausflugsziel der Wiener. Die Landschaftsarchitekten Hansjakob und Kirchner ließen zwischen alter (1,2) und neuer Donau (3) die Auenlandschaft aufleben, die vor der großen Donauregulierung Ende des 19. Jahrhunderts existierte (gegenüber), mit Flachuferbereichen (5), Mäandern (8), Kiesbänken (9), Altarmen (10) und Biotopen (11). 1988 gewannen sie in einem Team mit Architekten und Wasserbauingenieuren den Wettbewerb für ein neues Donaukraftwerk. Es verbindet heute die Insel mit dem rechten Donauufer (18). Zeichnung Büro Hansjakob (Christine Stüber): 1 aufgestaute Donau, 2 Donau-Unterwasser, 6 Umgehungsbach, 7 Fischaufstieg, 12 Wehranlage, 13 Krafthaus, 14 Kraftwerksinsel, 15 Schleusenanlage, 16 Oberhafen, 17 Unterhafen. Perspektive: Atelier Wimmer

Danube Island (4) is Vienna's most popular place for excursions. Between the river (1, 2) and the canal (3), the landscape architects Hansjakob and Kirchner revived the riparian landscape that existed before the late-19th-century regulation of the river, creating level shorelines (5), meanders (8), gravel banks (9), ox-bow lakes (10) and biotopes (11). In 1988, a team of architects and hydraulic engineers that included the Hansjakob brothers went on to win a competi-

ndicates that the institutes of architecture and ngineering have an urgent need to give up their arrow, guild-like approach for a more complex vay of thinking and working. This in turn has to ind expression in the way that the professions are rganised, as in the way that landscape planners or cologists are admitted to practice."

After the successful outcome of the environmental impact assessment and an opinion poll eld in Vienna in January 1991, a water rights earing was held. The Danube was dammed on November 28, 1997, resulting in a mean water evel of 8.32 metres, and the power plant was taken into operation on June 2, 1998. The power lant mainly consists of a power station, an island vith service buildings, a spillway, a lock and a diversion channel surrounded by a leisure area designed to be near-natural in effect.

What distinguishes the Freudenau power plant from previous power station concepts? First nd foremost, the fact that it is located within a city and thus had to be integrated in urban development terms. Situated between the Prater nd Lobau floodplains, the power plant is a care-

der sich das Betriebsgebäude befindet. Der so entstandene Umgehungsbach ist ein mit typischen Elementen von Seitengewässern des Donaustromes naturnah gestalteter Erholungsraum auf der Donauinsel, der außerdem ungehinderte Fischwanderung ermöglicht. Der rechte Uferbereich, den wir frei von jeglicher Bebauung gehalten haben, dient als Erholungsraum.

Im Unterschied zu konventionellen Kraftwerken wollte unser Planerteam ein für die Wiener Bevölkerung benutzbares, beschaubares, begehbares und begreifbares Kraftwerk bauen. Dazu errichteten wir eine Fuß- und Radwegbrücke, die sich von Ufer zu Ufer über das gesamte Kraftwerk spannt, integrierten eine unterirdische Ausstellungshalle zwischen Betriebsgebäude und Krafthaus, von der aus man einen Blick in die Krafthaushalle werfen kann, sowie einen Ausstellungshof im Betriebsgebäude. Darüberhinaus betonen Formen und Material unser besonderes Herangehen: Wesentliche Konstruktionsteile des Kraftwerkes sind in Stahl ausgeführt, etwa die beiden Kranbahnträger, das Krafthausdach und die Zufahrtsbrücke zur

tion for a Danubian power plant. Today it links Danube Island and the right river bank (18). The drawing by Christine Stüber of the Hansjakob office shows: 1 dammed river, 2 tailwater, 6 diversion channel, 7 fish ladder, 12 spillway, 13 power house, 14 power plant island, 15 lockage, 16 upper chamber and 17 lower chamber. Perspective view above: Atelier Wimmer

Im Unterschied zu herkömmlichen Kraftwerken wollte das interdisziplinäre Team in Wien-Freudenau ein benutzbares, beschaubares, begehbares und begreifbares Kraftwerk schaffen. Eine Fuß- und Radwegbrücke spannt sich heute von Ufer zu Ufer. Eine unterirdische Ausstellungshalle ermöglicht den Blick in die Krafthaushalle. Eine Terrasse mit Panoramafenster setzt die umgebende Landschaft in Szene. Um die Ufer weitgehend öffentlich nutzbar zu machen, reduzierten die Planer die Ausmaße des Kraftwerks so weit wie möglich und setzten das Betriebsgebäude auf eine eigens angelegte Kraftwerksinsel. Wesentliche Teile der Konstruktion führten die Planer in Stahl aus und erhielten so filigrane und expressive Formen.

In contrast to conventional power plants, the interdisciplinary team wanted to build a power station that would be largely accessible to the public, something they can look at, touch and even enter. To this end, the planners erected a bank-to-bank pedestrian and cycle bridge above the power plant and created a view into the interior of the power house from a subterranean exhibition hall. A panorama terrace provides sweeping views of the river and its banks. In order to enable a fair degree of public use of the banks, the planners reduced the dimensions of the power plant as far as possible and placed the service buildings on an island expressly created for the purpose. Important structural elements are made of steel, enabling filigree and expressive forms.

fully organised but elegant structure in which architecture and nature juxtapose each other in a interplay of tension. In order to ensure public us of the banks to a large extent, our team planne the power plant so that it would not impinge too considerably on the riverine landscape. This ha been achieved by means of two decisive measures namely by only installing six powerful turbines and by creating an island for the service build ings. The diversion channel created as a resul acts as a fishway and as a leisure area, and ha been given the character that is typical of Danub tributaries. We also kept the right bank free o buildings to make it suitable for recreation pur poses.

In contrast to conventional power plants, ou planning team wanted to build a power station that would be largely accessible to the public something that they can look at, touch and even enter. To this end, we erected a pedestrian and cy cle bridge above the power plant from bank to bank, integrated a subterranean exhibition hall to provide a view of the interior of the power hous between the service building and the powe house, and incorporated an exhibition court into the service building. Above and beyond this, th shapes and materials underscore our particula approach. This is evidenced by important struc tural elements, such as the two gantry girders, th roof of the power house and the access bridg leading to the power plant island, which are al made of steel. The high design quality is a resul of the precise collaboration between the archi tect, civil engineer and landscape architects.

At the inauguration of the power plant, th Mayor of the City of Vienna was visibly im pressed by the positive effects it has created: th

Danube now flows more lazily, thus hiding ripped rock banks, while the hydrological conditions in Prater bottom lands have improved considerably. The plant provides almost half the households of Vienna with environmentally-friendly power, the bridge is a welcome shortcut to Danube Island, thus making the cycleways along the river more attractive, and shallow areas of water and islands have come about, resulting in new living space for flora and fauna. The power plant operator planted 200,000 trees and shrubs all in all, and last but not least, an average of 4,000 people per year were directly or indirectly employed in connection with the construction site.

In our opinion, Freudenau is in keeping with the principle of a sustainable and ecological form of energy production, and is also the visible expression of the ideal partnership between architecture, construction, hydraulic engineering, landscape architecture and design that characterised the project from its basic concept to its final realisation.

Kraftwerksinsel. Das erlaubt einerseits einen sparsamen, den Kräften folgenden Umgang mit dem Material, andererseits expressive und filigrane Formen. Die hohe gestalterische Qualität entstand in der exakten Zusammenarbeit von Architekt und Bauingenieur.

Der Bürgermeister der Stadt Wien, Michael Häupl, zeigte sich bei der Inbetriebnahme des Kraftwerkes beeindruckt von den positiven Auswirkungen: Die jetzt gemächlicher dahinfließende Donau überstaut die früher sichtbaren Steinwurfböschungen, und die Wasserverhältnisse in den Wiener Prateraueen haben sich wesentlich verbessert. Wien bekommt mit dem Kraftwerk Freudenau umweltfreundliche Energie aus der Donau, die den Bedarf von fast der Hälfte der Wiener Haushalte abdeckt. Ein neuer Fuß- und Radweg über das Kraftwerk verkürzt den Weg zur Donauinsel; die Radwege entlang der Donau werden dadurch noch attraktiver. Flachwasserzonen und Inseln vergrößern den Lebensraum am Donauufer für Fauna und Flora. Insgesamt pflanzte die Donaukraft AG 200 000 Bäume und Sträucher. Und nicht zuletzt fanden 4000 Menschen im Durchschnitt pro Jahr auf der Baustelle direkt oder indirekt Arbeit.

Aus unserer Sicht steht Freudenau für das Prinzip einer nachhaltigen und ökologischen Form der Energieproduktion. Die einzelnen Disziplinen Architektur, Konstruktion, Wasserbau, Landschaftsarchitektur und künstlerische Gestaltung spielten in unserem interdisziplinären Team ideal zusammen und prägten den Entwurf entscheidend, von der Konzeption bis zur Ausführung.

Danubian Power Plant at Freudenau, Vienna, Austria
Client and general contractor: Österreichische Donaukraftwerke AG, Vienna
Planning: Österreichische Donaukraftwerke AG in collaboration with
Albert Wimmer, architect; Herwig Schwarz, engineer and Gottfried and Toni
Hansjakob, landscape architects
Construction period: 1988 – 1998

Barcelona: der wiedergewonnene Horizont

Barcelona: the regained horizon

Vom Klima begünstigt und in außergewöhnlicher Landschaft gelegen, lebte die Stadt Barcelona seit ihrer Gründung am und vom Meer. Bis zu dem Zeitpunkt, da der große Handelshafen, seine Eisenbahngleise, Fabriken und Lagerhallen eine Barriere zwischen der Stadt und dem Meer errichteten. Von da an war den Stadtbewohnern der Zugang zum Wasser verwehrt, und nur an wenigen Stellen, wie am Ausgang der berühmten Ramblas, öffnete sich der Blick auf das geschäftige Treiben im Hafen. Die nahegelegenen Strände freilich gaben ein trauriges Bild ab: Verschmutzt und verlassen lagen sie da, keine Spur von Strandidylle, wie man erhofft hätte. Allein der Aufstieg auf die stadtnahen Hügel ermöglichte den Blick auf das offene Meer, auf den sich in der Ferne verlierenden Horizont.

So geriet das Meer für die Einwohner von Barcelona zu einer Attraktion, die man während der Freizeit und in den Ferien genießt, zu einem Ort, an dem sie ihre Zweitwohnungen errichteten und all die angenehmen Seiten des Wassers wiederfanden, die die Stadt eingebüßt hatte. Bald zierten unzählige Wohnhäuser, Siedlungen und Campingplätze die gesamte katalanische Küste, alle mit Uferpromenaden, Sporthäfen, Molen und uniformen Bauten ausgestattet, wie man sie überall an Stränden und Steilküsten findet. Erst in den 30er Jahren realisierte die GATCPAC-Planergruppe unter dem Einfluß des CIAM und Le Corbusier in Barcelona einige Projekte, die darauf abzielten, das Meer wieder in der Stadt und im Alltag erfahrbar zu machen. Die Planer entwickelten damals neue Modelle der städtebaulichen Ordnung, und in der architektonischen Formensprache der Moderne erarbeiteten sie Entwürfe wie den »Plan Macià para Barcelona«, der mit kraftvoller Geste die Wasserfront der Stadt umgestaltete, oder die »Ciudad de Reposo para Barcelona« in den Pinienwäldern bei Llobregat.

Der »Plan Macià« von Le Corbusier, Pierre Jeanneret und der GATCPAC-Gruppe aus dem Jahre 1934 teilte die Stadt in Zonen auf und sah vor, den Handelshafen aus der Stadt an einen Bereich jenseits des Montjuic-Hügels auszulagern. Anschließend sollten auf dem freigewordenen Gelände Parks und ein Freizeithafen gestaltet werden. Auch ein riesiges Einkaufs- und Handelszentrum war Teil des Plans – es sollte in die Höhe gebaut werden, so daß an der Wasserfront möglichst viel Platz für öffentliche Einrichtungen blieb.

Enric Batlle
Joan Roig

Riesige Hafenanlagen zwängten sich in Barcelona zwischen die Stadt und das Meer – jetzt gelang die Rückeroberung des Strandes.

Huge harbour structures used to be wedged between the city and the sea in Barcelona – the reconquest of the beach has now succeeded.

LDEFELS

Gavà

Als sich Anfang des Jahrhunderts der Frachthafen vor Barcelona immer mehr ausdehnte suchten die Bewohner im Umland der Stadt Zugang zum Wasser. In den dreißiger Jahren entstanden die ersten geplanten Projekte, um der Stadt das Meer zurückzugeben. Oben: »Ciudad de Reposo« GATCPAC 1934, rechts: »Plan Maciá« von Le Corbusier, Pierre Jeanneret und GATCPAC

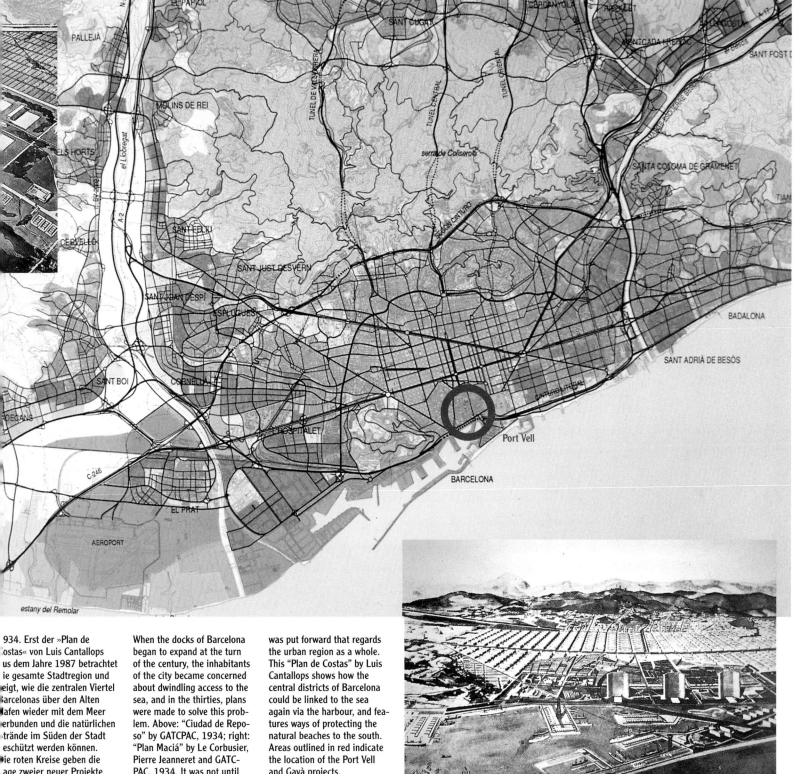

Various place labels visible on the map: PALLEJÀ, EL PAPIOL, SANT CUGAT, CERDANYOLA, RIPOLLET, MONTCADA I REIXAC, EL BOSC, SANT FOST, MOLINS DE REI, ELS HORTS, el Llobregat, TUNEL DE VALLVIDRERA, TUNEL CENTRAL, TUNEL ORIENTAL, serra de Collserola, SANTA COLOMA DE GRAMENET, TIAN, SANT FELIU, CERVELLÓ, SANT JUST DESVERN, SEGON CINTURÓ, SANT JOAN DESPÍ, ESPLUGUES, BADALONA, SANT ADRIÀ DE BESÒS, SANT BOI, CORNELLÀ, L'HOSPITALET, DEGANS, CINTURÓ LITORAL, Port Vell, C-245, BARCELONA, EL PRAT, AEROPORT, estany del Remolar

When the docks of Barcelona began to expand at the turn of the century, the inhabitants of the city became concerned about dwindling access to the sea, and in the thirties, plans were made to solve this problem. Above: "Ciudad de Reposo" by GATCPAC, 1934; right: "Plan Maciá" by Le Corbusier, Pierre Jeanneret and GATCPAC, 1934. It was not until 1987, however, that a plan was put forward that regards the urban region as a whole. This "Plan de Costas" by Luis Cantallops shows how the central districts of Barcelona could be linked to the sea again via the harbour, and features ways of protecting the natural beaches to the south. Areas outlined in red indicate the location of the Port Vell and Gavà projects.

101

Favoured by the climate and situated in an extraordinary landscape, the city of Barcelona lived by and from the sea ever since its foundation. That is, until the point when the large commercial port, its railway tracks, and storehouses created a barrier between the city and the sea. From then on the residents were prevented access to the water. Only in a few spots, such as the exit of the famous Ramblas, did a view of the industrious activity of the harbour open up. The nearby beaches certainly presented a sorry sight. There they lay, polluted and abandoned, without a trace of the idyllic scene one would have wished. Only the climb up the hills near the city allowed a perspective of the open sea and the horizon disappearing in the distance.

Thus the sea became an attraction to be enjoyed during leisure time and vacations for the residents of Barcelona. It was a place for building second homes, where all the pleasant aspects of the water that the city had lost could be found. Soon countless residences, settlements and camping sites adorned the whole Catalan coastline. All were equipped with coastal promenades, sport harbours, moles, and uniform buildings like those along beaches and steep coastlines everywhere. Only in the thirties did the GATCPAC planning group, influenced by CIAM and Le Corbusier, realize a few projects aiming to make the experience of the sea in the city and in daily life possible again. In the architectural language of modernity they elaborated designs such as the "Plan Macià para Barcelona", which reshaped the waterfront of the city in a bold gesture, or the "Ciudad de Reposo para Barcelona", in the pine forests of Llobregat.

Während der Nachkriegsjahre schossen an den Stränden von Castelldefels südlich von Barcelona Campinganlagen, Golfplätze, Freizeiteinrichtungen in chaotischer Aneinanderreihung aus dem Boden (oben). 1957 gestaltete E. Giralt zum ersten Mal innerhalb Barcelonas eine Uferpromenade, und es erwachte der Wunsch, die gesamte städtische Wasserfront Barcelonas neu zu formen.

During the postwar years, a chaotic huddle of golf courses, camp sites and other leisure facilities sprung up behind the beaches of Castelldefels, south of Barcelona (above). The city did not gain a waterfront promenade for itself (designed by E. Giralt) until 1957, a measure that soon led to calls to reshape the whole of Barcelona's shoreline in a similar manner.

The "Plan Macià" by Le Corbusier, Pierre Jeanneret and the GATCPAC group, dating from 1934, divided the city into zones and transposed the commercial port from the city to a region beyond the Montjuic hill. Parks and a leisure harbour were subsequently created on the vacated terrain. A huge shopping and trade centre was also part of the plan. It was to be tall, thus leaving as much room as possible along the waterfront for public facilities.

Also in 1934, the "Ciudad de Reposo" was erected in the south of Barcelona on the beaches of Castelldefels and Gavà. The town plan corresponds to a chess board pattern and is oriented to the straight line of the coast. Typical seaside elements, such as a promenade or private lots by the water, were rejected in order not to destroy the landscape character of the place. The beach could be reached by a connective path, embedded in a green belt. No further paths were made and the residents were free to look for their own spontaneous routes to the beach.

During the postwar years, several projects were realized in greater Barcelona along the coast. The majority, however, developed without any planning whatsoever and were of remarkably poor architectural quality. The inland behind the coast was increasingly subdivided into private properties and indiscriminately built upon. Thanks to the economic and social upswing, as everywhere in Europe, the residents of Barcelona could of course afford cars and second residences on the outskirts of the city now. Castelldefels and Gavà became the main attractions. A chaotic accumulation of camping sites, golf courses, and recreational facilities shot up along a coastal strip over ten kilometres long.

Die »Ciudad de Reposo« wurde ebenfalls 1934 im Süden von Barcelona an den Stränden von Castelldefels und Gavà errichtet. Der Stadtgrundriß entspricht einem Schachbrettmuster und orientiert sich an der Gerade der Küstenlinie. Auf typische Küstenelemente wie Promenade oder Privatparzellen am Ufer wurde verzichtet, um den landschaftlichen Charakter des Ortes nicht zu zerstören. Zum Strand gelangte man über einen Verbindungsweg, der in einen Grüngürtel eingebettet war. Weitere Wege wurden nicht angelegt, und die Bewohner waren frei, sich ihre eigenen, spontanen Pfade zum Strand zu suchen.

Während der Nachkriegsjahre wurden im Großraum Barcelona mehrere Projekte an der Küste realisiert. Die Mehrzahl entstand jedoch ohne jegliche Planung und zeichnete sich durch eine schlechte architektonische Qualität aus. Das Hinterland der Küste wurde immer mehr in Privatgrundstücke aufgeteilt und wahllos bebaut, denn natürlich konnten sich die Einwohner Barcelonas durch den wirtschaftlichen und sozialen Aufschwung nun – wie überall in Europa – Privatautos und Zweitwohnungen in der Peripherie der Stadt leisten. Castelldefels und Gavà entwickelten sich zu Hauptattraktionspolen. In chaotischer Aneinanderreihung schossen dort auf einem Küstenstreifen von über zehn Kilometern Länge Campinganlagen, Golfplätze und Freizeiteinrichtungen aus dem Boden.

1957 baute E. Giralt zum ersten Mal innerhalb Barcelonas ein kleines Stück Uferpromenade – eine schüchterne Annäherung der Stadt an den Strand von Barceloneta, zwischen dem Hafen und den Fabrikanlagen. Jenseits der Grenzen des Freihafens diente die Promenade dazu, das Stadtviertel mit dem offenen Meer zu verbinden, gewissermaßen als Verlängerung

Bei der städtebaulichen Neuordnung, die in den vergangenen 15 Jahren in Barcelona stattfand, stand die Öffnung der Stadt zum Meer auf dem Programm. Eine besondere Rolle spielte der Entwurf von Martorell, Bohigas, Mackay und Puigdomenech für das Olympische Dorf aus dem Jahre 1986. Mit diesem Viertel erhielt die Stadt eine neue Fassade zum Meer.

One of the main objectives in the urban reorganization of Barcelona of the past 15 years has been to open up the city to the sea again. The Olympic Village design drawn up by Martorell, Bohigas, Mackay and Puigdomenech in 1986 made a particular contribution in this respect.

In 1957, E. Giralt first built a small section of shoreline promenade within Barcelona, a cautious approach to the beach of Barceloneta, between the port and the factories. Beyond the limits of the free port, the promenade served to connect the urban district with the sea. In a way it was an extension of the harbour's mole, which had always been used by the residents for fishing and walking. Here they experienced the horizon, awakening the desire to fashion the whole urban waterfront of Barcelona along similar lines.

José Antonio Coderch developed new models for seaside recreational facilities with the example of his golf club "del Prat", as did Francesc Mitjans with the camping place "La Ballena Alegre", both outstanding arrangements in the pine forests of Gavà and Castelldefels.

Port Vell
Location: Paseo de Juan de Borbón, Moll de la
Barceloneta, Pla del Palau, Plaça Pau Vila
Client: Port Authority of Barcelona, City of Barcelona
Design: Jordi Henrich, Olga Tarrasó, Rafael de
Cáceres, architects
Project architects: Pere Mateu, Joan Romero,
Josep Maria Serra
Construction period: 1990–1993

Certainly among the greatest accomplishments in new city planning since the beginning of the eighties in Barcelona are the numerous new urban spaces. Opening the city out to the sea was on the programme from the beginning. The "Moll de la Fusta" project by Manuel de Solà-Morales marked the start of reclaiming the harbour area in 1982. In the 1987 "Plan de Costas", Luis Cantallops suggested readapting four kilometres of beach in the area of greater Barcelona. His urban development plan was the first since the beginning of democracy to take all the communities around Barcelona, which had grown considerably in the previous years, into consideration. Furthermore, he demonstrated how the inner city could have access to the sea via the old harbour, and how the natural aspect of the

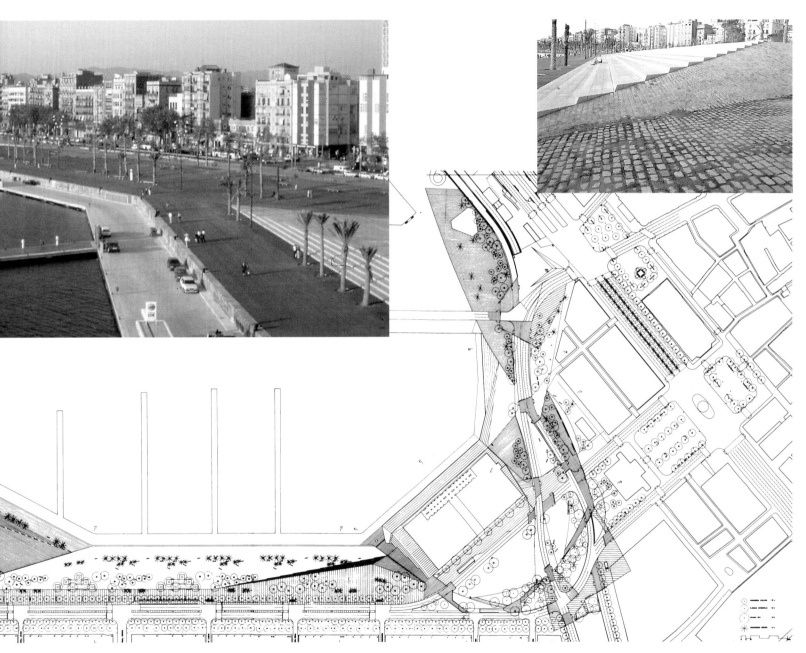

Zu den neuen Wasserfront-
Projekten Barcelonas gehört
die Umgestaltung des Port
Vell. Mit der Moll de la Fusta
bildet er eine öffentliche Uferzone und den Abschluß der
städtischen Hafenareale. Auf
den Kais wurden mit Treppen,
Rampen und Stützmauern
verschiedene Ebenen geformt.
Zur Stadt hin stehen dichte
Baumgruppen, zum Ufer hin
unterbrochene Baumreihen.

One of the Barcelona waterfront projects involves the
alteration of Port Vell, a long
stretch of waterfront that -
leads on to Moll de la Fusta at
one end and the harbour at
the other. Ramps, steps and
buttresses now divide the
old quays into various levels
and trees have been planted
in broken rows near the
waterfront and in groups
closer to the city.

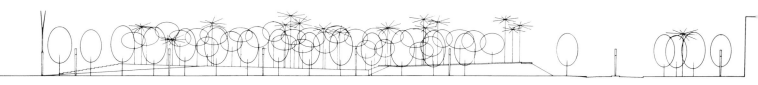

der Hafenmole, die von den Bewohnern seit jeher zum Angeln, Spazierengehen und Diskutieren benutzt wurde. Hier erlebten sie den Horizont, und es erwachte der Wunsch, die gesamte städtische Wasserfront Barcelonas auf ähnliche Weise zu gestalten.

Neue Modelle der Freizeiteinrichtungen am Meer entwickelten José Antonio Coderch am Beispiel seines Golfclubs »del Prat« und Francesc Mitjans mit dem Campingplatz »La Ballena Alegre« – beides herausragende Anlagen in den Pinienwäldern von Gavà und Castelldefels.

Zu den größten Errungenschaften der städtebaulichen Neuordnung, die seit Beginn der 80er Jahre in Barcelona stattfand, gehören sicherlich die zahlreichen neugestalteten Stadträume. Von Anfang an stand dabei auch die Öffnung der Stadt zum Meer auf dem Programm. Das Projekt der »Moll de la Fusta« von Manuel de Solà-Morales markierte im Jahre 1982 den Beginn der Rückgewinnung von Hafenarealen; 1987 schlug Luis Cantallops im »Plan de Costas« vor, vier Kilometer Strand im Bereich des Großraums Barcelona neu zu gestalten. Cantallops erarbeitete zum ersten Mal seit dem Beginn der Demokratie einen Stadtentwicklungsplan, der alle in den vorhergehenden Jahren stark angewachsenen Gemeinden um Barcelona berücksichtigte. Zudem veranschaulichte er, wie der Innenstadt über den Alten Hafen ein Zugang zum Meer verschafft und der natürliche Charakter der Strände im Süden der Stadt bewahrt werden konnte.

Schließlich trugen die Olympischen Spiele von 1992 entschieden dazu bei, daß solche Planungen in die Tat umgesetzt wurden. So änderten bis 1992 viele alte Hafenareale ihr Gesicht, die Gleisanlagen der Eisenbahn verschwanden von der Küste, die Strände wurden neu angelegt und das Wasser geklärt, die großen Fabriken wurden verlagert. Markante Orte entstanden: der »Port Vell«, der Olympische Hafen und der »Parque del Poble Nou.«

Eine besondere Rolle spielte dabei der Entwurf von Martorell, Bohigas, Mackay und Puigdomenech für das Olympische Dorf. Die Planer setzten ihre Vorstellung durch, das Dorf nicht als isolierte Siedlung zu betrachten, sondern als Stadterweiterung. Die strenge Geometrie der Innenstadt verlängerten sie über die ungenutzten Industrieareale bis zur Küste – dort entstand eine neue Fassade zum Meer.

Die neuen Freiräume des Port Vell in Barcelona, zwischen 1990 und 1993 von den Architekten Jordi Henrich, Olga Tarrasó und Rafael Cáceres gestaltet, nehmen eine Fläche von mehr als dreizehn Hektar ein und bilden

beaches to the south of the city of Barcelon could be preserved.

Finally, the 1992 Olympic Games contribut ed decisively to the realization of such plans Thus many old harbour areas changed their ap pearance. The railway tracks disappeared from the shore, the beaches were reconstructed, the water detoxified, and the large factories relocated Striking landmarks developed, such as "Por Vell", the Olympic port, and the "Parque de Poble Nou", introduced in TOPOS 1.

The design for the Olympic village by Marto rell, Bohigas, Mackay and Puigdomenech playec a special role in these changes. The planners im plemented their concept of considering the vil lage an urban expansion rather than an isolatec settlement. They extended the strict geometry o the inner city through the abandoned industria district towards the coast, where a new front fac ing the sea arose.

At "Port Vell" in Barcelona, built betweer 1990 and 1993 by the architects Jordi Henrich Olga Tarrasó and Rafael de Cáceres, the nev open spaces cover an area of over thirteen hec tares. Together with the "Moll de la Fusta" they constitute the limits of the city port. A kilomet re-long promenade runs next to the water. Pedes trians have a view of the city along it as if from the sea. They experience the space as a long path belonging to the Barceloneta district and provid ing access to it, while at the same time having the character of a shoreline pier. At this point the nar row city streets run into the wide, open space o the harbour. The vegetation underlines this tran sition. The closely planted trees on the urban side gradually thin out towards the harbour. The planners used only limited means in this projec

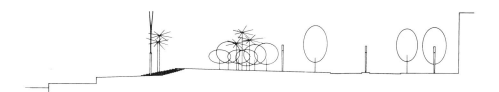

in order to emphasize the spatial and conceptual unity of place. They made a few points or lines stand out through small topographic changes. These shifts and layers in the terrain are framed by variously shaped supporting walls.

The delta of Río Llobregat has for centuries had a powerfully distinctive landscape. Today it is part of the metropolitan area of Barcelona and largely settled. Intensive planting of pine trees, stabilizing the dunes, and a few lagoons still testify to the old delta landscape. These landscape elements determine the appearance of the "Paseo Marítimo de Gavà" built in 1992/1993. As in the projects of the GATCPAC group in the thirties, the architect Imma Jansana similarly resigned from reinforcing the coastline with construction. Rather, she tried to direct pedestrians through a sequence of free spaces, from constructed to natural settings, without enforcing the route upon them or oppressing them with massive forms of construction. Everything about this project is minimal: the area, the materials invested, and the costs. In this way the character of the extraordinary coastal landscape is maintained, and the ecological system of water, beach, dunes, dune vegetation, and pines remains balanced.

Despite their apparent differences, the projects for Port Vell and Gavà have several aspects in common. Both had the motto of using simple forms and a minimal investment of means. Both are oriented towards the water. Natural dunes direct pedestrians towards the coast in one case, planted slopes in the other. There the view sweeps across the unchanging surface of the water in the open sea or in the harbour, as far as the horizon, which had been invisible to the city for so long.

zusammen mit der Moll de la Fusta den Abschluß des städtischen Hafens. Eine Promenade von einem Kilometer Länge führt am Wasser entlang – die Spaziergänger überblicken von dort aus die Stadt, wie vom Meer aus gesehen. Den Raum erfahren sie als langgestreckten Weg, der zum Stadtviertel Barceloneta gehört und es erschließt, aber gleichzeitig den Charakter eines Uferkais behält.

Die engen Stadtstraßen münden an dieser Stelle in den großen, leeren Raum des Hafens, die Vegetation unterstreicht den Übergang, indem die dichte Baumbepflanzung stadtseits sich zum Hafen hin stufenweise lichtet. Bei der Realisierung setzten die Planer nur wenige Materialien ein, um die räumliche und gestalterische Einheit des Ortes zu betonen. Einige Punkte oder Linien hoben sie heraus durch kleine topographische Veränderungen. Diese Versprünge und Stufen in der Fläche sind durch verschieden geformte Stützmauern gefaßt.

Starke landschaftliche Prägung besaß über Jahrhunderte das Delta des Río Llobregat, heute Teil des Stadtgebiets von Barcelona und zum größten Teil besiedelt. Intensive Pinienpflanzungen, mit denen die Dünen stabilisiert wurden, und einige Lagunen zeugen noch von der alten Delta-Landschaft.

Diese landschaftlichen Elemente bestimmen die Gestalt des 1993 fertiggestellten »Paseo Marítimo de Gavà«. Ähnlich wie in den Projekten der Gruppe GATCPAC aus den 30er Jahren, verzichtete die Architektin Imma Jansana darauf, die Küste durch ein Bauwerk zu befestigen. Vielmehr versuchte sie, die Spaziergänger über eine Sequenz von Freiräumen vom Gebauten ins Natürliche zu führen, ohne ihnen einen Weg aufzuzwingen oder sie mit massiven baulichen Formen zu erdrücken.

Alles an diesem Projekt ist minimal: Fläche, Materialeinsatz, Kosten. Auf diese Weise bleibt der Charakter der außergewöhnlichen Küstenlandschaft erhalten und das Ökosystem aus Wasser, Strand, Dünen, Dünenvegetation und Pinien in der Balance.

Die Projekte für Port Vell und Gavà in Barcelona haben trotz ihrer offensichtlichen Verschiedenartigkeit einige Aspekte gemein: Beide entstanden unter dem Motto der einfachen Gestaltung und des minimalen Einsatzes von Mitteln. Beide wenden sich zum Wasser – im einen Fall geleiten natürliche Dünen, im anderen baumbestandene Schrägen die Spaziergänger zum Ufer. Dort schweift ihr Blick über die unveränderliche Wasserfläche des offenen Meeres oder des Hafens bis zum Horizont, den die Stadt so lange nicht erblicken konnte.

Die Schnitte durch die neugestalteten Uferkais des Port Vell in Barcelona zeigen, daß unterschiedliche Baumarten und -kombinationen sowie die sanften Niveauversprünge den öffentlichen Raum definieren.

The sectional view of the converted quays at Port Vell, Barcelona, reveals how differing tree species and gentle changes in elevation have been used to define public space.

Paseo Marítimo de Gavà
Location: between Riera dels Canyara and Calle
de Sitges
Client: City of Gavà
Design: Imma Jansana, architect
Assistants: Jaume Vendrell, Santi Juan Navarro, Jordi
Navarro, architects; Beth Figures, landscape architect;
Francesc Giró, botanist; Pepa Marínez, Julia
Torregrosa, architecture students; Fernando Benedito,
project architect
Construction period: 1992/1993

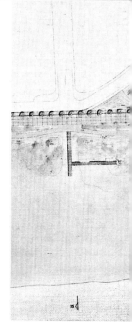

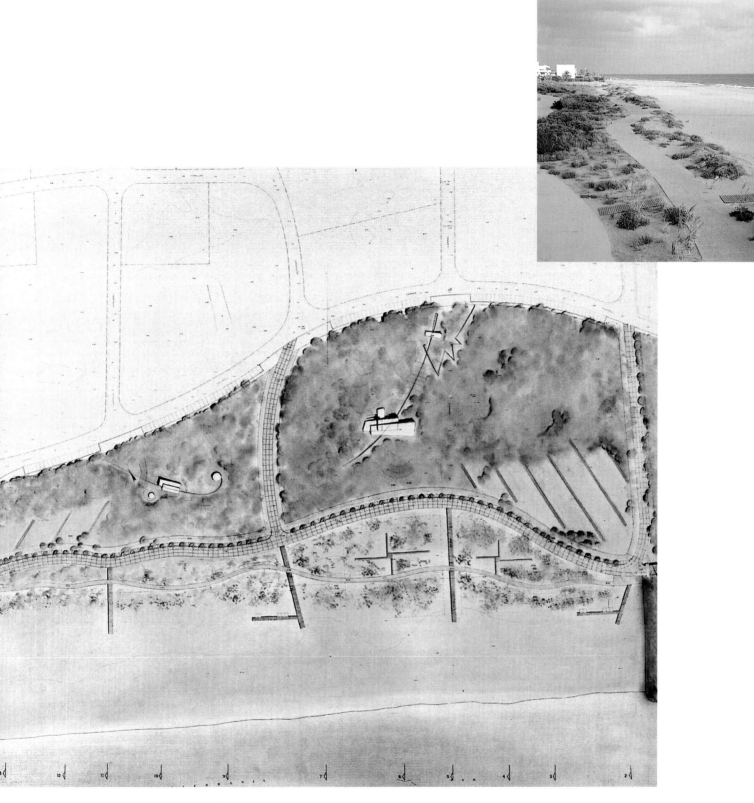

Die Dünenlandschaft des Río Llobregat sollte beim Bau der Promenade in Gavà bei Barcelona möglichst unberührt bleiben. Die Küste sollte nicht durch ein Bauwerk befestigt werden. Auf einen geschwungenen, asphaltierten Weg am Dünenrand folgt ein Pfad aus Holzplanken, Holzstege führen von dort aus zum Meer und enden im Sand – vom Gebauten zum Natürlichen.

The dunes of the Río Llobregat delta were not to be fortified or changed in any way by the design of the new Paseo Marítimo de Gavà, near Barcelona. A curved asphalt path now skirts the edge of the dunes, followed by a path of wooden planks that leads towards the sea, disappearing into the sand beforehand – in a transition from the man-made to the natural.

La Fosca-Strandpromenade in Palamós, Spanien

La Fosca seafront promenade, Palamós, Spain

Josep Fuses
Joan M. Viader

Die Strandpromenade sollte mittels Kombination von harten und weichen Oberflächen und der Anordnung der Bäume so in die Landschaft und die unmittelbare Umgebung integriert werden, dass sie natürlich wirkt. Ein zu städtischer Charakter wurde vermieden. Die Promenade gliedert sich in vier unterschiedlich gestaltete Abschnitte:

Der erste Abschnitt schließt an die Straße nach La Fosca und die existierende Häuserreihe an. Die bestehende Steinmauer wird erhalten und mit einem abgerundeten Abschluss aus dem gleichen Material – dem Banyoles-Stein – ergänzt. Sie ähnelt nun den niederen Schutzmauern, die die Straßen der Costa Brava säumen. Die Oberfläche besteht aus Mastix auf den Straßen und aus Waschbeton mit sichtbaren Steinen auf den Gehsteigen.

Im zweiten Abschnitt sind nur Fußgänger zugelassen. Gelbliche Natursteinplatten an den Rändern der Grundstücke und am Zugang zum Strand werden mit grobkörnigem Sand auf den restlichen Flächen kombiniert. Wo die gekrümmten Formen der unterschiedlichen Oberflächen aneinanderstoßen, wurden Pflanzinseln für Bäume wie Pinie, Zypresse, Olive und Tamarinde geschaffen. Sitzbänke sind linear angeordnet. Die Mauer, die die Promenade vom Strand trennt, ist zwar niedriger, aber auch mit Banyoles-Steinen abgeschlossen. Am Beginn der Promenade wird die gekrümmte Form der Mauer unterbrochen und geschwungene Treppen aus demselben Material wie die Platten führen an den Strand.

An der kleinen Landenge am Roca Fosca wurde der Küstenpfad zwischen den Stränden von La Fosca und Sant Esteve mit Hilfe einer Betonstützmauer, verkleidet mit Stein, befestigt. Die Mauer folgt der kurvigen Topographie des Geländes und am Ende nimmt ihre Höhe ab und geht in den Plattenbelag über. Die Steigung des Pfades beträgt unter sechs Prozent. So können auch behinderte Menschen den Pfad nutzen, um von einem Strand zum nächsten zu gelangen. Außerdem passt sich der Pfad sanft in das unebene Gelände. Der Belag besteht aus alten hölzernen Eisenbahnschwellen, die eine Schicht aus grobkörnigem Sand fassen.

Eine Plattform im nördlichen Bereich erleichtert den Zugang zum Strand vom Wohngebiet, ordnet den existierenden Geschäftsbereich und verleiht dem Küstenpfad in der Nähe der Fe-

Harmonisch fügen sich die einzelnen Abschnitte der Promenade in ihre Umgebung und beweisen trotzdem eigenständigen Charakter.

The individual sections of the promenade merge in harmoniously with the surroundings yet are independent in character.

In tackling this recent project in a picturesque village on Spain's Costa Brava, it was decided to integrate the promenade into the landscape by means of arrangements of trees and a combination of hard and soft surfacing. In the process, approaches with an excessively urban character were avoided to achieve a natural effect.

The promenade itself is divided into four sections, whereby the first runs next to the road to La Fosca and an existing row of houses. A rounded coping of Banyoles stone was added on to an existing wall of the same material, with the result that the wall now resembles the low guard walls that used to line the roads of the Costa Brava. The road was sealed in mastic, and washed concrete with visible aggregate was used for the promenade itself.

The second section uses stone fossil paving in a yellowish hue for the edges of properties and the entrance to the beach, and a softer solution of coarse sand has been employed for the remaining surfaces. These two zones meet along a sinuous line, creating islands for plantations of trees (pine, cypress, olive and tamarind) and lines of wooden benches. The curved wall separating the promenade from the beach is lower than the one in the first section, but is also coped in Banyoles stone. The wall is interrupted at the beginning by curved steps, which lead down to the beach in the same stone as the paving.

The third section, which faces the small isthmus of Roca Fosca, consists of the coastal path connecting the beaches of La Fosca and Sant Esteve. This path has been provided a concrete retaining wall faced in stone. The wall, which follows the sinuous form of the topography, decreases in height towards the end until it levels

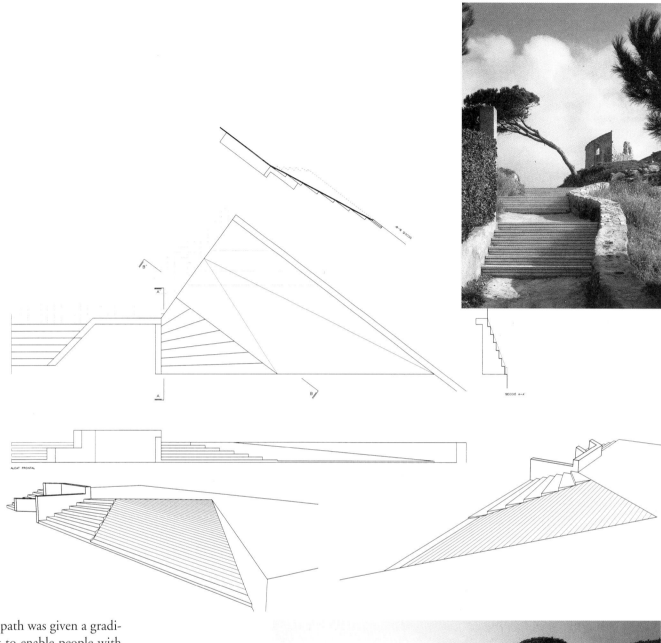

Bei der Restaurierung des Küstenpfades zur Festung Sant Esteve wurde die »pi tort« besonders berücksichtigt – eine als örtliches Naturdenkmal geschützte Drehkiefer.

In restoring the coastal path to the Sant Esteve fortification, emphasis was given to the 'pi tort', a natural monument in the form of a twisted pine.

out with the paving. The path was given a gradient of less than 6 percent to enable people with disabilities to pass from one beach to the other and adapt it more smoothly to the uneven relief. The paving consists of old wooden railway sleepers flanking beds of coarse sand.

In the northernmost section, a platform was installed which provides access to the beach from a nearby housing estate while organising the commercial zone and leading on over to the coastal path to the Sant Esteve fortification. A geometric platform adapted to the topography

Die Architekten haben die geometrischen Formen der Plattform ideal in die Küstentopographie eingepasst. Treppen und Rampen führen zum Strand.

The architects have created a geometric platform that merges in perfectly with the coastal topography. From here stepways and ramps lead down to the beach.

La Fosca seafront promenade, Palamós, Spain
Client: Municipality of Palamós
Architects: Josep Fuses and Joan M. Viader, Jordi López-Vives, Ingeniero C.C.i.P.
Direción General de Costas / Dirección obras
Collaborators: Nicolás Ruíz, Antoni Blázquez, Lluís Guanter, Jaume Frigola and
Ricard Turon
Planning: 1993
Construction planning:
Construction: 1994 – 1996
Costs: ESP 185,000, 000

stung Sant Esteve Kontinuität. Trotzdem verliert der Weg die Funktion als Promenade nicht. Die geometrisch konstruierte Plattform fungiert auch als Abschluss der Straße. Angepasst an die Topographie etabliert sie einen Dialog zwischen dem angrenzenden felsigen Bereich und dem natürlichen Charakter der Szenerie.

Außerdem wurde der Pfad zur Festung Sant Esteve verbessert. Ein leicht modifiziertes Längsprofil mit einer Reihe neuer Treppen erleichtert den Zugang. Die Treppen bestehen aus drei Steinen, der Auftritt aus einer Lage grobkörnigem Sand. Als Höhepunkt der Route und symbolische Besonderheit wurde ein Schwerpunkt auf eine Drehkiefer gelegt – die »pi tort« von Sant Esteve, die im kommunalen Katalog schützenswerter Güter enthalten ist.

ends an existing street and establishes a dialogue with the rocky zone and the natural character of the setting.

Finally, the path to the Sant Esteve fortification was improved by building a series of stairways to facilitate access by slightly modifying the longitudinal profile. The steps consist of three stone slabs, and the landings are made up of coarse sand. Emphasis was given to the Sant Esteve 'pi tort' (Beach Pine), a natural monument, to underscore its role as a symbolic feature of the site and to mark the end of the promenade.

Die Aussichtsterrasse ist Aufenthaltsort an der Promenade Strandspaziergänger können hier rasten und die Bucht und den Strand überblicken.

The viewing terrace is a favourite resting place on the promenade. People walking along the coast use it to enjoy views of the bay and the beach.

Telecom in der Lehmgrube Binz, Zürich

A telecom complex in a clay pit, Zurich

In 1988, work began on the western section of a clay pit in Binz, a district of Zurich, where a new building was to be erected for the Swiss phone corporation Telecom PTT. The actual area where landscaping measures could be carried out consisted solely of the floor of the pit since the gently sloping walls could not be touched, being part of a nature conservation zone. The brief specified the creation of an easily recognizable entrance area, fencing all around, an outdoor seating area for the staff, a fire-service access route, an evaporation basin for surface runoff and a retention pond for roof runoff. Nature conservation demands were also made, the most important being the preservation of spawning grounds and habitats for toads and other amphibians. In terms of planning, these latter elements are located at the right place, namely at the deepest point of the site, where the slopes run into the ground, thus blurring the boundaries between the construction site and the nature conservation zone. Since we were unable to run a fence through this moist area, we gained permission to shift it to the top of the slope, which not only trebled the amount of outdoor space but also gave the large building room to breathe. Moreover, since the wild character of the slope naturally had to be retained, the nature conservation zone now reaches right up to the walls of the building.

Nature and architecture are the two design protagonists at the site, and water is the keynote theme. Ecological considerations have been taken into account, but the design is architectonic and austere in approach. The tension arising from this contrast of natural growth and the geometry lends coherence to the individual elements, despite the fact that the slow erosion of the pond banks will

Mit dem Telecom PTT-Neubau wurde der westliche Bereich der ehemaligen Lehmgrube Binz neu strukturiert. Das Gelände umfaßte zuerst nur den Grubenboden, die Grubenwände liegen in der Naturschutzzone. Die betrieblichen Vorgaben beinhalteten einen gut erkennbaren Eingangsbereich, die strikte Einzäunung, einen Personalaufenthaltsbereich, eine Feuerwehr-Zufahrt, ein Verdunstungsbecken für das anfallende Oberflächenwasser sowie Retentionsbecken für das Dachwasser bei geringem Pflegeaufwand. Die wichtigste Forderung des Naturschutzes waren Laichgewässer und Lebensräume für Kreuzkröten und Unken. Gestalterisch richtig sind diese am Böschungsfuß, dem tiefsten Bereich des Geländes, wo die ehemalige Grundstücksgrenze verlief. Sie und damit auch der Zaun konnten aus gestalterischen Gründen an die Hangkrone verschoben werden. Dadurch verdreifachte sich der Außenraum, das große Gebäude gewann Luft. Das Naturschutzgebiet reicht nun bis zur Fassade.

Natur und Architektur sind die beiden entwerferischen Gegenspieler. Das Wasser ist das Leitthema. Die geforderte naturnahe Gestaltung wurde der Künstlichkeit des Ortes angemessen artifiziell interpretiert. Die aus dem natürlichen Bewuchs und den geometrischen Formen entstehende Spannung hält die einzelnen Elemente zusammen, auch wenn Eingriffe wie die langsame Erodierung der Ufer die ursprüngliche Exaktheit brechen wird, Kraft und Zeit sichtbar werden. Das Bauwerk kann altern, langsam und ohne künstlich erzeugte Patina. Dieses große Bauwerk und die ehemalige Deponie bekommen ein grünes Mäntelchen, das nicht beschönigt, sondern Fragen offen läßt.

Der im Quartier charakteristische Einschnitt der ehemaligen Grube mit den terrassierten Grubenwänden und dem freien Grubenfuß sind in den Entwurf übernommen worden. Die drei Grubenwände erscheinen nach Exposition verschieden: Gegen Norden der bestehende Wald, gegen Osten Strauchhecken in den Böschungen und Streuwiesen in den Bäumen, gegen Süden offene, wechselfeuchte Streuwiesen mit wenigen Einzelbäumen. Der Grubenfuß bleibt frei von Bäumen, nur die Grenzen sind markiert.

Das gesamte Oberflächenwasser fließt in fünf kaskadenartig angeordnete Teiche. Die Abflußmenge vermindert sich durch die Stauung von 111 Liter je Sekunde auf 27 Liter je Sekunde. Die

Guido Hager

Das Post- und Telekommunikationsgebäude in Zürich-Binz erhielt naturnah gestaltete, jedoch artifiziell interpretierte Außenanlagen.

The design for the grounds of the Swiss building may be architectonic in approach but it takes ecological requirements into account.

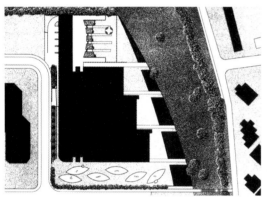

exakte Uferausbildung markiert den Hangfuß. Sie verbindet das Gebäude mit dem Naturschutzgebiet. Weder das eine noch das andere hat Vorrang: Natur bis zur Fassade, architektonische Struktur bis ins Naturschutzgebiet. Das Dachwasser wird in sechs linsenförmige Becken von 480 Kubikmeter Inhalt eingeleitet, die 168 Liter je Sekunde werden dem Vorfluter mit 5 Liter je Sekunde, also stark verzögert, abgegeben. Bei trockener Witterung sind diese Becken leer und liegen erdskulpturartig vor dem Betriebsgebäude.

Der Grubenfuß wurde nach der Stillegung des Lehmabbaus bis in die 70er Jahre als Abfalldeponie genutzt. Das Deponiematerial mußte am Ort stabilisiert und abgedichtet werden, damit weder Oberflächenwasser noch Luft eintritt. Die Abdichtung erfolgte im Bereich der Tiefgarage mit kalkstabilisiertem Lehm, im Bereich der Feuerwehrzufahrt mit zwei Schichten Zementstabilit als Druckplatte mit einer Bentofix-Dichtungsmatte B als Wasserdichtung. Die Teiche wurden mit der Bentofix-Matte, der Bereich der Retentionsbecken mit Lehm abgedichtet. Über den verschiedenen Abdichtungstypen liegt die Vegetationsschicht mit zehn Zentimeter Recyclingkies und fünf Zentimeter Straßenkies mit Schotter- und Geröllstreifen. Diese erzeugen mikroklimatische Unterschiede. Beide Seiten der Teiche erscheinen auf den ersten Blick als Wiesen. Die Grubenwand ist anstehender Lehm mit Schilfbewuchs, der gesamte Grubenfuß ist als Kiesfläche ausgebildet, auf der eine Magerwiese wächst. Eine freiwachsende Strauchhecke grenzt das Gebiet zur Grubenstraße hin ab. Säulenpappeln und vier geschnittene, hintereinander gestaffelte Hainbuchenhecken gliedern die Zone zwischen der Erschließungsstraße und der Eingangsfassade mit dem Bürotrakt. Der Haupteingang öffnet sich platzartig. Unter den Stützen des Restaurants- und Wohnungstraktes liegen Parkplätze sowie die Tiefgaragenzufahrt. Einige Stufen führen zum Aufenthaltsbereich über der Einstellhalle durch einen Vorhang aus Bambus, der in seiner Exotik die Arbeitspause einleitet, den künstlichen Standort widerspiegelt und gleichzeitig dem angrenzenden

disturb the exquisite precision of the design an demonstrate the action of time. The building an the pit itself will gain a green cover that does no seek to conceal either but which rather demor strates their very presence.

The way the pit is cut into the land, quite typ ical for the area, has been left as it is; this also ap plies to the empty sole and the three terrace walls, each of them different in character; th northern emnbellished with a wood, the easter featuring bushes growing down the sides an wetland grasses on moist sills and the souther with open areas of moderately well-drained litt meadows and a few occasional trees. We hav designed all surface water to run into five pond

Der Boden der ehemaligen Lehmgrube im Züricher Stadtteil Binz wurde Baugrund, die Böschungen erhielten Naturschutzstatus. Vor allem Laichgewässer und Lebensraum für Kröten und Unken waren gefordert, als die Telecom ihr neues Gebäude plazierte. Der Landschaftsarchitekt legte fünf kaskadenartig aneinandergereihte Teiche an, die zum Hang hin natürlich gestaltet wurden, zum Gebäude hin harte Kante aufweisen. Architektur und Naturschutzgebiet sind verbunden und stören sich dennoch nicht. Der Aufenthaltsbereich befindet sich hinter Bambuspflanzungen und wird beherrscht von einem runden und luftigen Pavillon – eine elementare Kleinarchitektur als Zitat aus der Gartenkultur

ined up in a cascade arrangement, which slows down flow from 111 litres per second to 27 litres. The rear banks of the ponds, which create a link between the building and the nature conservation zone, are formed by the slope. Neither the one nor the other are allowed to take precedence: nature runs up to the facades of the building while manmade structures intrude into nature. For its part, roof runoff is captured into six elliptic basins, 480 cubic metres in size, that reduce the flow rate from an initial 168 litres per second to a mere five litres when the water issues into the receiving canal. In dry weather, these basins are naturally empty and lie in front of the building like earth sculptures.

Schilf der Streuwiesen im Aussehen verwandt ist. Die Sitzbänke stehen an heißen Tagen bis in den Nachmittag im Schatten von Bambus, geschützt vor neugierigen Blicken aus dem Restaurant. Sie laden zum Ausruhen und stillen Betrachten des Naturschauspiels ein, die extensiven Flächen lassen Spiele wie Boccia oder Federball zu. Den Osthang trennt eine Mooswand vom Gebäude. Aus Sicherheitsgründen wurde ein Holzzaun für die Kinder errichtet. Der zentrale Pavillon liegt als traditionelles Element der Gartenkultur im Brennpunkt der Anlage und spielt als elementare Kleinarchitektur mit dem Licht. Das Artefakt und die Natur treten in eine sich gegenseitig durchdringende Beziehung: die Natur braucht den Betrachter, um als Natur erkannt zu werden.

Die gesamte Anlage ist unterhaltsextensiv angelegt, wobei die Eingangs- und Aufenthaltspartien aufwendiger sind als die rückwärtigen, dem Naturschutzgebiet zugeordneten Flächen. Den Unterhalt der Hangseite besorgt die Naturschutzgruppe Binz. Dazu gehört das Mähen der Wiesen, der ab-

The bottom of the former clay pit in Binz, Zurich, was designated building land but the slopes had already been declared a nature reserve, meaning that when the Swiss phone corporation Telecom PTT decided to erect a building at the site, it had to fulfil requirements regarding the preservation of spawning grounds and habitats for toads and other amphibians. In response, the landscape architect created five ponds lined up in a cascade arrangement, giving the ones close to the building hard perimeters and the ones further away natural banks, thus providing a link between nature and architecture in which the one does not intrude upon the other. A recreation seating area concealed behind bamboo plantings is predominated by a round and airy pavilion.

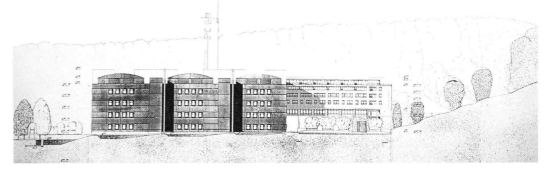

Client: PTT Executive board
Landscape architect: Guido Hager, Zurich
Collaborators: Brigitte Nyffenegger, Patrick Altermatt, landscape architects, Zurich
Architects: Fischer Architekten; Marcel Barth, Rudolf Reichling, Zurich
Size: 9,000 square metres
Planning: 1988
Construction: 1993–1994

Once the pit was abandoned, it was used as landfill until the seventies. This meant that the waste material had to be stabilized, in other words, it sealed off to ensure that neither surface water nor air could reach it. This was performed in various ways, depending on the area concerned and the function it fulfills; in the case of the underground garage, lime-stabilized clay was employed, while two layers of cement stabilizing material and a compression slab with a Bentofix B mat to seal off water have been used in the area of the fire brigade access route; ponds are sealed with Bentofix mats and the retention basin are with clay. A ten-centimetre layer of used gravel and a five-centimetre layer of road gravel have been laid on the respective sealants in areas of vegetation, and interspersed with strips of rock fragments and pebbles, thus creating different microclimates and the impression, particularly in the area of the ponds, of naturally growing meadows. Reeds grow on level stretches of the loam pit walls, a low-nutrient meadow has been created on a bed of gravel at the bottom of the pit trees mark the boundaries.

A wild hedge borders the pit road, and fastigiate poplars and clipped hornbeam hedges articulate the space between the access road and the entrance to the office wing. The main entrance area opens up into a small precinct, and parking space is provided for visitors' cars and bicycles under the columns of the restaurant and residential wing, which is also where the entrance to the underground garage is located. Several steps lead to the seating area via the covered parking area, passing through a curtain of bamboo, which with its hint of the exotic, symbolizes the transition from work to recreation while reflecting the

schnittsweise Stockschnitt der freiwachsenden Hecken, das alternierende Ausräumen der Teiche und das Abführen des Schnittgutes. Für Kreuzkröten und für verschiedene Pionierpflanzen werden jährlich offene Lehmflächen freigeschürft. Für Spezialarbeiten wie den Schnitt der Hainbuchenhecken und den Winterschutz für den Bambus werden Gärtner beigezogen. Die Bambuströge und Hecken werden automatisch bewässert. Den Schnitt der Magerwiesen erledigt der Hauswart. Ein Pflegeplan sichert langfristig den kontinuierlichen Unterhalt der Anlage.

Der Außenraum ist öffentlich nicht begehbar. Die punktuelle Einsicht schafft jedoch einen Öffentlichkeitsgrad, der alten Herrschaftsgärten anhaftet. Bei anhaltender fachgerechter und liebevoller Pflege wird eine gartenhafte Atmosphäre entstehen, die mehr als nur Natur in der Stadt darstellt, die durch die vielfältige Überformung der Natur durch den Menschen geschaffen worden ist. Über den Zaun hinweg wird im verbotenen Garten etwas von der Sehnsucht nach dem Paradies spürbar.

Das Dachwasser wird in sechs linsenförmige Becken geleitet. Sie dienen als Rückhaltebecken, geben das Regenwasser stark verzögert an den Vorfluter weiter. Sind die Becken leer, schmücken sie als Erdskulpturen den Außenraum.

Roof runoff is captured into six elliptic basins, which both serve as stormwater retention ponds while slowing down the flow rate when the water issues into the receiving canal. The basins form attractive earth sculptures in dry weather.

rtificiality of the site. The bamboo, which is
milar in appearance to the reeds growing in the
butting litter meadow, also serves to shade the
eating area on hot days and screens off curious
lances from the restaurant. The seating area it-
elf is inviting in character and is a pleasant place
o while away the time and contemplate nature
nd the extensively-managed areas, which are
uitable for boccie or shuttlecock. A wooden
ence has been erected to prevent children from
crambling from the restaurant precinct to the
onds beyond. A central pavilion, a traditional
lement of garden culture, forms the focus of the
ite in a fascinating play of light and shade. Here
he manmade and the natural interact in a way
/hich makes it clear that nature needs to be seen
o be recognized as such.

The whole grounds are designed for extensive
naintenance, whereby greater attention is paid to
he entrance and seating areas than to the rear ar-
as facing out towards the nature conservation
one. The loamy ground is shallowly excavated in
ertain areas each year to provide ideal conditions
or amphibians and pioneer plants, and the local
ature conservation group takes care of the main-
enance of the slopes. The low-nutrient meadow
s cut by the janitor, gardeners are hired to per-
orm special tasks, such as clipping the hornbeam
edges and wintering down the bamboo, and a
nanagement plan has been drawn up.

The grounds are not accessible, but the fact
hat they can be seen from certain points furnish-
s them a degree of public familiarity reminiscent
f the gardens of nobility from other times. Giv-
n continued expert care, the site will develop a
arden-like atmosphere and will come to repre-
ent more than just a piece of nature in the city.

Gegenüber der temporären
Nutzung als Abfalldeponie hat
die ehemalige Grube Binz
gewonnen, wie der Blick über
die Teiche zur Rotunde im Aufenthaltsbereich und auf
den nördlichen Hang zeigt. Das
gesamte Areal ist unterhal-
tungsextensiv angelegt, wobei
die Pflege der Hänge und
Laichgebiete von einer Naturschutzgruppe übernommen
wird.

Compared to the days when it
was used as a landfill, the clay
pit at Binz has definitely bene-
fited from the landscaping
measures, as a view over the
ponds to the round pavilion in
the seating area and the pit
walls proves. The whole site is
designed for extensive maintenance, whereby the slopes and
spawning areas are to be tend-
ed by a local nature conservation group.

Die Kolonisierung der Leere: Duindoornstad

The colonisation of emptiness: Duindoornstad

Harm Tilman

Eine Weile vernachlässigt, steht die Frage der zukünftigen Organisation der Niederlande wieder ganz im Zentrum des Interesses. Die Revitalisierung der Innenstädte, der Ausbau der ökonomischen Mainports, zu denen der Flughafens Schiphol und der Rotterdamer Hafen zählen, die Errichtung einzelner großer Infrastrukturprojekte, wie der Hochgeschwindigkeitsbahn nach Paris und der Betuwelinie, und nicht zuletzt die Planung neuer Wohn- und Gewerbegebiete werden das Gesicht der Niederlande in Zukunft prägen. Die Projekte von West 8 bieten dabei einen aufsehenerregenden Beitrag in der Debatte über die Rolle des Städtebaus in der Gesellschaft und über die Möglichkeiten der Steuerung des zukünftigen Wachstums der Städte. Mehrere spezifische, räumlich begrenzte Eingriffe bilden zusammen eine Strategie für städtebauliche Veränderungen – sowohl flexibel, als auch auf lange Sicht hin angelegt.

Transformationen der Landschaft. Adriaan Geuze hat zusammen mit seinem Büro West 8 ein umfangreiches Œuvre geschaffen, zu dem große Landschaftsentwürfe, Parks und Gärten, Plätze, aber auch mehrere städtebauliche Pläne zählen. Viele Entwürfe wurden inzwischen ausgeführt oder befinden sich gerade in der Ausführungsphase. Hierzu gehören unter anderem die Landschaftsgestaltung von Schiphol und der VSB-Garten in Utrecht, die ehemalige Bahntrasse Binnenrotte, der Theaterplatz Schouwburgplein in Rotterdam sowie das Viertel Borneo-Sporenburg im östlichen Hafengebiet von Amsterdam.

Die Landschaftsarchitekten von West 8 sind von der niederländischen Landschaft fasziniert – und davon, sie für die Gestaltung des städtischen Raums einzusetzen und produktiv zu machen. Damit führen sie die niederländische Tradition der Landschaftsgestaltung fort und erneuern sie gleichzeitig. Ihre Architektur des großen, offenen Stadtraums will nicht, wie manch andere Entwürfe für den städtischen Außenraum, die Stadtbewohner in ihrem Verhalten gängeln. Die eigentliche Stärke von West 8 liegt in der konkreten Analyse eines Projektgebiets, seiner Eigenarten und den dort möglichen authentischen Erfahrungen. Enric Miralles beschreibt die Arbeitsweise von West 8 als »Transformation einer Landschaft vermittels starker Kartographie von der Hand eines sensiblen Kartographen«.

After suffering neglect for some time, the future organisation of the Netherlands is once again the focus of interest. The revitalisation of inner cities, the expansion of major economic ports, including Schiphol airport and Rotterdam harbour, the installation of large-scale infrastructures, such as the high speed train to Paris and the Betuweline, and last but not least the planning of new residential and commercial districts are going to change the face of the Netherlands to come. The projects by West 8 make a sensational contribution to the debate on the role of urban architecture in society and on possibilities for controlling urban growth. A combination of several spatially restricted interventions forms a strategy for urban planning changes – designed to be both flexible and on a long-term basis.

Transformations of the landscape. Adriaan Geuze and his office West 8 created a substantial body of work that includes large-scale landscape designs, parks and gardens, squares, as well as several urban planning designs. Many designs have been carried out by now or are still in the process of being executed. These include the landscape design for Schiphol and the VSB garden in Utrecht, the former Binnenrotte railway tracks, the Schouwburgplein theatre square in Rotterdam, and the Borneo-Sporenburg quarter in the eastern part of Amsterdam harbour. The landscape architects of West 8 are fascinated by the Dutch landscape, applying it to the design of urban space and making it productive. In this way they are both carrying on and renewing Dutch tradition. Unlike some designs for the urban periphery, their architecture of large open urban spaces does not wish to dictate behaviour to the residents.

Bei Hoek van Holland entwirft das Büro West 8 eine neue Stadt als Teil der Rotterdamer Stadtregion – auf einer Düne im Meer.

Adriaan Geuze and his office West 8 designed a new town as part of greater Rotterdam near Hoek van Holland – on a dune in the sea.

The real strength of West 8 is the concrete analysis of a project area and its unique features as well as the authentic experiences possible there. Enric Miralles described the working methods of West 8 as "the transformation of a landscape by means of vigorous cartography at the hand of a sensitive cartographer". On the basis of a design for open urban space, West 8's landscape architects are evidently able to ask the disciplines of architecture and urban planning questions the way no other office with their specialty does. Their work is therefore an incentive to redefine the boundaries between and points of contact of the two disciplines.

Colonisation (Alexanderpolder). West 8 sees the city as a settlement in which town and country, settlement and free space unavoidably coexist. But to what extent can the design of landscape and the growth of cities be directed and

Ausgehend vom Entwurf des offenen Stadtraums zeigt es sich, daß die Landschaftsarchitekten von West 8 in der Lage sind, wie kein anderes Büro ihres Fachgebiets, Fragen an die Disziplinen Architektur und Städtebau zu stellen. Ihre Arbeiten sind daher Ansporn, die Grenzen und Berührungspunkte zwischen den beiden Gebieten neu zu definieren.

Kolonisierung (Alexanderpolder). West 8 betrachtet die Stadt als Ansiedlung, bei der zwangsläufig Stadt und Land, Siedlung und Freifläche gemeinsam auftreten. Doch inwieweit können Gestaltung der Landschaft und Wachstum der Städte gesteuert und kontrolliert werden? Diese Frage stand im Zentrum einer Studie zur Randstad, die West 8 im Jahr 1993 anfertigte. In dieser Studie wird die Verstädterung des sogenannten Grünen Herzens als ein unvermeidlicher Prozeß akzeptiert. Angesichts der zukünftigen Verstädterungsaufgabe sei es unrealistisch, das Grüne Herz offenzuhalten. Außerdem wurden bereits wegen der immer geringeren Rentabilität der Landwirtschaft Böden verkauft. West 8 hält nichts davon, über Baugebiete und Bauverbote Städte so zu organisieren, daß sie kontinuierliche und homogene Einheiten bilden. Statt die Außenbezirke von der Stadt aus zu betrachten, schlagen sie vor, die Perspektive umzukehren und von der Landschaft auf die Stadt zu schauen.

Die Landschaftsarchitekten von West 8 betrachten die Stadt als Ort, an dem sich Siedlung und Freiraum, Städtisches und Ländliches zwangsläufig mischen. Statt den Stadtrand vom Zentrum aus zu betrachten, schlagen sie vor, die Perspektive umzukehren und von der Landschaft auf die Stadt zu schauen.

The landscape architects of West 8 see the city as a place where developed areas and free space, urban and rural elements are necessarily mixed. Instead of considering the periphery from the point of view of downtown, they propose reversing the perspective and looking at the city from the landscape.

The colonisation of the Dutch
landscape: in the Middle Ages

in the 17th century

Von diesem Blickpunkt aus untersucht West 8 die mögliche Kolonisierung des Leerraums in der Randstad. Die Randstad besitzt ein Magnetfeld, das von den Faktoren Lage, Erreichbarkeit und Erschließungsgrad aufgebaut wird und starke regionale Unterschiede bezüglich der Dichte und der Kultur zur Folge hat. Die Projektion dieses Magnetfelds auf den bestehenden landschaftlichen und ökologischen Reichtum des Grünen Herzens führt zu einem neuen Verstädterungsmodell. In diesem Modell bleibt die »Wildnis« nicht mehr auf das Gebiet zwischen den Städten beschränkt, sondern erstreckt sich auf die bestehenden städtischen und suburbanen Regionen. Diese Umgebung entspricht eher den Ansprüchen, die der heutige Städter an sein Lebensumfeld stellt.

Der Prozeß der Kolonisierung wird von einfachen Spielregeln gesteuert, die je nach Gebiet bestimmte Entwicklungen stimulieren, oder auch einschränken. Diese Regeln stimmen die städtische Entwicklung auf die landschaftlichen Qualitäten eines bestimmten Bereichs ab. Sie variieren von der Definition eines Gebiets, das durch die Erreichbarkeit über Autobahnausfahrten bestimmt wird, bis hin zu Vorschriften zur Begrenzung des Lärmpegels in bestimmten Zonen. Diese Spielregeln können laut West 8 verschiedene städtische Milieus mit verschiedenen Dichten und Nutzungen

controlled? This question was the focus of a study of the Randstad that West 8 completed in 1993. In this study, the urbanisation of the Green Heart was accepted as an unavoidable process. In view of the future urbanisation project it seemed unrealistic to keep the Green Heart open. Besides, agricultural land was already being sold off due to declining profitability. West 8 does not care to organise cities around a combination of areas with and without construction so that they form continuous and homogeneous units. Instead of viewing urban peripheries from the point of view of the city, they suggest reversing the perspective and looking at the city from the country.

From the latter point of view, West 8 is exploring the possible colonisation of empty space in the Randstad. The Randstad constitutes a kind of magnetic field composed of factors such as location, accessibility and degree of development, and

from the 19th century to
World War II

postwar suburban
development

consequently considerable regional differences in density and culture. The projection of this magnetic field onto the existing landscape and ecological wealth of the Green Heart leads to a new urbanisation model. It no longer restricts the "wilderness" to the area between the cities but extends it across existing urban and suburban regions. This kind of environment corresponds better to the contemporary city dwellers' requirements.

The process of colonisation is governed by simple rules which, depending on the area, either stimulate or inhibit certain developments. These rules adapt urban development to the landscape qualities of the area in question. They vary from zone to zone depending on the area's definition, which is determined by factors ranging from accessibility via motorway access routes to regulations limiting the noise level. These rules can, according to West 8, create various urban environ-

erzeugen. Dies wird an einem konkreten Vorschlag zum Rotterdamer Stadt-viertel Alexanderpolder illustriert. Die ökologische Verbindungszone, die sich an der Ostseite dieses Stadtteils entlangziehen soll, wurde als Plantage entwickelt, in der drei Wohnungen pro Hektar gebaut werden können, während die Zone entlang der Autobahn eine beträchtliche Bebauungsdichte verträgt. Diese Studie legt die Potentiale der zukünftigen Randstad offen dar. Das Experiment, »Wildlife« genannt, basiert auf einer gründlichen Beobachtung dessen, was sich in den Zonen zwischen den Städten abspielt. Es zeigt, daß der moderne Städter das Grüne Herz auf eine andere Art nutzt, als die Bezeichnung es suggeriert. Das Projekt regt an, nachzudenken über Möglichkeiten zur Steuerung städtischer Entwicklungsprozesse. West 8 zufolge besitzt die offene Mitte der Niederlande genügend Struktur und Zusammenhang, um den Sprung zu wagen und hier neue Entwicklungen zu initiieren. Auf der Grundlage von einfachen und eindeutigen Spielregeln ließe sich diese Aufgabe schließlich lösen.

Dieser Glaube an Regeln steht in gespanntem Verhältnis zur heutigen Raumordnungspraxis in den Niederlanden. Denn wer garantiert, daß die größtenteils schon vorhandenen, doch bisher nicht befolgten Regeln später einmal nutzen werden? Das große Verdienst des Vorschlags von West 8 ist,

Seit dem Mittelalter formen die Niederländer ihr Land um. Die Landschaftsarchitekten von West 8 sind fasziniert von der so entstandenen Landschaft und setzen sie zur Gestaltung des städtischen Raums ein. Damit führen sie die niederländische Tradition fort und erneuern sie.

People in the Netherlands have utilised the land since the Middle Ages. The landscape architects of West 8 are fascinated by the landscape this has created and they incorporate it into their design of urban space. Thus they are both continuing and renewing Dutch tradition.

Duindoornstad, die Sanddornstadt, soll nach den Plänen von
West 8 im Norden des Rotterdamer Hafens, zwischen Hoek
von Holland und Scheveнin-
gen, entstehen. Vor der Küste
wird eine 160 Meter breite
und 17 Kilometer lange Düne
als Deich aufgeschüttet. Ein
schmaler See trennt sie vom
Festland. Im südlichen Teil der
Düne planen die Landschaftsarchitekten 80 Meter hohe
Sandkegel, die der Wind zu
einer natürlichen Dünenlandschaft verweht. Ihre Konturen
sind vorläufig unbekannt. Die
eigentliche Kolonisierung
beginnt mit der Aussaat von
Sanddorn. Die Pflanzen ver-
breiten sich im Dünengebiet
und formen es – wie, ist un-
vorhersehbar. Anschließend
kommen die Menschen. Sie
bauen Verbindungen zum
Festland und die Quartiere
einer neuen Stadt.

Duindoornstad (Buckthorn
city) is to develop north of the
port of Rotterdam between
Hook of Holland and Scheveningen according to West 8's
plans. A dune 160 metres
wide and 17 kilometres long
will be piled up off the coast
as a dike. A narrow lake separates it from the mainland.
A mound of sand 80 metres
high, planned by the landscape
architects at the southern end
of the dune, will be blown by
the wind into a natural dune
landscape. Its contours are unpredictable. The actual process
of colonisation will begin with
the seeding of sea buckthorn.
The plants will spread over the
dunes and shape the landscape
in unforseeable ways. The people will follow and build the
new city and its links with the
mainland.

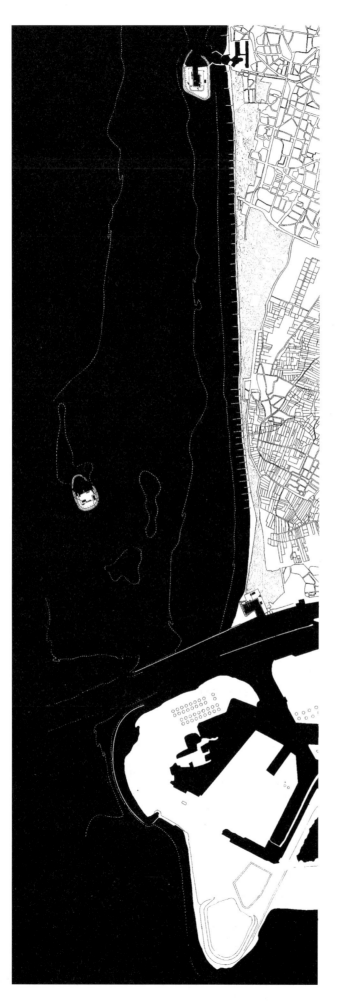
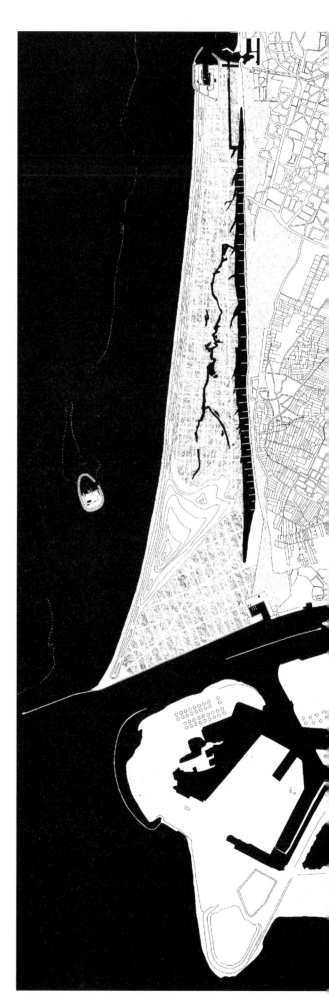

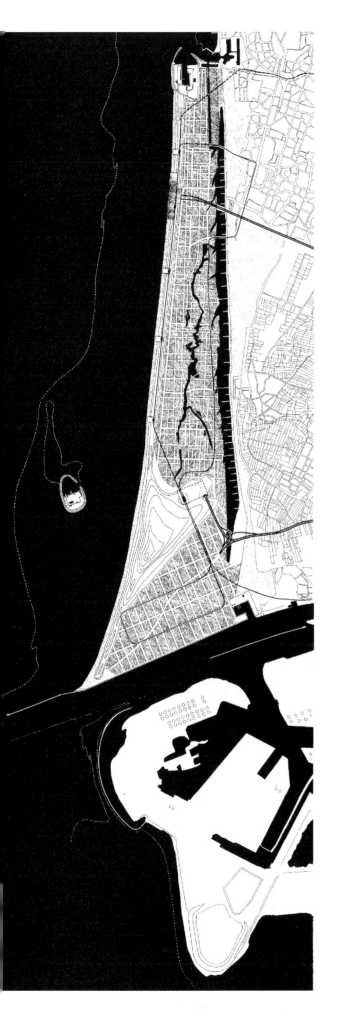
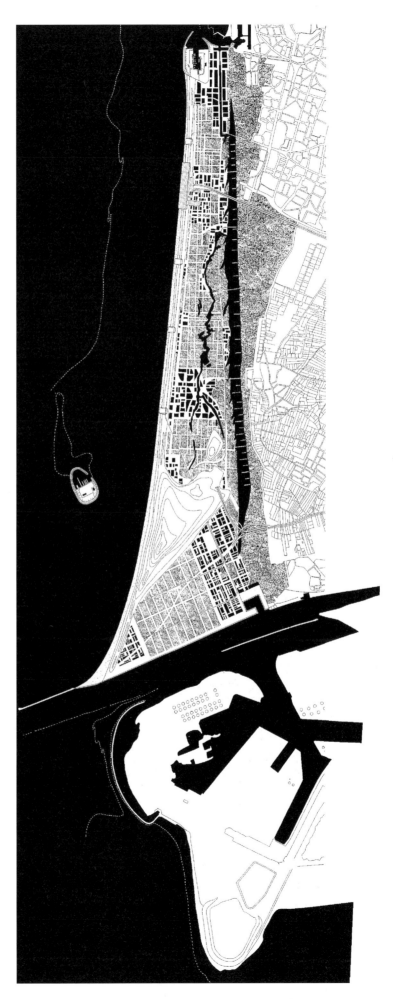

Landschaft und Stadt mischen sich in der geplanten Duindoornstad vor der Küste Rotterdams: 1 Catamaran Drive, 2 Scheveningen Marina, 3 An den Bächen, 4 Sanddornfelder, 5 Grasforum, 6 Villen-Wald, 7 Dorf am Kap, 8 Dünen-Downtown, 9 Rotterdam Europort
Landscape and city blend in Duindoornstad, planned off the coast of Rotterdam: 1 Catamaran Drive, 2 Scheveningen Marina, 3 Brookside, 4 Buckthorn Fields, 5 Grass Forum, 6 Villa Forest, 7 Cape Village, 8 Downtown Dunes, 9 Rotterdam's Europort

daß uns durch die Umkehrung der Perspektive die Augen für die Qualitäten und die Charakteristiken der suburbanen Landschaft geöffnet werden. Die Frage, ob diese Landschaft als Ganzes auch befriedigend ist, wird in dieser Studie nicht beantwortet.

Duindoornstad (Sanddornstadt). 1995 entwickelte West 8 einen Entwurf für die Stadtregion Rotterdam, bei dem vor der Küste von Hoek van Holland eine völlig neue, fast ideale Landschaft entsteht. In diesem Szenario erscheinen die Niederlande als ein Land der lokalen Gemeinschaften, in das Gebiete mit großer Dynamik und kontinuierlicher Beschleunigung aufgenommen werden. Ein gutes Beispiel für letzteres ist der Hafen, der unter dem Einfluß der Entwicklung von Containerdistribution, Schüttguttransport und Recycling noch großmaßstäblicher und arbeitsextensiver wird. Nördlich des Hafens liegen das Westland und die Küstenregion. Hier soll zwischen Hoek van Holland und Scheveningen eine neue Stadt entstehen, die sich durch ihre großen landschaftlichen Qualitäten auszeichnet. Sie wurde von West 8 als eine autonome Küstenstadt mit verschiedenen Wohnmilieus und einem kleinen Arbeitsangebot skizziert. Die Küstenstadt soll nach dem Prinzip des Entwerfens mit der Natur angelegt werden. Vor der Küste wird eine 160 Meter breite Düne als Deich aufgeschüttet, hinter der ein 17 Kilometer langer, künstlicher See entsteht. Der im südlichen Teil geplante, 80 Meter hohe Sandkegel verweht durch den Wind zu einem natürlichen Dünengebiet mit vorläufig noch unbekannten Konturen.

Mit der Aussaat von Sanddorn nimmt der Prozeß von Invasion und Sukzession seinen Anfang. In dieser Küstenlandschaft wird unvorhersehbarer Wandel stattfinden. Durch die verschiedenen landschaftlichen Bedingungen, aber auch durch die Anschlußpunkte ans Festland können sich mannigfaltige Kulturen entwickeln. So entstehen in der Küstenstadt Surfzonen, ein Stadtzentrum, Villenviertel und Dörfer. Die Raumnutzung auf lokaler Ebene ist auf die großmaßstäbliche Gebietsentwicklung abgestimmt. Hierbei kann man an die typischen niederländischen Feuchtgebiete denken, aber auch an den Rotterdamer Hafen und das Gewächshausgebiet Westland. Ausgehend von der Autonomie des Lokalen, aber ohne dabei die Wirkung der globalen Netzwerke zu unterschätzen, hat West 8 ein äußerst attraktives Zukunftsbild entwickelt. Dieses Bild bietet nicht nur eine adäquate Beschreibung unserer heutigen Lebenswelt, sondern könnte ebenso den niederländischen Planungsverantwortlichen als Zielvorstellung für die Randstad dienen.

Duindoornstad, Rotterdam
Client: Manifestation "50 Years of Reconstruction – 50 Years of Future",
Rotterdam 1995
Design: Adriaan Geuze, Edzo Bindels, René Marey, Arno de Vries, Guido Marsille,
Gricha Bourbouze, Cyrus B. Clark, Erik Overdiep, Wim Kloosterboer,
Katrien Prak, Ramon Jansen, Marc McCarthy; landscape architects

ments with different densities and uses. This is illustrated by the concrete proposal for the Alexanderpolder district in Rotterdam. The ecological zone along the eastern side connecting this district to the city is designed as a plantation, with three houses per hectare, while the zone alongside the motorway can support more substantial building density. West 8's study demonstrates the potential of the future Randstad. The experiment, called "Wildlife", is based on a thorough observation of what happens in the zones between cities. It shows that the modern city dweller uses the Green Heart in a different way than the designation suggests. The project stimulates thinking about possible means of regulating urban development processes. According to West 8, the open centre of the Netherlands possesses sufficient structure and coherence to risk the step of letting new developments loose in it. This could be accomplished on the basis of simple and definite rules.

This belief in rules conflicts with current principles of spatial organisation in the Netherlands. Who can guarantee that the rules, largely existent but not followed so far, will some day be of use? The great merit of West 8's proposal is that by reversing the perspective it opens our eyes for the qualities and characteristics of the suburban landscape. The study does not answer the question of whether this landscape as a whole is also satisfactory.

Duindoornstad (Sea buckthorn town). In 1995 West 8 developed a design for metropolitan Rotterdam for a completely new, almost ideal landscape off the coast of Hoek van Holland. The scenario represents the Netherlands as a land of local communities, dynamically and increasingly

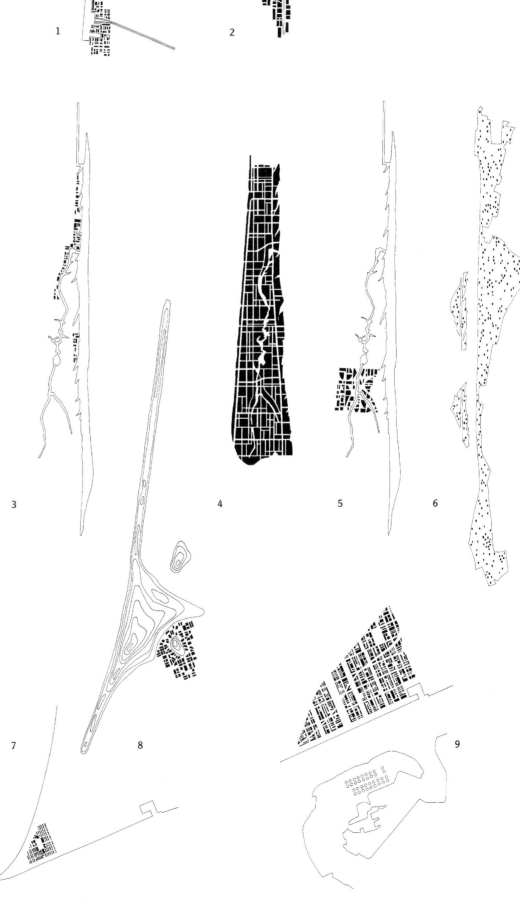

rapidly absorbing new areas. A good example of this is the harbour, becoming bigger and busier than ever due to the development of container distribution, bulk carriers and recycling. The Westland and the coastal region are north of the harbour. Between Hoek van Holland and Scheveningen, the new city is to be distinguished by considerable landscape and recreational qualities. It was sketched by West 8 as an autonomous coastal city with various residential environments and a small number of job opportunities. The coastal town is to be executed according to the principle of designing along with nature. A dune 160 metres wide will be piled up off the coast as a dike, creating a 17-kilometre-long artificial lake. The wind will blow a mound of sand 80 metres high piled up in the south into natural dunes with as yet unpredictable contours.

The seeding of sea buckthorn will begin the process of invasion and succession. Unforseeable changes will take place in this coastal landscape. Multifarious cultures can develop thanks to the various landscape conditions and the points of contact with the mainland. Hence the coastal town will have surfing areas, a city centre, suburbs with villas, and villages. This use of space on a local level is attuned to large-scale areal development covering the typical Dutch wetlands, the Rotterdam harbour, and the greenhouse region of Westland. Taking local autonomy as a point of departure, without underestimating the effect of global networks, West 8 developed a most appealing concept of the future. It provides not only an adaquate description of our contemporary world of experience but also a potential objective for the Randstad to be used by the planning authorities in the Netherlands.

Authors
Photo credits
Translations
Impressum

Authors

Stig L. Andersson, who was born in 1957, is a landscape architect and founded his own office for urban and landscape design in Copenhagen in 1991. He is an associate professor at the Royal Academy of Fine Arts in Copenhagen. Since 1992 he has been a member of the Academy Council Committees.

Sven-Ingvar Andersson, who was born in 1927, is a landscape architect. He succeeded C. T. Sørensen as the Professor of Landscape and Garden Arts at the Architecture School of the Art Academy in Copenhagen in 1963. As a landscape architect he has completed several projects in Copenhagen, Vienna, Amsterdam, and Malmö. He has published numerous articles and books, among them Havekunst i Danmark (1991).

Enric Batlle Durany was born in 1956 and studied architecture at ETSAB. After working with various architects, he founded an office together with the architect Joan Roig Duran in 1981. He has been teaching landscape architecture at the Technical University of Architecture de Vallés since 1982.

Henri Bava, who was born in 1957, studied biology and set design in Paris as well as landscape architecture at the Ecole Nationale Supérieure du Paysage (ENSP) in Versailles. In 1986 he was a joint founder of the Agence Ter landscape architecture office in Paris with Michel Hoessler

and Olivier Philippe. From 1987 to 1998 he was a lecturer at ENSP; since 1998 he has been a professor at the Technical University of Karlsruhe. He has been running the Karlsruhe office of Agence Ter since 2001.

Susana Canogar, who was born in 1961 in Madrid, studied biology at the University of Madrid. She gained a master's in landscape architecture at the University of California at Berkeley in 1993. After graduating, she set up practice in Madrid, where she works on a variety of landscape projects, mostly on a commercial scale. She publishes occasionally in the specialized press and has taught a number of courses on landscape design. She is president of the Spanish Landscape Association.

Christian Drevet, who was born in Lyon in 1951, studied architecture. He has been a free-lance architect in Lyon since 1980. From 1990 to 1994 he was a consultant town planner for Greater Lyon. He has been a consulting architect for the ministry of public building in Paris since 1992, and a teacher with civil service status at architecture schools since 1994.

Alfredo Fernández de la Reguera March studied architecture at ETSAB, graduating in 1967. He is a winner of the national award for urban planning and a member of the Beca Fundación Paul Getty. Since 1987 he has

shared an office partnership with Ignacio Salvans Terredemer and Jordi Solé Ràfols in Barcelona. They specialise in architecture, urban planning and landscape architecture.

Josep Fuses was born in Barcelona in 1954. He gained his degree in architecture at the School of Architecture of Barcelona in 1977 and pursued further studies at the Architectural Association in London in 1984-1985. He was in Rome in 1980 with a grant from the Spanish Academy. He is a professor of contemporary art at the University of Girona.

Adriaan Geuze, who was born in 1960, studied at the Agricultural University in Wageningen and graduated with a Masters in Landscape Architecture. He is the director and head designer of West 8 urban design and landscape architecture, which he founded in 1987. He teached at Delft Technical University in the Department of Architecture and Harvard University in the Graduate School of Design, Department of Landscape Architecture. In 2002 Adriaan Geuze won the Veronica Rudge Green prize for urban design for the project Borneo Sporenburg (Amsterdam, The Netherlands).

Kathryn Gustafson studied fine arts at the University of Washington in Seattle until 1970, and fashion at the Fashion Institute of Technology in New York until 1971. In 1979 she gained her diploma at the

Ecole Nationale Supérieure du Paysage, Versailles. She has had her own practice as a landscape architect in Paris since 1980, with offices in London and Seattle today.

Guido Hager was born in 1958. After being apprenticed as a gardener and florist, he studied landscape architecture at the Interkantonale Technikum (Swiss Technical University) in Rapperswil. He has had his own landscape architecture office in Zurich since 1984. He has had various teaching jobs, been a jury member, won several competitions, and has lectured and published at home and abroad.

Pascale Hannetel, who was born in 1959, studied landscape architecture at the Ecole Nationale Supérieure du Paysage in Versailles, where she graduated in 1983. In 1985 she founded her own office and worked as a free-lance landscape architect. She was a joint founder of Agence Hannetel & Associés SA in 1997, a practice that changed its name to HYL – Hannetel/Yver/Laforge in 2001.

Gottfried Hansjakob was born in 1937. He completed an apprenticeship as a gardener. From 1956 to 1969 he trained at Schönbrunn in Vienna. He gained practical experience working for Günther Schulze in Hamburg from 1960 to 1962. He founded his own office in Munich in 1962.

Toni Hansjakob was born in 1943. He works for Gottfried Hansjakob's office and has been a partner in the firm since 1974.

Eva Henze, who was born in 1965, studied geography at the University of Hamburg and landscape architecture at the University of Hannover, gaining her diploma in 1993. She worked for leading practices in Germany and England (landscape and property planning, garden monuments preservation). She has been a free-lance landscape architect in Hamburg since 2002. She is also a free-lance journalist and lectures at home and abroad.

Jacqueline Osty, who was born in 1954, studied at the Ecole Nationale Supérieure du Paysage in Versailles until 1982. She founded her own office in 1983 in Paris. She also teaches at the national landscape architecture school of Versailles as a visitor lecturer.

Agneta Persson has practised as a landscape architect for 16 years, specialising in landscape design and urban planning. She has had her own practice since 1993. For the last five years she has been the Director of Exhibition Planning at the Bo01 housing exhibition "City of Tomorrow" in Malmö.

Joan Roig Duran was born in 1954 and studied architecture at ETSAB in Barcelona. After working with various archi-

tects, he founded an office with Enric Batlle Durany in 1981. He has been teaching landscape architecture at ETSAB since 1989.

Ignacio Salvans Terredemer studied architecture at ETSAB and graduated in 1986. Since 1987 he has shared an office partnership with Alfredo Fernández de la Reguera and Jordi Solé in Barcelona. They specialise in architecture, urban planning and landscape architecture.

Jordi Solé Ràfols graduated in architecture from ETSAB with a master's degree in landscape architecture in 1968. In 1987 he founded an office partnership with Alfredo Fernández de la Reguera and Ignacio Salvans. They specialise in architecture, urban planning and landscape architecture.

Harm Tilman, who was born in 1954, is the editor-in-chief of de Architect, the monthly architecture journal from the Netherlands. He is the author of countless articles on modern architecture and town planning, and has contributed to various publications on the present-day city. He has been a visiting professor at different educational institutions at home and abroad.

Maria Cristina Tullio, who was born in 1958, has a doctorate in architecture and works on a free-lance basis in northern Italy, focusing on open space planning. She is a

orrespondent for trade jour-
als and performs research
work for universities and pri-
ate institutions.

oan M. Viader was born in
Bescanó, Spain, in 1953. He
graduated with a degree in architecture from the Architec-
ure School of Barcelona in
977 and studied for his mas-
er's degree in landscape architecture at ETSAB in
984-1985. He worked as a
ity planner on the rehabilita-
ion of the historic quarter of
Girona from 1983 to 1985
nd is currently a free-lance
architect in Barcelona.

Kolbjörn Wærn, who was
orn in 1949, studied at the
Swedish University of Agri-
culture and at Cornell University in New York State. He
s working as landscape archi-
ect at WSP Group in Göte-
borg and with historical parks
and gardens in his own firm,
Landskapsarkitekt Kolbjörn
Wærn.

Rasmus Wærn was born in
961. He studied architecture
at Chalmers University of
Technology, where he also became Ph.D. in history of architecture in 1996. He has
been curating exhibitions for
the Swedish Museum of Ar-
chitecure and is currently an
editor at the Swedish review
of Architecture, Arkitektur.

Photo Credits

Photo credits:
Gérard Dufresne: 9, 10, 11
Arnauld Duboys Fresney: 12,
14, 15, 17 (3)
Vimagen S.A.: 18, 19, 21, 22
(9)
Sven-Ingvar Andersson: 25,
26, 27, 28
Lise Schou: 29
Lisa Diedrich: 34 (3), 35 (3)
Ignacio Salvans: 37, 38, 40,
41 (3)
Göteborg (plan): 42
Hans Wretling: 44, 45, 48, 49
Kvalitetsbeskrivning Stads-
byggnadskontoret: 47
Kolbjörn Wærn: 50 (3)
Kim Wilkie: 51, 53, 56 (2),
58 (2)
François Guy: 59
Stéphane Couturier: 60, 61
Kathryn Gustafson: 64, 65,
66 (2)
Tavisa: 67
Yann Mercader: 68, 69, 70,
71
Jeppe Aagaard Andersen: 73
(4), 74
Lotta Swahn Karlsson, mima
arkitekter ab: 75
Ingvar Andersson: 76 (4), 77,
78
Åke E:son Lindman: 83, 85,
86
Stig L. Andersson: 84 (2) top
Jens Lindhe: 84 (2) bottom
Luis On: 87, 88, 89, 93 (2)
Büro Hansjakob: 94
Gerald Zugmann: 97 (2), 98
Enric Battle i Joan Roig: 102
Julià Espinàs: 104, 105 (2)
Lourdes Jansana: 108 (2), 109
Duccio Malagamba: 111 (2),
112
Guido Hager: 114, 115
Christian Müller: 114/115,
116
Wolfgang Glutz: 117
Olaf Probst: 119

Translations:

German/English:
Judith Harrison: pp. 6, 34,
37, 94, 113
Almuth Seebohm: pp. 5, 12,
80, 100
Beate Rupprecht: pp. 64
Valerie Mader: pp. 72

English/German:
Ursula Poblotzki: pp. 18
Cora Lorke: pp. 24
Peter Zöch: pp. 30, 110
Tino Schlagintweit: pp. 42

Dutch/German:
Beate Rupprecht: pp. 118

French/German:
Lisa Diedrich: pp. 34
Olaf Probst: pp. 59

Spanish/German:
Catrin Möhler: pp. 37
Lisa Diedrich: pp. 100

Swedish/German:
Ursula Killguß: pp. 72

French/English:
Almuth Seebohm: pp. 59

Impressum

Editor: Topos – European
Landscape Magazine
(www.topos.de)
Robert Schäfer, Claudia Moll
Layout: Boris Storz, Heike
Frese-Pieper

Das Werk einschließlich aller
seiner Teile ist urheber-
rechtlich geschützt. Jede Ver-
wertung außerhalb der engen
Grenzen des Urheberrechts-
gesetzes ist ohne schriftliche
Zustimmung des Verlags un-
zulässig und strafbar. Das gilt
insbesondere für Vervielfälti-
gungen, Übersetzun-
gen, Mikroverfilmungen und
die Einspeicherung und Verar-
beitung in elektronischen Sys-
temen.

This work is subject to copyright. All rights are reserved,
wether the whole or part of
the material is concerned,
specifically the rights of trans-
lation, reprinting, re-use of il-
lustrations, recitation, broad-
casting, reproduction on mi-
crofilms or in other ways, and
storage in data bases. For any
kind of use, permission of the
copyright owner must be ob-
tained.
© 2002 Verlag Georg D. W.
Callwey GmbH & Co. KG,
Munich,
P.O.Box 80 04 09,
D-81604 München,
Germany
in cooperation with
Birkhäuser – Publishers for
Architecture,
P.O.Box 133,
CH-4010 Basel,
Switzerland

A CIP catalogue record for
this book is available from the
Library of Congress, Washington D.C., USA.

Deutsche Bibliothek Cata-
loging-in-Publication Data
– CIP-Einheitsaufnahme

Wasser: Gestalten mit Wasser:
Von Uferpromenaden zu
Wasserspielen = Water: De-
signing with water: Prome-
nades and water features. -
München : Callwey, 2002
ISBN 3-7667-1554-2

Printed on chlorine-free pulp.
TCF

Printed in Germany

ISBN Callwey
3-7667-1554-2
ISBN Birkhäuser
3-7643-6976-0

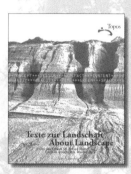